U0458535

本书获长春师范大学学术专著出版计划项目资助

邹艳丽 著

语料库与学术语篇作者身份短语研究

CORPORA AND WRITER IDENTITY PHRASE
IN ACADEMIC DISCOURSE

上海三联书店

前　言

近年来，随着英语写作能力，尤其是学术英语写作能力在加强我国传播能力建设和提高国家软实力开放战略中重要性的显著提升，培养我国大学生及青年学者在国际学术界的对话能力、竞争力和影响力，促进中国学术走出去、获得学术独创性和权威性认可的需求愈发突出。

作为社会文化的重要组成部分，学术语篇是学术知识交流与构建的重要途径、是作者与外界的学术对话、是学术共同体的规约范式。在学术语篇中，为推荐自己的研究成果、获得学术声誉和学术共同体的认可，写作者在对潜在读者充分预测和认知的基础上，在遵循学科话语规范的同时构建学术语篇作者身份，其中包括语篇组织者，具有创新能力的研究者，具有学术权威的专家型学者等。在英文学术语篇中，写作者们大量使用程式化或半程式式词汇语法结构，即英语短语，以实现语篇功能和构建作者身份。

基于语料库语言学的短语理念认为短语是语言的主要意义单位。这一观点强调了"语言的表意单位是短语而非孤立的单个词汇"（何安平 2013：6）。语料库驱动研究通过分析海量语料证明短语在话语中大量存在。尽管目前的短语研究定义各不相同，提取标准存在差异，但有一点不可否认，即作为在语言使用中大量存在的最小意义单位，短语对于语言学习者非常重要，如果短语掌握得不好，即使是语法正确的句子，听起来也不自然，不达意。

本书是本人从事基于语料库的英语学术语篇研究的一个阶段性小结。在博士研究期间，我有幸师从国际著名语料库语言学与应用语言学学家 Susan Hunston 教授,以包含第一人称代词的短语为研究切入点探索学术语篇中的作者身份建构话语,包括其相关的语篇功能和身份建构策略等。通过自建中国学习者多学科学术语篇语料库,我检索了自建语料库中的第一人称代词,描写并归纳了含有这些代词的短语结构,总结了这些结构的相关语篇功能,如:组织语篇功能、构建知识共同体功能、汇报研究内容及阐释研究结果功能等;在此基础上,我发现这些短语结构、语篇功能和语篇作者身份呈现一定的对应关系,形成了相对固定的矩阵组合。同时,我对比了含有第一人称代词的短语在不同学科学术语篇中的差异,以及从本科到研究生阶段频次及语篇功能的变化。通过对比,我发现提取出的相关短语在不同学术阶段的使用差异比学科间的差异更为显著。基于以上发现,我提出重视学习者学术语篇中第一人称代词,尤其是包含第一人称代词短语的使用、提高学习者对于其语篇功能及作者身份构建认识的重要性。我们还需要在教学中注重学科差异的引导,加强学习者学术写作能力的培养。

  本书共包含 8 个章节,从语料库语言学的概念、文献评述、研究方法、学术语篇中包含第一人称代词短语的描写、语用功能、作者身份构建和数据驱动学习与学术英语教学八个方面探索语料库与学术语篇中的作者身份短语。第一章为绪论,简要介绍了语料库语言学、学习者语料库、学术语篇及作者身份构建的概念及相关研究概况,探讨基于语料库和语料库驱动范式下的学术英语研究,包括其研究目的、方法优势以及应用价值。第二章综述了基于语料库的学习者学术语篇研究,包括短语学、学科间差异,不同教育阶段的教学目标,以及学习者文本与专家型文本之间的差异等。并以此为研究背景,提出基于语料库探索学习者在学术文本中的短语使用及身份构建问题。第三章重点介绍了"中国以英语为外语学习者学术文本语料库"的建设过程和架构。书中汇报的研究发现和相关讨论几乎都是基于这一语料库开展研究所得。

在第四章到第六章中,我将与读者共同分享学习者文本中包含第一人称代词短语的学科差异和不同学术阶段差异。研究结果和讨论分别从含有第一人称代词的短语结构、其相应的语篇功能和所映射的作者身份展开。第七章概括了学术语篇中含有第一人称代词短语的主要研究成果,探索了学术文本中短语—功能—身份的对应关系和在学术写作中影响人称代词及相关短语选择的7个原则。第八章总结全文,重点讨论研究成果如何反哺我国英语学习者的学术写作教学和后续研究建议。

归国后,本人入职长春师范大学,主讲学术写作相关课程,并在外国语学院的英美语言文学研究中心开展研究工作,攻读博士期间的研究发现和基于语料库的数据驱动学习方法得以运用到本科生和研究生的学术写作教学与研究中。同时,还作为负责人建设省级研究生精品示范课程《学术阅读与写作》。通过教学研究发现,作为学术写作的任课教师自身须对学术话语中的自我表征问题保持敏感,同时,利用语料库辅助学术英语写作教学可以有效提高学生在学术话语中的短语使用、注重语用功能及构建作者身份意识,这些内容在本书相关章节均有呈现。

由于笔者水平有限,书中难免有不足之处,恳请各位专家和读者不吝赐教,有不妥之处,敬请批评指正。

Contents

List of Figures

List of Tables

CHAPTER 1
INTRODUCTION

1.1 Introduction

"Instead of 'I' and 'We', I would rather use 'the author' or 'the writer' in my thesis. As a student, using 'I' in my paper seems too 'loud' to me".(Civil Law)

"My supervisor told me to remove all 'I' in my thesis and replace them with passive voice".(Computer Science)

The two comments cited above are made by two non-native speakers of English on using 'I' and 'We' in their graduation theses. Both of them are PhD students. One is studying Civil Law and the other Computer Science. The student of Civil Law thinks that using the first person pronouns (FPPs) 'I' and 'We' is too authoritative and face-threatening. The student of Computer Science was cautioned by her supervisor that no 'I' or 'We' is allowed in her thesis. In comparison to expert writers, the EFL learners' use of the FPPs in academic texts has been found to be problematic(Hyland 2002). I, as an EFL academic writer, also do have problems when using 'I' and 'We' in my academic writing. Before this research was undertaken and whilst I was in the process of writing this dissertation, whenever I was faced with a choice between the FPPs and available alternatives, I was inclined to avoid using 'I' and 'We'. Both the two PhD students and I have had the same experience as most novice academic writers from a Chinese cultural background. I have taught students who are novice academic writers drawn from a wide range of different academic disciplines in China. Although these two comments, coupled with our educational background and my professional status are all pieces of personal information and cannot be used as evidence of any kind, a few issues concerning the use of the FPPs are made apparent in a novice EFL writer's academic discourse. These issues are listed as follows:

● **The authoritativeness of 'I' and 'We' in academic discourse**

'I' and 'we' could be interpreted as offering authority in academic discourse. For instance, if a statement is attributed to a researcher(e.g. 'Ivanič says that …'), that researcher is being used as an authority. One interpretation of attributing a statement to self is that self is being allocated a similar status of authority. This implication of the authoritativeness of 'I' and 'We' may lead to the reluctance on the part of students in using the most apt FPPs in academic discourse. The tentativeness in using the FPPs is not uncommon in EFL writing practice. For example, both the PhD student of Civil Law and I subscribe to the notion that the FPPs 'I' and 'We' carry too much responsibility and commitment and are hence cautious about using them in our theses. From this perspective, it would be valuable to know when, where, and how novice writers inject themselves into their texts to claim authority; and how tentative and authoritative EFL students are in their academic texts. The resultant findings would shed some light on the appropriate use of 'I' and 'We' in academic writing.

- The visibility of the writers presented by the use of 'I' and 'We' in the academic text.

As 'I' and 'We' are the most visible forms of self-representations in a text, the visible writer's interpretations would result in two consequences. The writer could either be recognised as authoritative or be challenged by the readership. In a sense, visibility is partly related to the authoritative issue. It implies both commitment and threateningness. As a result, writers may choose to disguise themselves in their essays. For instance, the suggestion of removing 'I' and 'We' in the Computer Science student's essay, presumably, aims at keeping an objective tone by eliminating any visible trace of the writer. Here, the questions worth asking are: To what extent should a thesis writer choose to be visible? Is there a disciplinary difference that affects or influences visibility? For instance, the student of Civil Law chooses *the author* and *the writer* to represent himself/herself, whereas the student of Computer Science is advised not to present herself at all, at least not with the benefit of using the FPPs. The answers to these questions may provide more understanding of the writer's rhetorical strategy for self-projection when engaged in the process of writing academic text.

- The interactivity between writer and readership

The communicative goal of academic discourse is to share disciplinary knowledge with the writer's disciplinary community, by doing which, the writer also aims at being acknowledged and accepted in that society. However, unlike published articles, which are mostly read by the writers' peers, there is unbalanced power between the writer and the reader of students' theses. The readers of students' academic texts are always the student's supervisor (s) and the examiners who possess a greater degree of disciplinary expertise.

Consequently, the student writers may feel reluctant to assert their personal views in their writing. For example, the student of Civil Law considers 'I' and 'We' as expressions that allow the writer to boast in his/her thesis. From this perspective, it would be insightful and valuable if we know how the thesis writers interact with their readers with these constraints attached to them whilst attempting to create a certain degree of affinity with the reader.

● **The advice given to the students about the use of the FPPs in academic text**

Regrettably, the oversimplified instruction given to the PhD student of Computer Science is still widely practiced in Chinese EFL academic classrooms. Rather than simply instructing the removal of the FPPs, more specific and useful advice relating to the appropriate use of 'I' and 'We' would have helped the student in his/her future academic writing practice.

The three issues I have discussed so far, authoritativeness, visibility, and interactivity, shape the individual persona made manifest by an academic discourse writer's use of the FPPs. Indeed, 'I' and 'We' are the most obvious self-representative words of a writer in his/her academic text. Methodologically, the exploration of the FPPs is probably the most direct way of evaluating a writer's authoritativeness, visibility, and his/her ability to foster writer-reader interaction in his/her discourse. Further, these issues are probably most easily explored by examining what writers 'do' in their academic texts, which in essence, is the pragmatic function of their language. Since the verbs that collocate with 'I' and 'We' are what the writers 'do' in their academic texts, studying the choice of verbs seems to be a sensible way of examining those pragmatic functions(cf. Fløttum et al. 2006; Ivanič 1998; John 2005). Therefore, I decided to use a self-compiled computer learner corpus in this research. The corpus and the corpus tools would allow me to look for those repeatedly used expressions of 'I', 'We' and their verb collocates in the students' academic texts.

Motivated by the on-going development in English for Academic Purposes(EAP), Computer Learner Corpora(CLC), and phraseology, this study attempts to explore discourse functions and the phraseology of two most obvious self-representation FPPs, 'I' and 'We' in Chinese EFL students' academic discourse. The discussion focuses on the authoritativeness, visibility and interaction reflected by the discourse functions of the phrases of 'I' and 'We'. Methodologically, the starting point of this research is 'I' and 'We'. After the FPPs are retrieved, the verbs that collocate with them are extracted. This leads to the identification of a fairly large number of phrases of two or more words containing either 'I' or 'We' (e.g. *I think*, *I believe*, *We found*). Some trigrams, such as *we have discussed*, *we know that*, and some longer phrases such as *we can see that*, and *as we have mentioned* were also extracted. These are all considered as instances of phraseology in this study.

As an EAP teacher myself, I am also interested in the disciplinary differences and language development of the students' rhetorical strategies affecting the choice of the FPPs in their academic texts. Therefore, in this study, I compared 'I' and

'We' across two disciplines (Business and Management and English Literature), and across two academic levels (undergraduate and postgraduate levels). It is hoped that the findings would offer a fuller understanding of the EFL learners' use of the FPPs in academic writing and add to our knowledge of the FPPs in academic discourse. This would further provide pedagogical implications for the teaching and learning of the FPPs in EFL contexts.

The rest of this chapter is organised as follows. Section 2 provides a brief review of the previous research that is briefly mentioned in this introductory section: the FPPs and their pragmatic functions in academic texts, the verbs that collocate with the FPPs, phraseology and CLC. The review serves as the background for the present study. Section 3 presents the aim and research questions to be addressed in this study. Section 4 introduces the learner corpus and methodology of this research. The last section outlines the organisation of the whole thesis.

1.2   Background of the study

This pedagogical oriented research has been motivated by previous research on EAP, CLC, and phraseology. A full literature review will be provided in Chapter 2. In this section, I describe the key issues raised by previous research.

1.2.1   The first person pronouns and the pragmatic functions of the FPPs in academic writing

Researchers have reported that academic writing has experienced a shift from being personal to impersonal and then to personal(Bazerman 1984; Kuo 1998; Hyland 2004; Hyland & Jiang 2017; Swales 1990). For instance, research articles from about 350 years ago were mainly letters exchanged between scientists. In these letters, there were many first person narrative expressions(Swales 1990). The FPPs in these early forms of academic writing "would project both personal honesty and modesty"(ibid:114). From the end of the 19th century to the 1980s, scientific papers were seen as "a matter of fact" reports (Swales 1990:111). Studies have shown that the academic text has become impersonal, defined as a "shift from description and narration to explanation and analysis"(Kuo 1999:122). Academic writing tended to report methodology and results of an empirical research in an objective way(Bazerman 1984; Swales 1990). This led to a convention of the text being 'author evacuated'(Geertz 1998). Recently, scholars have argued that writing cannot be genuinely impersonal because the writer expresses himself/herself in every aspect related to language choices in the text, for example, lexis, syntax, and organisation(Ivanič 1998; Ivanič and Camps 2001). Further, academic writing is seen as an interactive dialogue between writer and reader which involves a personal manifestation of the writer and a recognition of the reader's reception of the text(Candarlı et al. 2015; Fairclough 1993; Ivanič 1998; Swales 1990; Thompson 2009). The increasing use of the FPPs in academic texts is one of the signs of this interaction. Hyland and Jiang(2017), for example, show that the usage of FPPs has increased considerably in the last 50 years, 45% overall, in the published research articles of both hard disciplines(Biology and Engineering) and soft disciplines(Applied

Linguistics and Sociology).

As discussed above, the self-representation of the writer could achieve the interactivity between the writer himself/herself, the target readership as well as his/her academic community. Therefore, in academic discourse, beyond the functions of being modest and hedging in early scientific reports, FPPs in academic texts are now frequently used to organise text, to stress solidarity, to claim authority, originality, and newsworthiness(e.g. Ädel 2006; Fløttum et al. 2006; Ivanič 1998; Harwood 2005a, 2005b, 2006, 2007; Kuo 1999; Hyland 2001, 2002, 2004, 2015; Tang & John 1999). Consequently, the employment of the FPPs is considered as "a key element of successful academic writing"(Hyland 2002:1093—1094). In short, the FPPs, 'I' and 'We' as the most obvious expressions of self-projection in discourse are powerful means to assert the writer's claim and to establish his/her authority in the academic community(Quirk et al. 1985). Because of these important pragmatic effects, this study takes 'I' and 'We' as the entry point of looking at the writer-reader interaction from the perspectives of the discourse functions of the expressions of the FPPs and of the persona in the students' academic texts.

The changes in the use of the FPPs indicate a tension in academic discourse as shown by the research mentioned above. On the one hand, there has been a drive to encourage objectivity by the exclusion of 'I' and 'We'. On the other hand, there also has been a more recent drive towards the acknowledgment of personal representation in the research process. This balancing act causes difficulties for academic writers. Novice writers in particular may find it difficult to accommodate the disciplinary community. The factors that may cause this difficulty include the writers' uncertainty of the disciplinary conventions, their position as novice writers, the unbalanced power between the novice writer and the expert readership, and their lack of rhetorical strategy in establishing authorship. All of these would "place students at a rhetorical and interpersonal disadvantage, preventing them from communicating appropriate integrity and commitments, and undermining their relationship to readers" (Hyland 2002: 1092). It is interesting to see, therefore, the strategies that the novice writers use to negotiate that tension and find their middle ground by being both objective and personal appropriately. The exploration of the novice writers' texts could help to formulate some guidelines that enable the novice writers to use 'I' and 'We' in academic writing more effectively.

Most of the studies on FPPs in academic texts so far (e.g. Harwood 2005a, 2005b, 2006, 2007; Hyland 2001, 2002, 2004, 2005, 2006, 2007, 2012, 2015, 2017; Ivanič 1998; Kuo 1999; Tang & John 1999; Swales 1990) focus on self-projection in academic discourse to achieve the textual effects of establishing solidarity, authority, originality and hedging. However, my discussion in Chapter 2 will show that most of these studies focus on the FPPs in expert academic discourse. Although some of Hyland's (e.g. 2001, 2002) studies are on non-native speakers, there is room for further exploration of the pragmatic functions of 'I' and 'We' in EFL academic discourse by comparing the EFL learners' academic texts in their own right and exploring the quality of the usage of the FPPs.

1.2.2   Semantic categorisation of verbs and the phrases of 'I', 'We' and their verb collocates in this study

Having discussed the background of the usage of 'I' and 'We' in academic discourse, I shall now turn to another related issue of this research. This relates to the identification and categorisation of the semantics of verbs in the EAP context. As mentioned in the introductory section, the verbs that collocate with 'I' and 'We' are the student writers' actions in their academic discourse. The semantic-pragmatic meaning of verbs contributes to the writers' self-representation in the texts(Fløttum et al. 2006). Like Fløttum et al.(ibid), my starting point is the semantic and functional categorisation of the verbs that collocates with 'I' and 'We'. Reference examples of the semantic classifications of verbs are from Biber et al.(2002) and Fløttum et al.(2006). These will be discussed in more detail in Chapter 3 and Chapter 4. However, at this juncture, we can simply note that Biber et al. offer a general categorisation of verbs, including 7 semantic categories: *activity verbs*, *communication verbs*, *mental verbs*, *causative verbs*, *verbs of occurrence*, *verbs of existence of relationship*, and *verbs of aspect*. These verbs are collected from a mixed genre of academic texts, conversation transcriptions, fiction, and news texts. Therefore, the semantic categories are of reference value but need to be re-examined in my corpus. In order to investigate the writer's roles in academic discourse, Fløttum et al.(2006) propose 4 categories of verbs that collocate with 'I', labelled *research verbs*, *discourse verbs*, *argue verbs*, and *various evaluating and emotional construction*. These verbs are used to discuss what the writers' identities in the texts are. Therefore, the phraseological features and the functions of the FPPs were not included in their study.

In Chapter 2 and Chapter 3, like Fløttum et al., I started this research by extracting the verbs that collocate with 'I' and 'We'. I then examined the meaning and the function of the verbs when they collocated with the FPPs. However, I went beyond the semantic categorisation of the verbs, extending the examination to phrases of 'I' and 'We' and their verb collocates. Hence, the items examined in this study include the collocation of 'I', 'We' and the verb collocates(bigram) and observable multi-word phrases that include the FPPs and the extracted verbs. In terms of the meaning and the function of the verbs that collocate with 'I' and 'We', this study offers up the proposition that the meaning of a verb is not necessarily consistent. Taking the verb *read* as an example, it means *the act of reading* when it is used in the phrase *I read* + *object*, which is an *activity verb* according to Biber et al.(2002). In another research, according to Fløttum et al.(2006), *read* is a research verb when it collocates with 'I' and 'We'. As discussed later in Chapter 5 of this study, the meaning and the function of the verb *read* is *an activity verb* as proposed by Biber et al., for example, in the phrase *I read Shakespeare*. In another phrase, *I read it as a seduction*, it falls under a different category from that of both Biber et al. and Fløttum et al. It is argued in this study that in the phrase *read ... as*, the verb *read* implies the writer's understanding and evaluation of the material. In this sense, *read* can also be considered as a verb of interpretation.

Based on previous research on semantic categories of verbs, I started this research by looking at the semantics and categorisation of the verbs that collocate with 'I' and 'We' in my corpus. I then, look at the discourse functions and the phraseology of the FPPs and their verb collocates in the EFL students' texts across two disciplines and two academic levels. The next section introduces Computer Learner Corpora (CLC), the methodology underpinning this research on learner language.

1.2.3 Computer Learner Corpora

Like many studies on learners' academic discourse, this research uses self-compiled corpus to investigate the FPPs, 'I' and 'We' in the student writers' academic texts. In recent years, there has been an increasing recognition of the importance of CLC in second language and foreign language research. Granger et al.(2002:preface) define CLC as:

"Computer learner corpora are electronic collections of spoken or written texts produced by foreign or second language learners in a variety of language settings. Once computerised, these data can be analysed with linguistic software tools, from simple ones, which search, count, and display, to the most advanced ones, which provide sophisticated analyses of the data".

By using corpus tools the frequent words, collocation and phrases may be observed and compared between corpora. CLC has been widely used for contrastive purposes, which compare between two or more corpora, most likely, between corpora of native speakers' and corpora of a second language or foreign language learners'. The main areas of CLC studies are, language transfer(e.g. Paquot 2008), error analysis(e.g. Osborne 2008), over- or under-use of certain language features in a learner corpus(e.g. Chen 2013) and interlanguage development (e.g. Meunier 2015). Most recent CLC based research on 'I' and 'We' in academic discourse focuses on the following comparisons: novice writers as opposed to expert researchers(e.g. Wang 2018), ESL learners as opposed to native speakers(e.g. Candarli et al. 2015), and between texts of different disciplines (e.g. Hyland & Jiang 2017). Informative as these studies are, relatively few comparative studies have been done on the collocations of the FPPs and the verbs between EFL learners at different disciplines and across different academic levels. The comparison across the different disciplines will add to our knowledge of the disciplinary differences presented in the learners' texts. The comparison of different academic levels could describe the EFL students' developmental features related to academic writing. Both are valuable to the understanding of interlanguage and could have pedagogical implications in EAP teaching and learning practice.

With respect to disciplinary studies, Becher(1989) proposes four disciplinary categories: hard pure(e.g. Physics), soft pure(e.g. History), hard applied(e.g. Mechanical Engineering) and soft applied (e. g. Education). Studies have shown that language conventions and rhetorical strategies could vary considerably across the four permutations (e. g. Bazermen 1988; Charles 2004; Groom 2007; Hyland 2002, 2005; Swales 1991). There is also evidence that the uses of 'I' and 'We' differ significantly between disciplines both quantitatively and functionally(e.g. Başal & Bada 2012; Hyland 2001, 2005). In line with previous disciplinary studies, I am inclined to concur with Becher's categorisation. In this study, I shall compare two disciplines from two different categories, Business and Management as a soft applied discipline and English Literature as a soft pure discipline. The selection of these two disciplines is reported in detail in Section 3.2.2 of Chapter 3.

I have discussed briefly the different areas that underpin this research. Previous research on 'I' and 'We' in academic discourse has been carried out on either native speakers or on ESL writers who have been studying English for a long time, for example, in Hong Kong in Hyland's 2002 study. In this thesis, I extended this form of research to a different context where learners have had lesser exposure to English by virtue of their educational background in China. Methodologically, most of the recent research on the FPPs is quantitative in nature. These previous corpus based studies have extracted 'I' and 'We' by concordance methods and proceeded to examine the results qualitatively by close reading of the extended discourse. Relatively little research starts from the examination of the phraseologies of 'I' and 'We' and their verb collocates and discusses the functions of these collocates or phrases. There is also relatively little research on the quality of the uses of the FPPs in EFL students' academic discourse. John (2005) and Harwood (2007) are exceptions. But John focuses on the writers' identity and the effects of revision, not the phraseology and the discourse functions of the FPPs. Harwood interviewed the writers of published research papers and discussed the discourse functions of the FPPs in expert academic texts. In addition, the question of the appropriateness of individual uses of 'I' and 'We' has been insufficiently explored. To expand our knowledge on these aspects of the FPPs in academic discourse, this corpus-based study intends to explore the phraseology and pragmatic functions of 'I' and 'We' and the verbs collocating with them in EFL learners' academic texts.

1.3   Aims and research questions

This study uses self-compiled corpora to examine Chinese EFL learners' uses of 'I' and 'We' and the verbs collocating with them. The research compares texts between two disciplines, Business and Management, and English Literature, and between two academic levels, undergraduate and postgraduate students' academic writing. Focusing on phraseology and pragmatic functions, the students' progress and disciplinary differences of the usage of the FPPs in their academic texts are explored. This research provides a new perspective on looking at the expressions of 'I' and 'We' in the phrases as the units of meaning. Consequently, the practical outcome of this research provides pedagogical implications for EAP classrooms. My overall aim is to investigate how the EFL student writers project themselves by using the two FPPs, 'I' and 'We' in their academic texts. More specifically, the research questions to be addressed are:

RQ1. How frequent are 'I' and 'We' used in each subcorpus? What are the verbs that collocate with them? What phraseological sequences of 'I', 'We', and the verbs collocating with them can be identified?

RQ2. What are the pragmatic functions of the phrases containing 'I', 'We', and their verb collocates?

RQ3-A. Do the phrases and their functions show any differences across the two disciplines?

RQ3-B. Do the phrases and their functions show any differences across the two academic levels?

RQ4. What are the pedagogical and methodological implications of this research for further investigation of the FPPs in academic writing discourse?

1.4   Corpus and methodology

The Chinese Advanced English Learner Corpus of Academic Written English(CAEL-CAWE) built for this research comprises four sets of subcorpora compiled from academic texts written by undergraduate students majoring in Business and Management(UGBM), postgraduates in Business and Management(PGBM), undergraduates in English Literature(UGEL), and postgraduates in English Literature(PGEL) respectively. The texts are all submitted graduation dissertations written in English by Chinese students in China. To compare the disciplinary differences between Business and Management(BM) and English Literature(EL), the comparison was carried out between UGBM + PGBM vs. UGEL + PGEL; to compare the academic level difference between undergraduate(UG) and postgraduate(PG) levels, the contrastive analysis was between UGBM + UGEL vs. PGBM + PGEL. These comparisons facilitate the two-dimensional exploration of the disciplinary and academic level differences.

It may come as a surprise that I am not comparing the learner corpora with the corpora of native speakers of expert writers in this study. In other words, unlike most CLC researchers in EAP, I compare the two disciplines and two levels within the corpus without relying on a native speaker or an expert writer benchmark. I acknowledge that my approach is at odds with many previous learner corpus studies. However, I would argue that the learners' language is self-contained and does not need to be compared with an external norm. The comparison between the two disciplines, BM and EL, keeps us focusing on the exploration of how the learners present themselves through the usage of the two FPPs in their disciplinary academic discourse, including their unique phraseology and the discourse functions of these phrases. For undergraduate students, the level of competence of postgraduate students is their next achievable goal rather than the competence level of native speakers or experts. Therefore, a comparison of the undergraduate students' texts with the postgraduates' can provide valuable pedagogical information relating to the students' development in the use of 'I' and 'We' in their academic writing practice.

The major steps of this research are as follows. Firstly, the corpora were loaded into Sketch Engine(Kilgarriff et al. 2004). Then, the instances of the two FPPs, 'I' and 'We' in the corpus were extracted. Thirdly, the frequent verbs that collocated with the two FPPs were extracted. The threshold of the frequency of the verbs was set to no less than 5 times collocating with 'I' and/or no less than 10 times collocating with 'We'. At the same time, only those verbs that occurred at least in 3 texts were included for further analysis. The fourth step was to examine the extracted verbs with regard to their semantic features and pragmatics functions. On the basis of the analysis, these verbs were classified into 4 major categories. The analysis of the differences across the disciplines and academic levels were carried out based on this categorisation. The primary purpose of the classification of the verbs in this study is not to propose a new typology of verb categories. Rather, they are used for this particular study to explore the collocation, the phraseological features as well as the pragmatic functions of 'I', 'We', and their verb collocates.

1.5 An outline of the book

This chapter has briefly discussed the background of this research, including the FPPs in EAP, CLC, previous forms of categorisation of English verbs, phraseology, and disciplinary differences in the EAP context. The data and methodology have been introduced and the aims and the research questions discussed. The remaining 7 chapters of this thesis are organised as follows. Chapter 2 reviews previous research in the field of EAP, in particular, the uses of FPPs in academic discourse. The research background that has been briefly introduced in this chapter is further elaborated in Chapter 2. Chapter 3 reports the compilation process of the corpus. The method of extracting the two FPPs, 'I' and 'We', and the extraction of the verbs that collocate with the FPPs are also discussed in this

chapter. Chapter 4 explains how the extracted verbs are classified according to their meanings and functions when collocating with 'I' and 'We' in the corpus. In this chapter, categories of discourse function are proposed to facilitate the subsequent comparative analyses.

Chapters 5 to 6 present the analyses and results of this research. Chapter 5 reports the findings across the two disciplines, BM and EL. The phrases of 'I', 'We', and their verbs
collocates are observed and analysed quantitatively and qualitatively. The similarities and differences between the two disciplines are also discussed. It is found that there are more epistemic differences than pragmatic function differences of the
FPPs' phrases between BM and EL. Chapter 6 reports the comparison between the two academic levels, UG and PG. Comparatively, the texts of PG students present fewer instances of
the FPPs. Some of the phrases and their discourse functions
differ between the two levels as well.

Chapter 7 summarises the major findings of the study.
Choices between the FPPs and impersonal expressions, and
choices between 'I' and 'We' in these students' academic texts
are explored. A set of principles that influence the discussed
choices is proposed. Writer identities that are presented by the
phrases including the two FPPs are also discussed in this chapter. Chapter 8 concludes this thesis by discussing the implications and applications of this research. The study suggests that
teachers must be sensitive to the self-representation issue in
academic discourse. Strategic introduction in EAP classrooms
would raise the students' awareness of the uses of the FPPs in
their academic discourse. The introduction should include the

phraseology of 'I' and 'We', the discourse functions of these phrases, the writer identities reflected by the FPPs and the principles that influence the students' choice of the FPPs in their academic writing practice.

CHAPTER 2
LITERATURE REVIEW

2.1 Introduction

This chapter reviews previous studies on learner corpus research, phraseology, the first person pronouns (FPPs) in English for Academic Purposes(EAP), verbs and verb classification, the impact of both disciplinary difference and academic level difference in EAP. By reviewing these issues of language research, I shall attempt to underpin this corpus based study on the phraseology and pragmatic functions of the FPPs, 'I' and 'We' in EFL students' written academic texts. This chapter is organised as follows. After this introductory part, Section 2 discusses Computer Learner Corpora(CLC) and phraseology. This is to evaluate how a corpus linguistic approach facilitates the understanding of the learners' language and their multi-word expressions. In Section 3, the literature relating to two areas, previous research on personal pronouns and the study of verbs and the categorisation of the verbs in academic discourse, is reviewed. The discussion of FPPs focuses on the use of FPPs in the field of EAP. The study of the categorisation of the verbs introduces both semantic and functional classes of verbs in academic discourse. Section 4 synthesises the literature on the impact of disciplinary and level differences in academic discourse. Section 5 reviews the problematic employments of the FPPs and the phraseology in the EAP context, in particular, texts written by novice writers. Section 6 concludes the previously reviewed topics in this chapter and illustrates the gap between previous research and this study.

2.2 Learner corpora and phrases

This section reviews studies related to Computer Learner Corpora and phrases. These two research areas are closely related as the use of language corpora facilitates language description and makes the research on phraseology easier than the traditional manual examination of a large amount of material (Sinclair 1991, 2008; Hunston 2002, Hunston & Francis 2000).

2.2.1 Learner corpora

Learner corpora came into being with the development of Corpus Linguistics(CL). Researchers of CL primarily used this technique to collect and explore English texts that are produced by native speakers only. With the development and influence of CL, scholars in applied linguistics have used a corpus to study learners' languages, for instance, English as Second/Foreign Language (SL/FL), French as a Second/Foreign language. Thus, this subsection starts with a brief introduction of CL, then moves on to a more detailed review of the studies on Computer Learner Corpora.

2.2.1.1 Corpus linguistics

Corpus linguistics became possible with the development of

computer science. A corpus is defined as "a collection of pieces of language text in electronic form, selected according to external criteria to represent, as far as possible, a language or language variety as a source of data for linguistic research" (Sinclair, 2005:16). Corpus linguists collect a large amount of language samples and analyse them by computer programs that are specially designed for language exploration. The fact that CL is of importance or brings a new perspective of looking at languages is because before it came to the forefront,

> ... linguistics has been formed and shaped on inadequate evidence and in a famous phrase 'degenerate data'. There has been a distinct shortage of information and evidence available to linguists, and this gives rise to a particular balance between speculation and fact in the way in which we talk about our subject. In linguistics up till now we have been relying very heavily on speculation(Sinclair 2004:9).

With the assistance of language corpus and corpus processing tools, language researchers are now able to conduct their research and study languages more effectively. They are able to do so not only with a large number of available and representative samples but also with the benefit of more trustworthy statistics(Biber et al. 1998; Hunston 2002; Sinclair 2004; Biber 2009; McEnery & Hardie 2012).

Corpus Linguistics is an approach to studying or exploring language based on the information extracted from corpus. Hunston(2002:3) explains this point:

> If a corpus represents, very roughly and partially, a speaker's experience of language, the access software

re-orders that experience so that it can be examined in ways that are usually impossible. A corpus does not contain new information about language, but the software offers us a new perspective on the familiar. Most readily available software packages process data from a corpus in three ways: showing frequency, phraseology and collocation.

This definition of corpus may be better understood in light of the following three aspects: Firstly, corpus is only useful with corpus accessible software. Secondly, corpus software could assist us to look at language from a different perspective that was once difficult with manual calculation or mere observation before the advent of the computer. Thirdly, neither the corpus nor the corpus software is able to provide new information. It is the linguists who observe the data and examine the text who are in a position to offer an interpretation of the results.

2.2.1.2　Computer Learner Corpora

Since the late 1980s, informed by corpus linguistics studies on native speakers' language, researchers have been using Computer Learner Corpora(CLC) to explore the language of learners of various second languages(SL) or foreign languages (FL). In order to explore SL/FL that are produced by learners, to understand the mechanism of SL/FL acquisition, and to help improve EL/FL learning and teaching, CLC collects non-native speakers' language for SL/FL studies with unprecedented large databases, computerised query tools and is also able to analyse quantitative data.

The definition of Computer Learner Corpora

According to Hunston(2002:15), a learner corpus is,

A collection of texts—essays, for example—produced by learners of a language. The purpose of this corpus is to identify in what respects learners differ from each other and from the language of native speakers, for which a comparable corpus of native-speaker texts is required.

Adding more information, including the collection criteria and purpose of CLC, Granger(2007:45) defines CLC as "... electronic collections of authentic FL/SL textual data assembled according to explicit design criteria for a particular SLA/FLT purpose. They are encoded in a standardized and homogeneous way and documented as to their origin and provenance".

Granger(2007) stresses the principles of the compilation of CLC. She provides three criteria on the compilation of CLC: Firstly, a CLC should present **Authenticity**. It should collect naturally occurring language as its evidence to examine linguistic features. The data is authentic language produced by language learners instead of data obtained from a controlled experimental environment or elicitation-oriented tasks. Secondly, CLC should maintain **Homogeneity**. It means that a learner corpus should be collected according to a set of explicit criteria which should be adhered to strictly without fail to maintain integrity. This is fundamentally because a wide range of variable factors may affect the investigation of learner language. Therefore, these variables such as mother tongue, learning context, time exposure to the target language, proficiency level and data collection setting should be taken into consideration when building the corpus. Furthermore, though not explicitly stated by Granger, a homogeneous corpus would facilitate comparative studies within corpus or across corpora based on these clearly defined criteria. Thirdly, Granger stresses the goal of CLC. It is built purposefully for **SLA/FLA language exploration**. Compared with many large multi-purpose native language corpora(e.g. Bank of English, British National Corpus, Brown family corpora et al.), a learner corpus is highly purposive. It is assembled for second/foreign language acquisition research, which sets its goal of revealing SL/FL learning mechanisms and making a contribution to SL/FL learning and teaching in practice. However, the benefits of CLC are not limited to the exploration of cognitive mechanism of SLA but also a detailed description of the learners' language. The corpus of this study is made up with authentic texts written by EFL Chinese learners. CEAL-CAWE corpus for this study is homogeneous as all the student writers are from China. The collected texts are all accepted graduation dissertations from two academic levels, undergraduate and postgraduate taught. And these academic texts are of two disciplines, Business and Management, and English Literature. In Chapter 3, I shall show in detail, how my corpus collection meets these criteria that Granger suggests.

Using Computer Learner Corpora in ESL/EFL language research

At the early stages of CLC research, such research mainly facilitated two aspects pertaining to the exploration of learner language. One is error analysis and the other is contrastive interlanguage analysis(e.g. Granger 2003, 1994, 1998, 2007; Gui & Yang 2002; Kaszubski 1998). Both research methods draw on a native speaker corpus, for example, the Corpus of Contemporary American English(COCA) and the British Academic Written English Corpus(BAWE), as a reference corpus to investigate the inter-language proximity to the native language or what is commonly described as the 'norm'. This comparison is used to identify what is known as over- and underuse. If a feature occurs more frequently in the learner corpus than the reference native speaker corpus, it is said to be overused, and when a feature is less frequent in the learner corpus than in the native speaker corpus, this is referred to as underuse. For example, Chen and Baker (2010) found that L2 students overused the expression *all over the world* in their academic texts, whereas native academic writers rarely used the phrase. On the other hand, when compared with expert writers, the same learner corpus shows a considerable underuse of referential expressions, such as *in the context of*.

In contrast to these studies, there is an increasing number of studies that compare one group of learners with another, in particular, a less developed group of learners with a more advanced group of learners(cf. e.g. Bestgen and Granger 2014; Chau 2015; Vyatkina and Cunningham 2015). Therefore, CLC can also be used to compare different varieties of language. The investigation of inter-language features looks at learner's language in its own right. Meunier(2015:396) states that "learner corpora are solid and reliable data sources to trace learners' proficiency development in a L2" after discussing some core issues and representative studies on longitudinal language development of L2 learners. In general, comparing learners with other learners usually means comparing learners of differing language proficiencies or learners from different language backgrounds in order to evaluate the influence of their first language on their interlanguage. For example, a different language background is one variable of the many variables of the International Corpus of Learner English. In fact, learners' language from 11 different ESL/EFL background were collected in this corpus(Granger 2003).

However, it is also possible to compare learners of different disciplines and learners at different levels of academic achievement. This is the core issue to be explored in this thesis. Treating learner's language as self-contained avoids the assumptions based on native-speaker usage, a situation which is quite common in some of the other learner corpus based research. The advantage of comparing learners with other learners could be twofold. Firstly, comparing the learners' academic texts drawn from different disciplines allows us to focus on the epistemic differences between those two disciplines, without the complicating factor of differing educational backgrounds or the L1/L2 difference. Secondly, comparing learners' language of different academic levels can inform us what the learners' next attainable proficiency goal is. For the undergraduate student, what is achievable in terms of language proficiency might be better represented by the language of the comparable postgraduate student than by the native speaker. Moreover, this comparison between learners of different proficiency levels has the potential to tell us more about inter-language development. This information is not available from a comparison between the learners and the native speakers. Therefore, instead of comparing SL/FL learners' texts with native speakers' discourse, this research explores the disciplinary difference and academic level differences exhibited in the dissertations written by Chinese EFL learners.

2.2.2 Phrases

Phrases have been investigated under many different names in the field of linguistics. For example, they have been described as idiom(Liu, 2003), formulaic expression(Nattinger & DeCarrico, 1992), lexical bundle(Biber et al., 2004), formulaic sequence(Wray 2002; Erman and Warren 2000), phrase (Martinez & Schmitt, 2010), and formula(Vlach and Ellis, 2010). There is no consensus in relation to having an agreed name of these multi-word expressions, nor is there an agreement regarding the definition of what a phrase is. Wray(2002), for example, emphasises the prefabricated nature of the phrase, which is psycholinguistic in its definition. Biber et al. (2004), Biber and Barbieri(2007) and Gries(2008) use statistical tests to identify phrases or lexical bundles. In her book, *Corpora in Applied Linguistics*, Hunston(2002:138) provides the applied aspect of phraseology, which is the essence of what is known as "preference sequencing". As stated by Gries(ibid), phraseology is a very broad category.

In terms of collocation, one of the most frequent quotations in corpus linguistics is probably "[y]ou shall know a word by the company it keeps" by Firth(1957:11). This statement relating to collocation is often cited by corpus linguists given that with the assistance of computer technology, the calculation of collocation in a large dataset is much easier and statistically more reliable than it is with mere manual observation. And it is now well acknowledged that "collocations are indispensable elements with which our utterances are very largely made"(Kjellmer, 1987:140). According to Sinclair, collocation is(1991:170), "the occurrence of two or more words within a short space of each other in a text". In this definition, Sinclair points out the syntagmatic feature of a collocation; namely that it has no less than two words and that they should co-occur within a limited span in a text. Further, in corpus linguistics, the statistical aspect of collocation is stressed, that the co-occurrence has to be statistically frequent(Handl 2008; Hunston 2002; Sinclair 1991).

Although there is no standard frequency and the criteria of collocation could vary between researchers(cf. Granger & Bestgen 2014; Gries 2013; Handl 2008), collocation may be regarded as one subcategory of phrase. This is due to the fact that both collocation and phrase have to have no less than two words, with both of them needing to be frequently used in a corpus. Furthermore, there is also a limited span of these co-occurrences. All factors considered, in this research, collocation refers to those observable frequent co-occurrences being an integral component part of phrases. I will come back to this issue again shortly.

As mentioned, there is no agreed definition or name in relation to phraseology in the field of linguistics. Different scholars focus on different kinds of phrases and different aspects of phraseologism. However, there is general consensus that the phrase is pervasive in the English language. It is demonstrated by some studies that the percentage of multi-word units in running texts range from 30% in the form of lexical bundles in the conversation corpus(Biber et al. 1999) to 58.6% in the form of formulaic sequences in a spoken discourse data base(Erman & Warren 2000). In a nutshell, formulaic expressions constitute a significant portion of English discourse(Sinclair 1991; Nattinger & DeCarrico 1992; Biber et al. 1999; Leech 2000; Hunston 2002; Ellis et al. 2008). These pre-fabricated phrases are important to ESL/EFL learners as well as to native speakers. ESL and EFL learners need to be sensitive to the native speakers' preferences for certain sequences of words over others(Wray 2000). This is due to even the advanced learners of second language having great difficulty with native-like collocation and idiomaticity, and many of the grammatical sentences composed by these learners sound unnatural, which makes it difficult for native speakers to process(Granger 1998; Howarth 1998; Ellis et al. 2008; Millar 2011).

In summation, there is no agreed definition of what phraseology is in the field of linguistics. In fact, it is probably next to impossible to have one specific definition in the linguistic arena due to the different aims and purposes of various types of research. I would argue, however, that in the field of applied linguistics, all these forms of multi-word units can be recognised as phrases with specific meanings and pragmatic functions as mentioned above. These could therefore help ESL/EFL learners in their academic writing classrooms and practices. It is noted that there is a considerable variation in the way the definition of phrase is interpreted in corpus linguistics. The study of phraseology incorporates more than what I have here in this study, and in some cases, it defines phrases somewhat differently from how I interpret them for the purposes of my study. To some extent, this is similar to what others have said, and concurrently, it is also at odds with other scholars' definitions of what a phrase is. A broad definition that incorporates every form of multi-word units into phrases would be helpful and less confusing to EFL novices provided that they are used in the preferred sequences and connote unit meaning in text. It therefore saves the students from the trouble of having to distinguish the different terms and ambiguous boundaries of phraseologism.

The technique of corpus linguistics makes the exploration of phraseology easier. Prior to corpus linguistics being used as a mainstream research, it was time-consuming to identify phrases manually, especially when it came to the filtering of phrases with open slot(s). One of the most important functions of corpus linguistics is that the pattern of co-occurrence could now be identified in a large dataset with the help of corpus-based tools. In the study of corpus linguistics, scholars have proposed a criterion for determining the extraction of phrases including those derived from statistical tests. For example, t-test, mutual information, log-likelihood, all of which help to determine if a sequence is a phrase or not(cf. for example, Gries 2008; Ellis et al. 2008; Ackermann & Chen 2013). Thus, corpus linguistics is "at least is currently the single most frequently used method employed in the study of phraseology"(Gries 2008: 15). As proposed by Sinclair(2004: 10) "we should strive to be open to the patterns observable in language in quantity as we now have it".

In this study, one of the aims is therefore to critically examine the phraseology of the FPPs and the verbs collocating with them in the EFL students' academic texts. In order to do so, as previously discussed, I decided to include all the phrases over a certain threshold and to connote their unit meaning in the student's text as a phrase. I focussed particularly on the use of 'I' and 'We' in the context of phraseology. I set a pre-determined threshold in relation to the frequency, span and range of the extracted phrases. In other words, in this research I examined simple collocation as well as those recurring more specific phrases. Specifically, I looked at the following phrases:

- two-word phrases of *I/We* + *frequently occurring verbs* (*e.g. I worked, I/we found*);
- *I/we* + *verb class* which is also a two-word phrase, but one of the words is variable (e.g. *believe* and *think* of mental verbs, see Chapter 4);
- multi-word phrases, for example, fixed expression *as we all know*;
- more specific instances of the verb phrases, for example, *I/we* + *can, could* + *verb* (e.g. *we can/could see*);
- phrasal pattern *I/We* + *present perfect of the Textual organising verbs*.

The object of this study is of phrases interpreted as being one of the above-mentioned five things. Chapter 3 elaborates on the methodology issues relating to phrase extraction in this study, including the extraction of the two FPPs, 'I' and 'We' and the verbs collocating with them.

Two important issues that are directly related to each other are learner corpora and phrases, and these have been discussed in this part of the thesis. The next section, Section 3 reviews another two language areas related to this research, namely, previous studies on the use of the FPPs and the categorisation of English verbs.

2.3   FPPs and verbs in academic writing

This research brings the two classes of words, the FPP and the verb together and views them as collocates in the context of the academic text. By doing so, this study aims to add to our knowledge about the phraseology of 'I' and 'We', and to explore the pedagogical implications to EFL academic writing practice.

2.3.1   First person pronouns

There was a time when academic discourse was considered as monologic. This is no longer considered to be the case (Swales 1990; Ivanič 1998; Tang & John 1999; Hyland 2002, 2004, 2005, 2010b, 2015, 2017; Li & Ye 2023). Studies on academic discourse have shown that authors of academic discourse interact with their expected readers to achieve the interpersonal effects of seeking solidarity, hedging, declaring responsibility, claiming authority, and contributing to their own academic community(e.g. Çandarlı et al. 2015; Harwood 2005a, 2005b, 2006, 2007; Hyland 2002; 2005; Thompson & Ye 1991). The interaction between writer and reader may be explored by the examination of metadiscourse expressions, report structure, adjectives and self-representation in academic discourse (e. g. Crismore et al. 1993; Hyland 2005; Charles 2004, 2006). This section discusses previous research carried out on one of the approaches, namely, self-representation in academic discourse. This topic will be reviewed in light of the self-representation strategies, pragmatic functions of self-representation, and writer identity. The next subsection, Section 2.3.1.1 reviews the importance of self-mention strategy, particularly through the usage of FPPs in academic discourse. Sections 2.3.1.2 and 2.3.1. 3 are on two perspectives that are mostly investigated in the area of self-mention, i.e. pragmatic function and writer identity.

2.3.1.1 Self-representation in academic text

The strategic use of the FPPs to claim the writer's authority has been considered as a key element of successful academic writing(Hyland 2002). In a diachronic study, it is found that the usage of 'I' and 'We' in published journal articles has increased by 45% overall in four different disciplines at three periods during the course of the last 50 years, in 1965, 1985, and 2015(Hyland & Jiang, 2017). This growing usage of the FPPs shows an increasing emphasis on writer-reader interactivity in academic texts. By analysing how a writer presents himself/herself in academic discourse through the FPPs, the writer-reader interaction may be seen from the manner in which the writer organises reader-friendly discourse to achieve a good reading experience. It may also be seen from how a writer seeks alignment in the text with the intended readership and how a writer claims commitment and authority to establish his/her membership of an academic community. Kuo(1999:123) argues that,

> "the choice of a certain personal pronoun for a given context, or even the presence or non-presence of a personal pronoun in journal articles, and particularly in scientific journal articles, can often reveal how writers view themselves, their relationship with readers, and their relationship with the discourse

community they belong to".

Due to the different genres and purposes of academic texts, readers' identities vary correspondingly. For example, research articles are viewed by the editors of the submitted journals, reviewers, and if published, by peer scholars of a similar or related disciplinary community. The readers of research reports or theses in universities are viewed as teachers or supervisors. Therefore, the interaction between a writer and a reader could be multi-faceted as between a writer and a reader who is a reviewer or editor. It could be also between a writer and his/her peers, a writer and their instructors, or indeed between a writer and the academic community in which he/she belongs to or wants to be acknowledged in. During the writing process, the writers are aware of who their potential readers are and write accordingly. To reveal the complexity of the relationship between the writer and the readership through the exploration of FPPs in academic discourse, the studies mainly focus on two aspects: pragmatic functions (see, for example, Kuo 1999; Hyland 2001, 2002; Harwood 2005; Fløttum 2006a, 2006b), and writer identity (see, for example, Ivanič 1998; Ivanič & Camps 2001; Tang & John 1999; Hyland 2001, 2002, 2004, 2005; Harwood 2005; John 2005).

2.3.1.2 Pragmatic functions of 'I' and 'We' in academic writing

The definition of discourse function of personal pronoun adopted in this study is "the function that a sentence containing a personal pronoun performs the immediate discourse context of a journal article. It reflects the specific communicative purpose of writers-researchers in a certain part of a journal article"

(Kuo, 1999: 130). The discourse function of FPPs has been investigated in different academic genres. For example, Kuo (1999) and Harwood(2005) examined the functions of FPPs in published research articles; Hyland(2002) and John(2005) discussed the discourse function of FPPs in ESL learners' academic texts; and Hyland(2010) investigated the use of the FPPs in the published research articles, monographs and book chapters written by two leading scholars of applied linguistics, John Swales and Debbie Cameron. Of the many pragmatic functions of phrases including the FPPs in academic discourse, the recognised functions include, for example, organising discourse(e.g. *we have discussed*), hedging(e.g. *Personally*, *I think*), alignment seeking (e. g. *as we can see*) (Harwood 2005a, 2005b, 2007; Hyland 2001, 2002; Kuo 1999; Fetzer 2014). In the wider context, however, 'I' and 'We' may be seen to have different functions, such as self-promotion, for example, "[t]o provide structure for the empirical work, I developed a simple three-region model characterised by migration and transport costs.(ECON 8)"(cited in Harwood 2005:1224), and authority claiming(see, for example, "... *we believe that LEW satisfies better the important criterion of comprehensibility*" in Table 1). The following review covers three articles on discourse functions of 'I' and 'We' in academic discourse. One is conducted by Kuo(1999), one by Hyland(2002), and the last, by Harwood (2007). Each of them focuses on different material, aspects of writer-reader interaction, and research methods which provides guidelines from different angles of pragmatic categorisation for this study. Kuo (1999) identifies discourse functions in research articles of 3 different disciplines. However, the disciplinary difference is not investigated in this study. Hyland(2002) compares the ESL students' academic reports with experts' research articles, complementing with interviews. Harwood(2007) does a qualitative study by interviewing expert research article writers. The interviewees were asked to reflect on their own uses of the FPPs in their own published articles and evaluate the instances of 'I' and 'We' in their peers' published academic papers.

Kuo(1999) conducted an empirical study to explore the use of the personal pronouns from three perspectives, the writers' own perception of their roles in research, their relationship with readership and the academic community they belong to.

Material: a corpus of 36 scientific journal articles from 3 arbitrarily selected disciplines: Computer Science, Electronic Engineering, and Physics.

Methodology: in this study, the pragmatic functions of 258 instances of 'We', 23 'us' and 74 'our' are analysed. The discourse functions of the instances of the plural FPPs are assigned by qualitative analysis of the actual occurrences in the sample texts(Kou 1999:123).

Findings of pragmatic functions: 12 discourse functions of the plural FPPs, 'We', 'us', and 'our' are generalised by Kuo in this study. Among these functions, one function, that of *seeking agreement or cooperation*, is realised only by using 'us'. Table 2.1 lists all the functions and the examples given by Kuo in his article. The ultimate goal of using personal pronouns in journal articles, as stated by Kuo(1999:136) at the end of his paper, is "to emphasise their(*journal article writers*, interpretation mine) personal contributions to their fields of research and how to seek cooperation and stress solidarity with expected readers and their disciplines".

The discourse functions of the FPPs proposed by Kuo offer a new perspective to look at the relationships between the writer, reader and academic community of the academic texts. One argument made in this paper is that "... the communicative purpose of scientists ... can be revealed by the analysis of specific lexico-grammatical forms such as personal pronouns and their discourse function"(Kuo 1999:136). Drawing on this point, in my study I consider the dissertations as one genre of academic discourse and the communicative purposes of 'I' and 'We' are consequently explored in that light.

Table 2.1   Discourse function of plural FPPs 'We', 'us',
and 'our' proposed by Kuo(1999)

	Discourse Functions	Example(all cited in Kuo 1999:131—132)
1	Explaining what was done	*We* consider two specific instantiations of the generic problem, those of Texture segmentation and Gestalt grouping. (Reed & Wechsler, 1990:1)
2	Proposing a theory, approach, etc.	... *we* propose to use a statistical quality control procedure.(Constant et al., 1990:296)
3	Stating a goal or purpose	In this paper, *we* are concerned with the carrier collection necessary to support stimulated emission in ultrathin quantum wells.(Kolbas et al., 1990:25)
4	Showing results or findings	*We* found no correlation of failures between bonded and unbonded lasers, thus excluding the possibility of bonding stress. (Gfeller& Webb, 1990:15)
5	Justifying a proposition	Since *we* also consider negative cues, *we* use Mode to indicate whether a cue is positive or negative.(Constant et al., 1990:297).
6	Hedging a proposition or claim	*We* assume that the mistake in copying never gets too big ...(Shvaytser, 190:463).

continued

	Discourse Functions	Example(all cited in Kuo 1999:131—132)
7	Assuming shared knowledge, goals, beliefs, etc.	Let *us* consider a set of four cues ..., namely, *we* easily see that C1, C2 and C3 are in the same thread t1.(Constant et al., 1990:301)
8	Seeking agreement or cooperation	In this work, let *us* restrict ourselves to three-dimensional distributions of deposited ions only. (Fink et al., 1990:959).
9	Showing commitment or contribution to research	Finally, *we* believe that LEW satisfies better the important criterion of comprehensibility ... (Constant et al., 1990:306)
10	Comparing approaches, viewpoints, etc.	... this topic has been addressed for image processing applications by Wilson and Granlund [14]. *We* next address this issue from an analytical viewpoint, ...(Reed & Wechsler, 1990:4)
11	Giving a reason or indicating necessity	(31) *We* have to modify them instead, according to the peculiarity that ...(Fink et al., 1990: 959)
12	Expressing wish or expectation	... *we* wish to select a window that is of a specified size ...(Reed & Wechsler, 1990:6)

As stated in Kuo's article, the papers used for his research were collected arbitrarily from three different disciplines. The disciplinary difference is not the concern of Kuo's research. The disciplines were randomly chosen and there is no detailed account of disciplinary differences in his paper. However, it may be seen from the statistics presented in the article, that the normalised frequency of per million words of the investigated personal pronouns in the three disciplines presents differences in distribution. The specific figures are 1,033,858 and 677 in this study. This divergence in the distribution of the personal pronouns is typical of the predictable uneven spread of the different pragmatic functions associated with each discipline. In other words, the proposed discourse functions may or may not be distributed consistently in the three investigated disciplines, Computer Science, Electronic Engineering, and Physics.

It is clear that the 12 discourse functions proposed in Kuo's article are quite specific and serve the aim of facilitating theoretical discussion in relation to the usage of the FPPs in scientific articles. Nevertheless, some of these functions may be assembled into more general categories. For example, "explaining what was done", "proposing a theory, approach" and "showing results or findings" are all indicative of research procedures. "Showing commitment or contribution to research" and "giving a reason or indicating necessity" are both arguments for ownership or authority of the propositions. From a pedagogical viewpoint, more general categories with additional subcategories may benefit both teachers and students of academic writing alike. This point is elaborated further at the end of Section 3.

Furthermore, two briefly mentioned, yet very important issues of using the first personal pronoun in Kuo's study are worthy of further exploration. Firstly, in all of the 36 research articles, no instance of 'I' was found in Kuo's corpus. The personal pronoun with the most occurrences is 'We' across the three disciplines. Kuo also found in this study that 3 single-authored articles use 'We' to refer to the writer himself/herself. Kuo furnishes a very brief explanation relating to this replacement of using 'We' instead of 'I'. He suggests that it is the writers' "intention to reduce personal attributions" (1999: 125). No further discussion or analysis on this issue is put forward in the rest of the paper. Secondly, when discussing the textual function of *hedging*, Kuo mentioned that

'We' co-occurs with verbs like *suspect* or *assume* in order to avoid being too assertive. These two issues raise two questions: (1) Is there a choice between the two FPPs themselves, 'I' or 'We' in academic text? (2) What are those verbs that co-occur frequently with the FPPs in academic discourse other than *we suspect* and *we assume*? And what other functions of the co-occurrences of 'I', 'We' and the verbs may be realised in academic discourse?

Most of Hyland's (2001; 2002; 2004; 2005; 2012; 2015) studies at the beginning of 21st century are on writer identity, visibility and authority of academic discourse. Hyland (2002) is chosen to be under discussion here because Hyland categorises 5 discourse functions of self-mention based on the analysis of the FPPs 'I', 'me', 'my', 'we', 'us', and 'our' across 8 disciplines. Additionally, the sample texts in his corpus are written by undergraduate ESL students in Hong Kong. The students of Hyland's study and my study share the same Chinese culture. Therefore, this work of Hyland's(2002) is of reference value.

Material: a 630,100 words corpus of 64 project reports written by final year ESL Hong Kong undergraduates. The reports were from 8 disciplines: Biology, Mechanical Engineering, Information Systems, Business Studies, TESL, Economics, Public Administration, and Social Science. Though Hyland does not mention the general differences between the 8 disciplines, he presents the divergence between the hard-pure (Biology), the hard-applied (Mechanical Engineering, Information Systems), the soft-pure (Social Science) and the soft-applied disciplines (Business Studies, TESL, Economics and Public Administration).

Methodology: the quantitative information is drawn by the extraction of the FPPs by corpus software. The categorisation of these FPPs is determined by the manual examination within the context of the texts. What should be noted is that, in this study, Hyland excludes the instances in which the FPPs are used for organisation of text. Only those occurrences in which the writers explicitly present themselves in their projects reports are investigated in this study.

Findings of pragmatic functions: Differing from Kuo's (1999) study, in which no instance of 'I' was found, Hyland found that the singular FPP 'I' is the most common self-representation device in these ESL students' project reports. However, plural forms of the FPPs are commonly used even in single-authored texts to refer to the writer himself/herself. Hyland broadly discusses the quantitative disciplinary differences between the 8 disciplines, stating that student writers use fewer self-mention devices than more experienced journal article authors. At the same time, those from soft disciplines use more instances of the FPPs than those from hard disciplines. He then focuses on the analysis of the 5 discourse functions across the whole corpus. Five functions are proposed in Hyland's (2002) paper and the following table, Table 2.2 illustrates those five functions.

The discussion on discourse functions is only one section in

Hyland(2002). Hyland's categorisation of the pragmatic functions of the FPPs in this paper is only partial because he mainly discusses the visibility and authority that the ESL learners present by the utilisation of self-mention FPPs in their academic writing. His study amalgamates the strength or the degree of assertiveness shaped by the FPPs with the discourse functions. Particularly, the choices of using the FPPs in these writers' project reports, are of different threatening levels. *Expressing self-benefits* is the least face-threatening and unique in the students reports only and *Stating results/claim* as the most face-threatening. The level of increase of the responsibility and commitment to the proposition is analysed by comparing the pragmatic uses of the FPPs in the students' reports with those in published journal articles. The reasons for choosing or not choosing the FPPs are also provided in his study.

In Hyland's examples, there are a few common verbs that collocate with 'I' and 'We', for instance, the verbs *say, interview, use, collect, examine*, and *think*. However, Hyland does not discuss the meaning and the function of these verbs that collocate with the FPPs. It would be interesting to explore whether the collocation of the verbs and the FPPs perform any discourse functions in ESL/EFL learners' academic discourse. For instance, what are the frequently used verbs that co-occur with 'I' and 'We'? What discourse functions are they used for? Are there any rules or principles relating to the choice of FPPs and the verbs that collocate with them in the students' academic discourses? These are the focus areas of my study.

Table 2.2   Discourse functions of FPPs 'I', 'me', 'my', 'We', 'us', and 'our' proposed by Hyland(2002)

	Discourse functions	Examples(all cited from Hyland 2002:1091—1112)
1	Stating a goal/purpose	*We* are interested in the strategy of Coca-Cola when it started to open the China market.(PR: Bus)
2	Explaining a procedure	*I* have interviewed 10 teachers, there were 10 teachers from different primary and secondary schools in Hong Kong.(PR: TESL)
3	Stating results/claims	Likewise, *I* have offered evidence that some critical thinking practices may marginalise sub-cultural groups, such as women, within U.S. society itself. (RA: AL)
4	Expressing self-benefits	After finishing the project, *I* found that Information System(IS) techniques can be applied to the real world. This helps *me* to be an IS professional in the future career.(PR:IS)
5	Elaborating an argument	*I* think it works something like this: suppose we start with a new, just-assembled ship S.(RA: Phil)

The paper authored by Harwood(2007) is one of the studies that did not use corpus tools as his research methodology. A brief recount of this research is as follows.

Material: Five published journal articles of the Political Science discipline written by five different scholars.

Methodology: This paper takes a qualitative approach of interviewing 5 experienced journal article writers. The participants were asked to comment on the instances of two FPPs, 'I' and 'We' in their own published articles and of those instances in the articles written by their colleagues. Differing from the analyses of the instances of the FPPs by looking at the context, in which researchers are only able to look at the concordances and decide the discourse functions of the FPPs, this qualitative study provides another perspective from the authors themselves as well as their peers on how 'I' and 'We' are used in academic texts.

Table 2.3   Discourse functions of plural FPPs 'I'
and 'We' proposed(adapted from Harwood 2007)

Discourse function	Examples(all cited from Hyland 2007:27—54)
1	Make the readership feel included and involved in the writers' argument (including the reader)	*We* can also assess the impact. (POL5)
2	Make the text more accessible (helping the reader)	*I* find it helpful to present the relevant information.(POL4)
3	Convey a tentative tone and hedge writers' claims(hedging an argument; tentativeness, judgement, authorial responsibility)	This conceptual alignment is, *I* think, the reason why ...(POL4)
4	Explicate the writers' logic or method regarding their arguments or procedures	*I* accordingly do not de-trend the various independent variable measures.(POL3)
5	Signal writers intentions and arguments	*we* have include, *we* turn again (POL2)
6	Indicate the contribution and newsworthiness of the research	It is this claim about the logic of political choice that *I* wish to concentrate on(POL4)
7	Allow the writer to inject a persona tenor into the text	NA

Findings of the pragmatic functions: Seven discourse functions are identified in this paper. Harwood pays more attention to the interactivity between the writer and the readers when he proposes these textual effects. This perspective is different from the two studies discussed above, which focus on discourse function of the instances of 'I' and 'We' from the writer's perspective. Table 2.3 illustrates the discourse functions of 'I' and 'We' in Harwood's study.

As the methodology is different from other studies on personal pronouns in academic discourse, this paper is chosen to provide another viewpoint on the functions of the FPPs in academic discourse. What is interesting to note is the acknowledgment by the participants that the choice of using the person pronouns in the investigated journal articles could be solely down to personal rhetorical choice. In other words, the use of the two FPPs could be due primarily to the intention of adding a personal tenor in the discourse.

In fact, in another paper of Harwood(2005a), which is based on corpus data, he discusses the discourse functions of the FPPs, particularly the inclusive and exclusive usages of 'We' in journal articles in four different disciplines. Harwood (2005b: 365) argues that the personal pronouns in academic texts "can help to create a sense of newsworthiness and novelty about their prose". Seven discourse functions of the FPPs are proposed in that study. They are (1) *moving between inclusive and exclusive pronouns to construct novelty*; (2) *describing disciplinary practice*; (3) *critiquing disciplinary practice*; (4) *elaborating an argument either with which the community would concur* or *out of politeness for helping the readers to interpret*; (5) *elaborating an argument by asking questions*; (6) *methodological description*; and (7) *discourse guide*.

Comparing the two studies(Harwood 2005b, 2007), there is fuzziness and overlap in relation to the pragmatic functions within each of the categorisation and also between the functional categorisations within the two studies. For example, in Harwood(2007), *make the text more accessible* and *explicate the writers' logic or method regarding their intentions or procedures* are both assisting readers to comprehend and digest the writers' description of methodologies, procedures, and arguments with less effort. In Harwood's(2005b) paper, *describing disciplinary practice*, *critiquing disciplinary practice* and *elabo-*

rating an argument with which the community would concur are all commenting on the disciplinary practices. The difference between the three is the degree of authoritativeness that each function implies. *Describing the disciplinary practices* may be neutral, whereas *elaborating and criticizing the disciplinary practices* may be construed as confrontational. The functions that overlap between the two papers can be seen, for instance, *signal writer's intentions or argument* in the 2007 paper and *discourse guide* in the 2005 article.

To summarise, the discourse functions of the FPPs in academic discourse are based on the writer's awareness of the disciplinary community and the intention to interact with the expected readers and the communal academic society at large. The most frequently used functions in academic writing may be summarised even though the discourse functions may go by different names whilst also falling under different categories in the range of articles under scrutiny. For instance, almost all the studies illustrate the discourse functions of *discourse organising*, *reporting or recounting research methodology*, *aligning with readership or disciplinary community*, and *claiming originality and authority*. As most of the research so far is based on expert journal articles or ESL academic texts, the questions that arise from these papers are as follows. Whether, and if so, to what extent are discourse functions presented in the EFL students' academic texts? Although almost all the reviewed research takes a quantitative method approach of looking at the discourse, the discourse functions however, are decided by the process of manual examination of the concordance lines. These not only vary in length but are also left unreported in most of the studies. This gives rise to the second question. Are we able to recognise the textual function by examining the occurrences of the FPPs and the verbs that collocate with them? In other words, can we identify the pragmatic functions of the phrases including the FPPs, in which the FPPs represent the novice writers and where the verbs denote the actions taken by these writers in the discourse?

2.3.1.3   Writer identity

Writer identity in various genres of academic discourse has been investigated recently. Hyland's(2001, 2002, 2004, 2005, 2010, 2012, 2015) studies are representative of such work. His investigation on writer identity includes texts written by expert writers (e.g. writers of journal articles, monographs, and scholars' homepages) and texts written by ESL learners(e.g. students' reports and thesis acknowledgment). The investigations carried out on writer identity are either about the process of writing, individuality, and conceptualisation(cf. Ivanič 1998), or link the concept of writer identity with specific words(cf. Hyland 2001, 2002, 2015), among which, the mostly investigated words are 'I' and 'We'(see, for example, Fløttum et al. 2006; Tang & John 1999). Hyland(2010:160) addresses the concept of writer identity in academic discourse as:

> *Who we are* and *who we might be* are built up
> through participation and linked to situations, to rela-
> tionships, and to the rhetorical strategies and posi-
> tions we adopt in engaging with others on a routine
> basis. This means that it is through our use of commu-
> nity discourses that we claim or resist membership of
> social groups to define who we are in relation to oth-

ers. Identity therefore helps characterize both what makes us similar to and different from each other and, for academics, it is how they achieve credibility as insiders and reputations as individuals.

Hyland(2012:22) defines identity as "a person's relationship to his or her social world, a joint, two-way production and language allows us to create and present a coherent self to others because it ties us into webs of common sense, interests, and shared meanings". In both interpretations, Hyland stresses the interpersonal aspects of identity: the relationship between writer and reader, and writer and his/her community. Even though Hyland discusses the authoritativeness, visibility, and the interaction between the writer and audience in many of his studies, he does not propose a set of categories of writer identity. After reading Hyland(2001, 2002), I have interpreted what he says as relating to the following writer identity categories: *student identity*, *discourse organiser*, *research procedure recounter*, *interpreter of results*, and *originator of ideas*(see Figure 2.2). However, Hyland himself does not do this. Where Hyland does propose categories, they are in relation to 'I' and 'We', which I have discussed under Hyland's(2002) categorisation of the discourse functions of 'I' and 'We' in academic discourse at length in the previous section. These discourse functions match the writer identities in L2 students' academic texts that are proposed in Figure 2 where the categorisations of Hyland's and Tang & John's are compared. Thus, in this section, the discussion of writer identity in Hyland's papers will not be repeated. I will focus on some other writer identity literature for now and come back to this textual function and writer identity correlation at the end of this section.

In the following, I mainly discuss four models of writer identity proposed by Ivanič(1998), Tang and John (1999), John(2005), and Fløttum et al.(2006) in the context of academic writing. These studies are discussed in detail because explicit categorisations of writer identities are proposed by these scholars in their works. The fundamental difference between the writer identities proposed by Ivanič(1998), Tang and John (1999), John(2005), and Fløttum et al.(2006) is that Ivanič's model is about the conceptualisation of writer identity in academic writing. More specifically, Ivanič(1998) focuses on the writer during the writer identity construction process instead of focusing on the actual discourse that the writer produces. In contrast, Tang and John(1999), John (2005), and Fløttum et al.(2006)use writer identity as tools for academic text analysis, to classify and quantify the occurrences of the FPPs in the texts for different language research purposes. Table 2.4 summarises the four different models of writer identity categorisations in academic writing as proposed in these four studies.

Based on a social-cultural constructive view, Ivanič(1998: 24) suggests three ways of "thinking about" writer identity. They are the *Autobiographical self*, *Discoursal self*, and *self as author*. The *autobiographical self* is the way the writer is shaped by his/her personal experience and social or life history. This identity is unique and dynamic to every writer because of its connection to the life-history of the writer. Ivanič(1998:24) argues that this form of writer identity is constantly changing as "a consequence of their developing life-story". The *Discoursal self* is the identity of the writer that comes across in a particular discourse. This identity is dependent on the discourse, in other words, the identity of the writer is formed by what the writer says or does in the text. The writer intends to impress the reader with this identity, and the reader remembers the writer as THE WRITER in discourse not the writer in real life, which is the autobiographical self. I would propose this identity could be considered analogous to an actor of a play or a movie in that the audience(*readers*) remember the character(*discoursal self*) that the actor(*the writer*) plays but not the actor himself/herself(*autobiographical self*). The *Self as author* identity, according to Ivanič(1998:26), is a "relative concept". Every writer in a certain sense is an author, however, it is the "authoritativeness" that determines the transformation from a writer to an author where he/she is 'voicing' his/her own "opinion, position or beliefs"(Ivanič, 1998:26). As such, this identity is considered as the most important form of identity in academic discourse.

Table 2.4　Writer identity proposed by Ivanič(1998), Tang and John(1999), John(2005), and Fløttum(2006) in academic writing

Ivanič(1998)	Tang and John(1999)	John(2005)		Fløttum(2006)
Autobiographical self	Representative	person		
Discoursal self	Guide	Academic	Organizer	Writer
	Architect			
Self as author	Recounter of research process		Scholar	Reseacher
	Opinion-holder			Arguer
	Originator			Evaluator

　　Ivanič's(1998) model of writer identity provides a theoretical basis for subsequent writer identity research. She provides a framework for conceptualising writer identity in academic writing genres. However, as mentioned, she focuses on the person in the academic writing process(cf. e.g. Harwood 2007) from a social constructivist viewpoint rather than investigating the text in which the writer identities are formed. She does not establish an explicit criterion to classify the writer identity in academic writing.

Tang and John(1999:23) propose a typology of six different writer identities by examining all the forms of the FPPs(*I*, *me*, *my*, *mine*, *we*, *us*, *our*, and *ours*) in academic writing" (see Figure 1 and Table 4). In discussing identity, they argue that "language does not serve merely as a tool to express a self that we already have, but serves as a resource of creating that self". By looking at the writer identities in samples, Tang and John also evaluate the degree of authorial power conveyed by these identities. The ideology of authorial power representation is developed from Ivanič's(1998:307) book, in which the continuum "from not using 'I' at all ... to using 'I' with verbs associated with cognitive acts". According to Tang and John, the least powerful authorial presence is *self as representative*. As stated in the paper, it reduces the writer identity into a non-entity. The most assertive and authorial identity is *self as originator*, where the writer expresses his/her own opinion and evaluation in the discourse. What should be noted is that no instance of the '*I*' *as recounter of research process* is found in Tang and John's data. In Table 4, I treat this identity as part of *self as author* as in Ivanič's classification and as the *Scholar* in John's. This is because the writer as *researcher* identity exemplifies the unique role that identity has in making decisions related to research procedures whilst adhering to disciplinary competence and authority(Hyland 2002; Harwood 2005b). The authorial strength of the six proposed writer identities is similar to the assertiveness or visibility of the writer identities in Hyland's (2002) study, see Figure 2.1 and Figure 2.2.

No, 'I'	'I' as representative	'I' as guide	'I' as architect	'I' as recounter of research process	'I' as opinionholder	'I' as originator

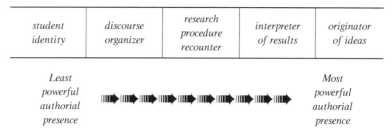

Least powerful authorial presence

Most powerful authorial presence

Figure 2.1   A typology of possible identities behind the FPP in academic writing as proposed by Tang and John(1999)

student identity	discourse organizer	research procedure recounter	interpreter of results	originator of ideas

Least powerful authorial presence

Most powerful authorial presence

Figure 2.2   A typology of possible identities behind the FPPs in academic writing proposed by Hyland(2001, 2002)

Based on a small-scale pilot study of the singular FPP 'I', and drawing on insight from Ivanič's(1998) categorisations of writer identity, John(2005) used the concept of *autobiographical self* but re-labelled it as the *self as person* identity, agreeing that a person's writing is shaped by his/her life experience. She also re-labelled Ivanič's *discoursal self* as the *self as academic* identity. Differing from Ivanič's categories to some extent,

John subdivided the academic category into *academic-organiser* and *academic-scholar*. She argues that the *academic-organiser* performs the metadiscoursal function of discourse organising, which in essence, is restricted to "rhetorical organization"(Hyland 2005:17) of a text. The *academic-scholar* identity is identified by what "the writers do in the text" by John(2005:123). Namely, in academic writing, five moves are considered as *academic-scholar* activities reviewing previous studies, niche creation, reporting methodology, and reporting and interpreting of research findings. Whenever a writer is carrying out one of these five activities, he/she is assigned the role of an *academic-scholar* in his/her study. John merged Ivanič's (1998) *discoursal self* and *self as author* into the *academic* category, and further divided it according to what a writer does in discourse into *academic-organiser* and *academic-scholar* groups.

Turning to the fourth model, Fløttum et al.'s(2006) categorisation of writer roles is proposed by identifying the verbs that collocate with the FPP, 'I'. According to Fløttum, the different types of writer identity may be categorised by the different groups of verbs that 'I' collocates with. To identify the writer's roles in published researcher articles, she examines 'I' and the main verbs that combine with it. Four writer roles are proposed according to the categorisation of the verbs, as illustrated in Table 2.5:

Table 2.5   Fløttum et al.'s(2006) categorization of writer roles

writer role	researcher	writer	arguer	evaluator
Type of verbs	research verbs	discourse verbs	argue verbs	various evaluating and emotional construction

continued

writer role	researcher	writer	arguer	evaluator
Example	*analyze*, *assume*, *find*, *study*, etc.	*illustrate*, *summarize*, *as begin by*, etc.	*argue*, *claim*, *dispute*, etc.	*be content to*, *be special about*, etc.

In summation, the categorisations of writer identity that are identified by Ivanič(1998), Tang and John(1999), John (2005) and Fløttum et al.(2006) focus on different aspects of the writer's self-representation in academic discourse. Ivanič (1998) considers the process of writer identity construction from a socio-cultural perspective. She discusses how writer identity is constructed through negotiation and instruction in the context of the higher educational environment. Concerning the methods of investigation, Ivanič(1998) does not provide a method of how to identify the writer identities she proposed. Tang and John(1999) and John(2005) examine indeterminate broader contexts to classify and quantify the writer identities because of the relatively smaller size of their corpora. Fløttum et al.(2006) use corpus tools to search for the verbs that collocate with the FPP 'I' and categorises the writers' roles according to the semantic groups of the verbs.

Similar to what Fløttum et al. carried out, I also looked at the collocations of 'I', 'We' and the verbs in the learner corpus complied for the purposes of this research. But in addition to this, I also examined multi-word units, i.e. phrases of 'I', 'We' and the verbs collocating with them with specific discourse functions. Further, like the previous researchers, each concordance line was read manually to ensure that the textual function classification is correct. It is found that in some cases, isolating the collocation of the FPPs and the verbs from the context could lead to an erroneous classification. This will be illustrated in more detail in the methodology section of this paper, Chapter 3.

As mentioned previously, when reporting the results of this research, I started with the process of identifying and classifying the discourse functions of the phrases of 'I' and 'We' and the verb collocates in my corpus. Whenever it comes to the discussion of writer identity, I match the two, the discourse functions with their corresponding writer identity. I propose that the writer's identity and the textual function are directly related. The connection between pragmatic function and writer identity may be seen from, for example, the function of *Stating a purpose* in Hyland(2002) and *Signalling intentions and argument* in Harwood(2007), could be the writer identity of a *Discoursal self* in Ivanič(1998), a *Discourse guide* in Tang and John(1999), and simply a *writer* in Fløttum(2006). It is noted in this study that the concept of writer identity involves more complex issues. For example, social and cultural factors also play a role in shaping writer identity. However, in this research, taking into consideration the overlapping of pragmatic function and writer identity from a discursive perspective, I will mainly discuss pragmatic functions, and will return to writer identity briefly in Chapter 8.

2.3.2   Verbs and verb category in academic text

This section reviews the different approaches of the categorisation of English verbs in academic texts. To serve the purpose of this research, the discussion focuses on semantic and pragmatic classifications, but not grammatical categories. Further, this section reviews the studies on the categorisation of the verbs that collocate with the FPPs. It is on the basis of this form of categorisation that I propose my categories for the phrases of 'I', 'We' and the verbs that collocate with them.

There are many different ways to classify verbs, ranging from very broad classifications such as those offered by Biber et. al(2002) or Halliday(2004) to a very specific classification of, for instance, reporting verbs in academic writing. Thompson and Ye(1991) propose two categories of reporting verbs. One class is the verbs denoting the author's stance, which presents the writer of the paper's point of view, examples of which are *accept*, *attack* and *assess*. The other is the verbs denoting the writer's stance, which reports the viewpoints of the cited writers in academic text, examples of which are *notice*, *disregard*, and *believe*. In relation to the sense of meaning, Biber et al.(2002:106—109) classify single-word lexical verbs into 7 semantic categories in the *Longman Student Grammar of Spoken and Written English*. They are *activity verbs*, *communication verbs*, *mental verbs*, *causative verbs*, *verbs of occurrence*, *verbs of existence or relationship*, and *verbs of aspect* (see Table 2.6). This reference book, according to Biber et al.(ibid), is compiled for students and teachers alike. The verbs and the samples are extracted from academic texts, conversation transcriptions, works of fiction and news texts. Indeed, these groups provide a general guidance on the semantics and the functions of the verbs in academic writing for novice writers. However, as will be discussed in the next few chapters, it is found in this study that it is difficult and possibly misleading to classify verbs in isolation and in a mixture of different genres. Classification of the meaning and function of a verb may be specific to a particular genre and the particular subject that it collocates with.

Table 2.6 Semantic categories of single-word lexical verbs(Biber et al. 2002: 106—109. The definitions and examples are all cited from the original book)

Category	Definition	Examples
Activity verbs	An action preformed intentionally by an agent or 'doer'.	*move*, *bring*, *buy*, etc.
Communication verbs	A special subcategory of activity verbs that involve communication activities, particularly verbs describing speech and writing.	ask, call, claim, etc.
Mental verbs	Mental states and activities, including mental states or process; emotions, attitudes, or desires; receptions; the receiving of communication.	think, love, see, read, etc.
Causative verbs	Verbs indicate that some person or thing helps to bring about a new state of affairs.	allow, help, require, etc.
Verbs of occurrence	Report events that occur without an actor	become, change, develop, etc.
Verbs of existence or relationship	Report a state of existence or a logical relationship that exists between entities.	appear, contain, exist, etc.
Verbs of aspect	Characterise the stage of progress of an event or activity. These verbs usually occur with a complement clause following the verb.	begin, continue, stop, etc.

By looking at the verbs that collocate with the FPPs, 'I' and 'We', Fløttum et al.(2006:207) propose another set of verb classification. Compared with the classes of the verbs identified without context, this categorisation classifies verbs in research articles only, which evades the noise of different genres. It also takes into account the subject of the verbs into consideration. In short, only verbs that collocate with the FPP, 'I' in research articles are classified in this research. In their project, Fløttum et al. examine the authors' roles and the author-reader interaction by dividing the verbs that collocate with the FPP into four groups. The first group is called '*Research verbs*', which includes 'actions and activities directly related to the research process, for example, *analyse*, *assume*, and *consider*. The second group is named '*Discourse verb*'. It is adopted from Hyland's (2000) classification of discourse act verbs, such as *describe*, *illustrate*, and *present*. Verbs that are 'denoting process related to position and stance' are assigned as the third group, called '*Position verbs*'. Examples of words that fall into this group are *argue*, *claim*, and *dispute*. The last group is called '*Evaluating and emotional constructions*'. This group contains not only verbs but semi-fixed or fixed phrases. Some examples are words such as *feel*, *be content to*, and *be sceptical about*. This category includes verbs and expressions by which the authors express their opinions, stance, and emotional reactions to entities or observations. The four groups of the different types of roles that match the four verb classes are Researcher, Writer, Arguer and Evaluator respectively.

This classification by Fløttum et al. (2006) is helpful, in that the verbs are classified with the two FPPs in the academic writings of the three different disciplines. This enables the categorisation of these verbs into a more specific, and a more focussed group for academic writing investigation. However, the boundary is ambiguous between the '*Position verbs*' and the '*Evaluating* and *emotional constructions verbs*' groups in Fløttum et al.'s project. In academic writing, writers evaluate and concurrently adopt a position. They argue for or against a proposition. They express their opinions or understanding in order to assert their authority either explicitly or by hedging. It is therefore difficult to separate instances of a writer taking a firm position and that of a writer going through a process of evaluation for the purposes of delivering a proposition in academic writing. The separation of this action in academic writing into two groups seems less than necessary. This point is acknowledged and justified in Fløttum et al.'s (2006: 85) later work, *Academic Voices*, claiming that the distinction is used to serve 'potential individual style' in the investigation of their projects.

As mentioned above, different researchers classify the verbs in different ways to serve different research purposes. A verb in academic writing is more complex in a longer unit than when it is examined as a single lexical unit out of context. It may present different meanings and has different pragmatic functions when collocating with different subjects and in varying forms of expression. Only looking at 'I' or 'We' alone in the text may not be revelatory about either textual function or writer identity, or visibility, or authority for that matter. Discussion of the categorisation of verbs without considering the frequent phrases in which they are used might thus be misleading, especially to ESL/EFL learners. In this research, quantitatively, I extracted 'I' and 'We' from the corpus, then checked the verbs that frequently collocate with them in the EFL students' texts (see Chapter 3). Qualitatively, the phrases including the two FPPs and their collocating verbs are examined. There are two aspects to this examination. The first relates to their meanings and the second, their discourse functions in the text.

To summarise Section 3, many previous studies on the FPPs in academic writing focus on the exploration of writer identity, textual function, visibility and authority in academic texts. Some of the studies discuss all the FFPs, some focus on the singular 'I', and some on the plural 'We'. Many of the previous research take either a qualitative approach to look at the context that 'I' and 'We' are located in(see, for example, John 2005), or use corpus tools to extract the FPPs, to look at the quantitative information. The research then proceeds to look at each instance manually to decide the pragmatic function of them in context(see, for example, Hyland 2002). The categorisation of the verbs is most frequently carried out by evaluating the verb itself. However, it is observed that the verb collocates of the FPPs may present different meanings and pragmatic functions in different phrases. This will be discussed in detail in the present study and this is a facet that has not been discussed in most of the reviewed studies.

2.4 The disciplinary difference and level difference of academic text

Literature on the disciplinary difference and the academic level/proficiency difference of an academic text is reviewed in this section. In general, in most of the previous studies on academic discourse, discrepancies are found both between different disciplines and between different academic levels(e.g. published research articles vs. students' essays and advanced students' texts vs. intermediate students' texts).

Becher(1989:42) divides disciplines into four large categories: hard pure(e.g. Physics), soft pure(e.g. History), hard applied(e.g. Mechanical Engineering), and soft applied(e.g. Education) with the consideration that discipline is the "basic intellectual organization". Since then, most of the comparative studies use this categorisation as the yardstick to differentiate between the rigours of various disciplines. As a linguist who focuses on the language of different disciplines, Hyland(2015: 33) defines disciplines as "language using communities which help us join writers, texts and readers together". In this definition, he points out three key elements that are fundamental in a disciplinary text: disciplinary text written by the writer, reader who reads the text, and the interaction between the writer and the reader through the text. It also implies that different disciplines practice different language conventions according to their own disciplinary epistemology. As argued further by Hyland and Tse(2007:247), "The resources which have developed in the sciences for construing reality as a world of logical relations and abstract entities are far removed from our routine ways of describing the world and so represent a more precise disciplinary lexical arsenal".

Besides the variation between disciplines, language use may also differ at different academic levels. Expert writers of journal articles write differently from apprentice writers, such as research students. Likewise, research students are not likely to write as undergraduate students do. Although there are many studies on the disciplinary and proficiency level differences of rhetorical strategies in academic discourse, the issue of 'I' and 'We' across disciplines and proficiency levels in EFL students' texts has not been adequately explored.

2.4.1　Disciplinary difference

Academic discourse varies in different disciplines due to the divergence of disciplinary conventions, knowledge construction strategies and approaches of evaluation alignment with community members (Swales 1990; Ivanič 1998; Hyland 1998, 2002, 2004, 2005, 2010, 2012, 2015).

When people question about the change from formal to less formal academic discourse over time, the usage of FPPs is one of the issues. It is reported that from 1965 to 2015 the usage of FPPs increased by 213% in published papers in Biology (Hyland and Jiang, 2017). On the other hand, they record a decrease of the utilisation of the FPPs in the discipline of Applied Linguistics. According to Hyland and Jiang, this change is due to the highly competitive nature of the hard science academic community that spurs the authors to establish authority, originality, and claim contribution. In the case of Applied Linguistics on the other hand, with an increasing awareness of the formality and convention of the disciplinary academic discourse, there is a drop in the usage of the FPPs. The overall increase of the FPPs however, is explained as there are an increased number of papers written by ESL or EFL authors who hail from different cultural backgrounds.

The soft vs. hard disciplinary differences of using the FPPs differ in quantity and pragmatic functions in the academic texts. It was noted that the soft disciplines such as Economics and Business and Management display the use of 'I' and 'We' three times more frequently in the published research articles than those of the hard disciplines such as Computer Science and Physics(Harwood 2005b). In the same paper, Harwood also proposes that writers of soft disciplines prefer to use 'I' over 'We' to refer to themselves, while authors of hard science use 'We' as self-representation in their texts. Authors of soft disciplines tend to use the two FPPs to emphasise their authoritative roles and contribution (Hyland 2002, 2004, 2005, 2015); whereas authors of hard science prefer to distance themselves from the discourse by using other rhetorical means, for example, "passive voice, dummy *it* subjects and the attribution of agency to inanimate things"(Hyland 2015: 34). Difference in the usage of 'I' and 'We' in published research papers between soft pure and soft applied disciplines has also been explored. For example, in Başal and Bada's study(2012), 16 articles from two journals, *Social Sciences Journal of Cukurova University* (SSJC) and *English Language Teaching Journal* (ELTJ), were compared to see the different usages of 'I' and 'We'. The result shows that writers of soft applied discipline (ELTJ) use more instances of the two FPPs. At the same time, 'I' is more frequently used by soft applied(ELTJ) and 'We' is more frequently presented in soft pure(SSJC). In both disciplines, the employment the FPPs are said to serve the purpose of establishing authority in the texts.

2.4.2   Academic level difference

In this section, academic level/proficiency difference is

discussed from two aspects, namely, the use of phrases and the employment of the FPPs in the texts written by writers of different proficiency. The difference between expert writer and student writer in using phrases is examined by Chen and Baker (2010). It is reported that student writers use many more 4-grams than expert writers. The students' discourses also contained more VP-based bundles and discourse organisers whereas the expert texts consist of more NP-based bundles and referential markers. This overuse of lexical bundles and choice of different categories of the lexical bundles in the student's discourse are considered as a "sign of immature writing". Meanwhile, compared to the students of the intermediate level with advanced non-native speakers of English, it was found that high frequency bigrams are overused and that low-frequency but highly-associated bigrams are underused in the intermediate NNS students' discourse(Bestgen and Granger, 2014).

When exploring the usage of the singular FPP 'I' in computing academic discourse, Harwood(2005) found that there is a significant difference between the uses of the FPPs in students' and experts' texts. It is reported that the students use about 80% of all the instances of 'I' in the corpus. Comparatively, there are only 3% of instances found in expert texts. At the same time, the functions of these 'I' differ in students' and experts' academic discourse. When 'I' is used to report methodology in the students' academic discourse, the pragmatic function of this FPP is to illustrate and present the students' capability and resourcefulness in carrying out research procedures competently. The interactive purpose is to "create a favourable impression on the reader by constructing them as

tenacious neophytes" (Harwood, 2005a: 244). The textual
function of the 6 instances of 'I' in the expert texts is implicit
in Harwood's paper. However, it is believed that the student
writer may be unaware that the use of the FPP in methodology
report is to display the writer's prominence and his/her unique
role in the choice of research method in expert discourse(Hyland 2002).

In summation, there is a difference in using 'I' and 'We'
in different disciplines and academic levels. Nevertheless, most
of the research on disciplinary difference uses published research articles as sample texts. The studies on academic level
differences compare the difference between texts written by
experts with those written by novices. Little research has been
conducted on the disciplinary and level difference of the two
FPPs, 'I' and 'We' in NNS's academic discourse. In the next
section, I turn to phraseology and the FPPs in EFL academic
texts to illustrate the significance of exploring the phraseology
of 'I' and 'We' in EFL students' academic discourse.

2.5   The phraseology and the FPPs in EFL aca-
demic writing

With increasing interest in formulaic expressions in SLA
and EAP, several lists of idiomatic expression are presented in
different registers, for example, American spoken idioms(Liu,
2003) and PHRSE List for ESL/EFL pedagogical purposes
(Martinez and Schmitt, 2012).The most recent one, the Academic formula list (AFL) for academic purposes (Simpson-
Vlach and Ellis, 2010) is extracted in response to the AWL

(academic word list) composed by Coxhead(2000). It includes formulas in both written and spoken academic context, as well as in academic written language alone and academic spoken language alone. They all attempt to list the most frequently recurrent corpus-derived data from a wide range of genres and for different purposes. Knowledge of phraseology is considered as an essential aspect leading to competence in learning English as a SL and FL. However, this epistemic knowledge seems rather difficult for NNSs. "Control of a language involves a sensitivity to the preferences of expert users for certain sequences of words over others, but students can have enormous difficulty distinguishing the idiomatic from the merely grammatical"(Hyland 2008:7). In writing academic discourse, another difficulty experienced by the NNSs is the appropriate employment of the FPPs. It is a firm view held by many academic instructors that academic discourse should be objective, detached, and impersonal. One principle of achieving this style is to avoid any use of the FPPs(Swetnam 2000). Arguably, with the demand for interactive function of academic discourse, the employment of 'I' and 'We' is now not considered as an informality but rather, a key element of self-representation rhetorical strategy. They are used by many contemporary expert writers in their academic papers. Consequently, the contradiction between traditional practice and lack of clarity in classroom instruction causes ambiguity and problems for the students, especially ESL/EFL students engaging in academic writing, as observed by Hyland(2002:1092)

> "While it is clear that the conventions of personality are rhetorically constrained in academic writing,

these constraints are uncertain, and the extents to which one can reasonable explicitly intrude into one's discourse, or assert one's personal involvement, remains a dilemma for novices and experienced writers alike. It is particularly problematic for students because they frequently feel positioned by the dominant disciplinary and institutional discourses they encounter in university studies, and the problem can be seriously compounded for NNS whose rhetorical identities may be shaped by very different traditions of literacy".

Phraseology is an obstacle for EFL students. Facing the phrases of 'I' and 'We', another layer of difficulty is added to the students due to the bewilderment of the usages of the FPPs in academic discourse. This lack of knowledge and understanding could therefore be a two-pronged problem which needs to overcome when engaging in academic writing tasks. Against the background of standard formula lists derived from native speakers, little has been done in relation to the formulaic expressions used by non-native speakers and the development of the phrases for academic purposes. This is the case for those from different disciplines and similarly applicable to advanced English learners, both undergraduate and postgraduate students. Previous studies on mixed academic levels and disciplines blur the EFL learners' continuum of the multi-word expression production at their different proficiency levels and the different stages typical of the academic community. To contribute to this arena, exploring the phrases of 'I' and 'We' by corpus linguistic techniques is of importance in applied linguistics, because "[a]s multiword units of all kinds ... are notoriously difficult for learners, and corpus linguistic techniques are an extremely powerful way of exploring them" (Paquot and Granger 2012:130).

2.6 Conclusion

In this chapter, I have reviewed the general literature on Computer Learner Corpus and English phrases. I have noted that my corpus meets the criteria for the purpose of corpus compilation. I shall be focusing on comparisons relating to different groups of learners rather than comparisons between learners and native speakers. With regard to phrases, I adopt a very general definition of phraseology that includes collocation as well as frequently occurring phrases. That said, it is however always in the context of 'I' and 'We' and their verb collocates.

I have also reviewed literature, in particular, studies of the FPPs, especially 'I' and 'We' in academic discourse, categorisations of verbs, and level and disciplinary variations of using the FPPs in academic discourse. Most of the sample texts used in these studies, except John's(2005), are published journal articles. The writers of sample papers are experienced researchers who are familiar with rhetorical skills and well aware of the disciplinary conventions. The usage of the FPPs in the academic texts written by those less skillful writers, for instance, EFL students in this research, have not been sufficiently explored. Methodologically, many of the studies mentioned in this chapter use corpus to extract the FPPs, read the extended texts of undetermined length manually and assign each instance of 'I' and 'We' a pragmatic function. There are few studies on the co-occurrence phenomenon of the first personal pronouns 'I', 'We' and the verbs in academic discourse. Their discourse functions, lexical and semantic features receive little attention. Thus, based on a self-built learner corpus, this research explores phraseology and pragmatic functions of the two most obvious self-representation FPPs, 'I', 'We' and the verbs collocating with them in EFL students' academic texts. Through this study, I seek to reveal the phrasal and pragmatic features of the collocations of the two FPPs and the verbs across academic levels and disciplines. The aim is to add understanding of the FPPs, 'I' and 'We', the co-occurrences of them and the verbs in EFL academic texts, and to provide pedagogical guidance to EFL students and teachers in academic writing classrooms.

CHAPTER 3
METHODOLOGY OF THE STUDY: CORPUS COMPILATION AND THE EXTRACTION OF 'I', 'WE' AND THE VERBS

3.1 Introduction

This study is designed to investigate how Chinese EFL learners use the two FPPs, 'I' and 'We' in academic discourse across two specific disciplines, namely, Business and Management(BM) and English Literature(EL) and across two different academic levels, i. e. undergraduate and postgraduate (taught). In line with most studies on FPPs in the field of EAP, this study uses a corpus approach to investigate the academic texts written by Chinese EFL learners. In this chapter and throughout the whole thesis, I use 'I' and 'We' in single quotation marks to indicate these pronouns in general and denote them in italics when quoting examples from the corpus.

This chapter discusses the methodology of how 'I', 'We' and the verbs collocating with them were collected for this study. In Section 2, I set out and explain the procedure undertaken during the process of data collection and the subsequent compilation of The Chinese Advanced English Learner Corpus of Academic Written English(CAEL-CAWE) that was used in this research. The ethical review for this study was completed in March 2015. Section 3 describes the extraction process of the instances of two FPPs, 'I' and 'We'. Section 4 reports on how the verbs that collocate with the two FPPs were collected in the corpus. Section 5 concludes this chapter.

3.2　Corpus compilation

Before describing the data collection procedure, it may be useful to introduce two pieces of background information relating to Chinese Higher Education (HE). The first, relates to the writing of a dissertation and how it is perceived as an integral constituent of the EAP genre (3.2.1). The latter relates to EFL teaching and learning background, specifically in higher education institutions in China (3.2.2). Both of these discussions seek to explain in greater detail, the representativeness of the corpus in relation to how the Chinese students' dissertations across the two disciplines, i.e. BM and EL, and the two academic levels, i.e. undergraduate and post graduate were chosen for the comparative analyses in this study. I then proceed to report in this subsection, the process of data collection, the data clean-up process and the corpus building procedures of this research.

3.2.1　Genre and representativeness of the corpus

Academic discourse includes many different genres. These include research articles, monographs, research reports, dissertations and oral presentations in seminars or in academic conferences (Biber 2006; Swale 1990). The body of written

work that goes on to make up the above genres would undoubtedly be authored by writers with varying levels of writing competence. Work that is produced by expert writers or researchers
could include material such as research papers and published
books. Material produced by novice writers or early career researchers could include research reports and presentations in
seminars. Written work produced by learners for instance could
include written work such as dissertations. In China, as in most
other countries, the dissertation work embarked upon for the
purposes of graduation is probably the most significant piece of
writing in the student's academic life. The award of a student's
degree depends on primarily whether or not his/her thesis is up
to the standard set by the university. To ensure their academic
degrees are granted, the students need to guarantee their dissertations are of high quality. Thesis of poor delivery would result in a resubmission or graduating without an academic degree
in China. Therefore, the sample dissertations that are included
in this research can be considered as of fairly good quality.
From the student's perspective, this is possibly the most comprehensive and difficult piece of writing in his/her academic
training experience. It is a comprehensive writing task that en-
tails the reporting of research that calls on the student's ability
to plan and carry out research. The exploratory task of interpreting the research findings and results, gives an indication of
the student's disciplinary knowledge. The argumentative discussion put forward by the student in relation to the findings and
results, displays the student's ability to think independently. It
is also indicative of the originality and the impact generated by
the research. The dissertation also investigates the student's in-

terpersonal rhetorical skill with regards to how readers are taken into consideration and addressed. For example, it displays how the text is organised to enable an unfettered reading experience, and how the ideas are presented to achieve the purposes of enhancing persuasion, solidarity and acknowledgement of the student's work. As a direct result of its comprehensiveness and complexity, the dissertation may provide a comparatively complete view of the phraseology and pragmatic function of the two FPPs, 'I' and 'We' in Chinese learners' academic discourse.

I started this research with an explicit purpose in mind, that is, to investigate dissertations of different disciplines written by Chinese EFL student writers. However, the decision made in relation to choosing the two disciplines, Business and Management and English Literature was decided primarily by taking into account, the education background in China. The choice of disciplines is limited by the availability of dissertations written in English in China. The next section explains this issue further.

3.2.2   The English-language dissertations of Business and Management and English Literature in Chinese higher education

The academic texts in CEAL-CAWE are all submitted dissertations written in English by Chinese EFL learners. The background of Chinese higher education is introduced to shed light on why the theses were written in English by Chinese student writers, particularly in the field of Business and Management. In China, most universities described as 'comprehensive' provide undergraduate English courses as a subject area. For these English major students, during the course of their four-year undergraduate education, the first two years' curriculum focuses on English language. The courses provided include Intensive Reading, Extensive Reading, Listening and Speaking, Writing, English Culture, and so on. At the beginning of the students' third academic year, they are asked to choose one specialty subject as their main field of interest. Most students select one of the following: English Literature, International Business Management, Interpretation, Cross-cultural Communication, or Applied Linguistics. These specialty subjects are designed to prepare the students for the competitive Chinese job market upon their graduation. With English as their major subjects, coupled with the specialties on one of the above areas, the students would be looked upon favourably when hunting for jobs. In those universities, where these specialty courses are provided, the students are asked to write their dissertations on topics of their chosen specialty areas in English. The dissertations that are authored in the undergraduate course of Business and Management were mainly collected from two comprehensive universities in China. Additionally, there are some dissertations that I collected from the students from 5 other universities in person. This information is furnished in Section 3.2.3.

The postgraduate taught program in China is a three-year Masters program. Like the undergraduate curriculum, the postgraduate taught program in English, also provides the students with the option of specialty subjects to develop their disciplinary knowledge. The aims of tailoring these disciplinary areas in English schools are twofold. Firstly to cultivate the students' cross disciplinary research ability for further academic pursuit. Secondly, it is to prepare the students for the job market upon their graduation. In some Chinese universities, the postgraduate program of International Business and Management is centered in their Business schools. No matter which school this International Business and Management program is affiliated with, the courses of this discipline are taught predominantly in English and the dissertations are required to be written in English as well.

As English Literature is a traditional program at most English universities, dissertations related to this discipline maybe easily collected, at both undergraduate and postgraduate levels.

Summing up, in the corpus of this particular study, all the undergraduate dissertations were written by English major students who undertook two years of either Business and Management or English Literature as their undergraduate disciplinary training during the course of their four years of education. The postgraduate dissertations could be sourced from either a Business school or an English department because most of the courses at this academic level of these disciplines are conducted in English and the final theses are required to be written also in English.

The dissertations of the two academic levels i.e., undergraduate and postgraduate taught courses are considered as academic texts of different stages of inter-language proficiency, namely, advanced-UG and advanced-PG. The UG/PG distinction corresponds to the stages similar to that of the Chinese higher education system: four years of undergraduate training for a Bachelor's degree and another three years of postgraduate

(taught) for a Master's Degree after the students have successfully passed their oral examinations and submitted their dissertations.

3.2.3   Data collection

To collect the texts written by undergraduate students for
this research, several English departments of different universities in China and some individual students from 5 other universities were contacted either by me or by my colleagues in
person. After a detailed explanation of my research project, I
obtained permission to use the dissertations of the English or
Business colleges from two Chinese universities. The students of
these two universities granted their institutes the right to use
their theses upon their graduation. In addition, 72 individual
students from the other 5 universities in China that were contacted in person by me or by my colleagues kindly signed the
consent letters and provided their undergraduate dissertations. I
had collected a total of 1,031 undergraduate dissertations at this
stage of the data collection. All of the collected dissertations
were in electronic form, so they were easily processed at the
data cleaning stage. As introduced above, the two universities
that agreed to provide the theses offer English major students
several different specialties: English Literature, International
Business and Management, Interpretation and Translation,
Cross-cultural Communication and Applied Linguistics at the
start of the students' third academic year. The English major
students of these two universities needed to choose their fields
of interests and compose their graduation dissertations in English on the specific fields they had chosen. The 1,031 academic

texts that were sent to me were drawn from the 5 different disciplines mentioned above.

After briefly dividing these papers into different disciplines by reading the English titles of each paper, two subject areas, Business and Management(168 texts) and English Literature(137 texts) were selected to serve the cross disciplinary investigation. These two disciplines were chosen because they belong to different disciplinary fields. Business and Management is a Social Science and represents a soft-applied discipline (Becher, 1989). English Literature is from an Arts and Humanities field representing a soft-pure discipline(ibid). The two disciplines therefore, may be used for a contrastive study. At a more practical level, this choice was made because there were a reasonable number of texts on these two subjects which made it possible to build a comparatively balanced corpus of a suitable size for the purposes of this study. The texts of the other three disciplines were not included mainly due to the following reasons: theses on Interpretation and Translation included too many examples of languages other than English in the texts, ranging from Chinese, Japanese and Spanish. If the texts of these disciplines had been chosen, the deletion of the examples would have brought about a significant drop in the quantity of the words in English at the data cleaning stage. The two other disciplines, Cross-cultural Communication and Applied Linguistics, did not have as many dissertations as those from Business and Management and English Literature. Comparatively, the words contained in the dissertations of Business and Management and English Literature are about the same in total, both of which are about 1,000,000 after the data was cleaned.

As mentioned by Hunston(2002:26), "[i]t is a truism that a corpus is neither good nor bad in itself, but suited or not suited to a particular purpose. Decisions about what should go into a corpus are based on what the corpus is going to be used for, but also about what is available". Although the choice of the two disciplines, Business and Management and English Literature is partly due to the ease of accessibility, the selection of Business and Management and English Literature should not in any way be construed as a compromise. The texts of both these two disciplines and the two distinct academic levels are most appropriate for the contrastive investigation purpose of this study.

The next step was to make sure that the collected dissertations from both the disciplines of Business and Management and English Literature genuinely belong to these two specific subject areas. In order to build the undergraduate Business and Management sub-corpus, I read the titles of the dissertations and identified the words that belonged to the Business and Management discipline. Two of my colleagues from a Business School in a university in China helped me to identify those terms at this stage. After reading all the titles, the dissertations identified by the following specific words(see Table 3.1) were included in the body of the undergraduate of Business and Management sub-corpus. As these words have been identified, it is possible to use them as search terms to enlarge the corpus, especially applicable at the stage of collecting postgraduate dissertations. To identify the appropriate theses for inclusion in the English Literature sub-corpus, I again read the titles and subtitles of the collected papers and identified words that belonged to the following categories: the title or the name of a specific character in a novel, poem or play, and the name of an author.

Table 3.1   Word list of Business and Management

Business and Management	Corporation (Corporations, Corporate)/Companies/Customer/Consumer/Enterprise (Entrepreneurship)/Industry/WTO/Producer (s)/Product(e.g. Cosmetics)/Brand/Market(Marketing)/Currency(e.g. Renminbi)/Capital(money invested into a business)/Bank/Custom/Business/Economic/Export/Import/Retail/Resale/Sales/Price/Exchange Rates/Banking/Accounting/Triffin dilemma/Investment/Venture(s)/ Profit/Consumption/Trade/Service/Anti-Dumping (Dumping)/Advertising (Advertisement, Advertisements)/Commercials/Tax/Ecommerce/Merger(s)/Acquisition/Financial Management/Motivation Mechanism/Recruiting/Employee (Employer, Unemployment)/Staff/Public Relations. Some specific companies' names, for example: Louis Vuitton, Carrefour, KFC and HSBC.

The same word list and selection criteria were then used to select the postgraduate Masters dissertations from the online source, CNKI(China National Knowledge Infrastructure) website. These dissertations are publicly available, and as an academic staff member working in one of the universities in China, I have permission to browse and download the academic papers, thus avoiding any copyright issues. All the collected and downloaded theses have been saved in electronic files and have been included in the database for further processing.

The design criteria of the CAEL-CAWE corpus can be summarised as follows:

1) The dissertations were written by Chinese EFL learners;

2) The dissertations were written for the completion of an academic degree, undergraduate(Bachelor's degree) and postgraduate taught(Master's degree);

3) The titles of the dissertations in the subcorpus of Business and Management contain at least one word from the Busi-

ness and Management word list;

4) The titles of the dissertations in the subcorpus of English Literature contain one of the following: the title or the name of a character of a novel, poem or play, and the name of an author.

Each thesis included in this study was annotated with a header that encodes the information about the participant's academic level, undergraduate(UG) or postgraduate taught(PG) as well as the disciplinary information of the thesis, Business and Management(BM) or English Literature(EL). In addition, each label is combined with a unique 4 or 5-digit reference number to anonymise, and concurrently identify every thesis in the CAEL-CAWE corpus. For example, dissertation UGBM 0045 is a thesis written by an undergraduate student of Business and Management discipline, and PGEL 0311 is a thesis written by a postgraduate student of English Literature.

3.2.4   Data cleaning

The primary focus of this research is to investigate the use of 'I' and 'We' in the main body of academic texts written by Chinese students. The papers sent to me are all complete versions of the dissertations including titles, abstracts, tables of content, references, etc. In order to retain the main bodies of the texts only, the following components of all the papers were removed from the database during the process of data cleaning. They are:

● titles

● footnotes

● captions

- content tables
- abstracts
- references
- acknowledgements

In Business and Management subcorpora, I also deleted

- tables
- charts
- graphs

By doing this, only the main body of each text was kept for further analysis.

As for the English Literature subcorpora, during the data cleaning work, I found that there were many quotes attributed to third parties, for example, words from primary resource book(s) were used for analysis. There were also reviews quoted from other critics. To ensure that the final texts for analysis were written by the student writers instead of other informants, I decided to remove quotations if they met the following conditions:

- The quotation comprised of an individual paragraph
- The quotation was more than one sentence or was at the beginning or end of a paragraph.
- The removal of the sentence(s) would not affect the structure of the text.

The following two extracts from UGEL 13809 are examples(quotations are italicised here):

Example 3-1: Moreover, Perowne is a calm, logical man willing to analyze and ask "why". He is a habitual observer of his own moods, and when he wakes up early in the morning of the Saturday, he wonders about this sustained, distorting euphoria:

Perhaps down at the molecular level there's been chemical accident while he slept—something like a spilled tray of drinks, prompting dopamine-like receptors to initiate a kindly cascade of intracellular events; or it's the prospect of a Saturday, or the paradoxical consequence of extreme tiredness (McEwan, 2006: 7).

Example 3-2: Professional jargons as well as terminologies are also parts of her vocabulary. When Perowne showed his love to her, Rosalind's attitude was unusual: she "*was responsive enough, though hardly abandoned, and for almost a week found herself too busy in the evenings to see him*" (McEwan, 2006: 47). Solitude and work were less threatening to her inner world than kisses.

The long quotation at the end of the paragraph of Example 3-1 was decided to be irrelevant for the purpose of this study. Thus, quotations such as this were removed and replaced with [quote] in the English Literature sub-corpora. The inserted quotation of Example 3-2 was cited in the middle of the sentence, and the deletion of it would affect the whole sentence structure. Quotations of this nature were retained in order to keep the smooth flow of the sentences.

3.2.5   Corpus construction and components

After all the texts were cleaned, they were uploaded to the online corpus tool, Sketch Engine (Kilgarriff et al. 2004). The words in the texts were all tagged for part of speech (PoS) automatically by Sketch Engine when the theses were uploaded. The

PoS tagging facilitates the making of queries when I looked for certain phrasal patterns of 'I', 'We' and the respective collocating verbs applicable to this piece of research. For example, when the phrasal frame $I/We + will + verbs$ was examined, I used the query[word = "I"] [word = "will"] [tag = "VV* "] | [word = "We"] [word = "will"] [tag = "VV* "] to extract all the phrases that matched this pattern. By doing so, all the verbs that present themselves in this phrasal frame in the corpus could be found and the discourse functions of these phrases in the discourse could be examined by looking at these retrieved concordance lines(see Section 5.3.1 in Chapter 5).

The CAEL-CAWE was designed to include 4 sub-corpora: undergraduate Business and Management(UGBM), undergraduate English Literature(UGEL), postgraduate taught Business and Management(PGBM) and postgraduate taught English Literature(PGEL). Table 3.2 presents the information of the four sub-corpora.

Table 3.2　Meta-information of CEAL-CAWE

	Number of texts	Total tokens	Total types
UGBM	168	991185	23301
UGEL	137	767648	24796
PGBM	73	1073130	21890
PGEL	78	1361450	37818
Total:	456	4193413	107805

To achieve the contrastive purposes of this research, these four subcorpora were then arranged into two sets. Figure 3.1 illustrates the sub-corpora arrangement for the purpose of cross-disciplinary investigation. The corpus was categorised according to different disciplines in order to investigate the disciplinary differences(i.e. BM vs. EL). Figure 3.2 presents the mapping of the 4 subcorpora into two different academic levels to facilitate the purpose of comparison in relation to the use of 'I' and 'We' across the academic levels(UG vs. PG).

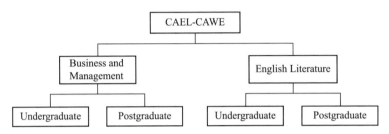

Figure 3.1   CAEL-CAWE cross disciplinary research structure

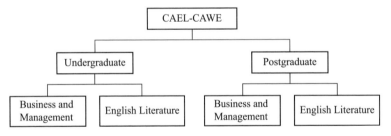

Figure 3.2   CAEL-CAWE cross academic levels research structure

3.3   The extraction of 'I' and 'We'

3.3.1   The method

As discussed in Chapter 2, the FPPs 'I' and 'We' are the most obvious and visible expressions of the writer in academic writing. In this research, I use corpus tools to investigate 'I' and 'We' and their verb collocates in the collected students' academic texts. Because the data has been cleaned and most of the quotations in the texts were removed before they were uploaded to Sketch Engine, the instances of 'I' and 'We' that are used as self-representation devices in the texts may be easily extracted by simply typing in *I* or *We* in the searching box of Sketch Engine interface. There are other forms of *I*, for example, *See Appendix I* and *World War I* which have to be removed manually. Additionally, 'I' and 'We' contained in short quotations are removed manually at the concordance stage. This step returned 1,730 instances of 'I' and 5,083 instances of 'We', 6,813 in total. The detailed quantitative information of 'I' and 'We' in each sub-corpus is reported in the next subsection.

3.3.2   Quantitative results of the FPPs, 'I' and 'We'

There are 6,813 instances of 'I' and 'We' in the CEAL-CAWE(see Table 3.3). It is found that most of the texts, i.e. 409 out of 456, accounting for 90%, across the four subcorpora contain one or both of the two FPPs. The other 47 texts in this corpus did not have either of the two FPPs at all after the data was processed. The average frequency of the two FPPs is 17 per text. The average use of 'I' is 4 times per text, and the average use of 'We' is 12 times per text. It is noted that the spread of the two FPPs in the CEAL-CAWE is disproportionate. One text, which has the most occurrences of the two FPPs, has 186 instances of 'I' and 'We' altogether, whereas the text with the fewest instances contains only 1 'I' or 'We'. However, the vast majority of the texts, (388 out of 409 or 95%) contain up to 50 instances of 'I' and/or 'We'. This diversity in the frequency of occurrence shall not be investigated further as my focus is on the phraseology and discourse functions of 'I', 'We' and the verb sequences in this study.

Table 3.3   Distributions of 'I' and 'We' in the CEAL-CAWE

	Hits of 'I'	Hits of 'We'	Hits of 'I' & 'We'	Number of texts that include 'I' and 'We'	Average number of 'I' and 'We' in each text	Normalized frequence per 1,000 words
UGBM	612	1,184	1,796	141	13	1.81
UGEL	419	1,305	1,724	125	14	2.25
PGBM	421	1,154	1,575	73	22	1.47
PGEL	278	1,440	1,718	70	25	1.26
Total:	1,730	5,083	6,813	409	17	1.62

It may be seen from Table 3.3 that there is no significant difference between the total occurrences of the two FPPs across the four subcorpora. The normalised frequency shows that the postgraduate writers use fewer 'I' and 'We' in their theses than their undergraduate counterparts. In the undergraduate texts, there are more uses of these two FPPs than those in the postgraduate texts. There is also clearly less frequent occurrences of the singular FPP 'I' in the postgraduates' texts than the undergraduates' dissertations. It is therefore quite apparent that learners of English Literature use fewer 'I' than those undertaking the Business and Management course. These differences across the academic levels and disciplines are presented and discussed in more detail both from a quantitative and a qualitative perspective in Chapter 5 and Chapter 6 respectively.

In this and the next three chapters, I will not be taking into consideration, the difference between the singular FPP 'I' and the plural 'We'. They are discussed only where necessary as both of the FPPs are obvious representations of the writers and expressions of subjectivity. I will come back to this in Chapter 7 where I discuss the different uses and principles related to the two FPPs, 'I' and 'We' in these academic texts in detail.

3.4   The extraction of the verbs that collocate with 'I' and 'We'

3.4.1   The method

One of the many advantages associated with the study of corpus linguistics is that, with the assistance of corpus tools, the comparison of language features may be made between large sets of data and the frequency of recurrence may be identified automatically with quantitative information(Biber et al. 1998; Hunston 2002; McEnery and Hardie 2012). Using corpus tool in this research facilitates the comparison of the phrases including the FPPs and the verbs collocating with them.

After the extraction of all the instances of 'I' and 'We', I used the collocation function of Sketch Engine(Kilgarriff et al. 2004) to retrieve all the verbs that collocate with 'I' up to R5, minimum frequency set at 5, with 'We' at R5, and the minimum frequency set at 10. The minimum frequency in the given range was set at 3 for both retrievals of the verbs collocating with 'I' and 'We'. The purpose of setting the collocation span on the right side of the two FPPs at R5 was to find out all the instances in which 'I' and 'We' are used as the grammatical subjects of the clauses, as these cases constitute the most obvious representation of authorial voice in academic discourses. Setting the minimum frequency at 5 with 'I' and 10 with 'We' was to examine those frequently recurrent verbs in each subcorpus. The setting of the minimum frequency in given range at 3 was to ensure that the extracted verb occurs at least in three different essays. This was to avoid idiosyncratic use, particularly the higher frequency of a verb usage due to many occurrences in only one or two essays in the corpus. In addition, the different forms of the verbs were counted and lemmatised to be included into the lists. For example, *tell*, *tells* and *told* are all word forms of the verb *TELL*. In UGEL, the base form of the verb *tell* collocates with 'We' on 6 occasions, and the past tense/past participial of this verb, *told* occurs 6 times, in this case, the lemma *TELL* was added to the list as this verb co-occurred with 'We' 12 times. It is obvious that if the word forms were lemmatised, there would be more occurrences of each verb.

After the extraction of all the verbs that collocate with 'I' and 'We', a further filtering process was performed. At this step, only the main verbs that collocate with the FPPs were taken into consideration. This filtering process excluded the modal verbs(e.g. *can*, *should*, *would*) or the auxiliary verbs (e.g. *BE*, *HAVE*). Where there was a catenative phrase, I included the second verb and not the first into the list. Another exception is the copular verb *BE*, where the meaning is made more apparent by the adjective than the verb. Therefore, *BE* was not included in the verb classification in Chapter 4. Examples of the verbs that are kept and removed are listed below:

Example 3-3: It is worth studying in the future, for *we are confident* that it will have an unexpected impact on the promotion of private brands and sales. (UGBM 05505)

Example 3-4: From above analysis *we can see* how M makes the best use of charity into its marketing strategy. (UGBM 10205)

Example 3-5: Also in direct marketing, as *we have mentioned*, the company should employ a sales team. This sales team is very important because it is the force who directly delivers the information of the company as well as its products to customers. (UGBM 05607)

Example 3-6: Keeping in mind the two concepts of market research and culture, *we then go on to discuss* several cases that involve in multinational marketing. (UGBM 06804)

In Example 3-3, *we* is counted in the quantitative statistics because it refers to the writer, however, the copular *are* in this discourse was not included into the verb list for discourse function categorisation. The modal verb *can* in the Example 3-4 and the auxiliary verb *have* in the Example 3-5 were also removed from the final list. In the Example 3-6, the second verb *discuss* was kept and the phrase *go on* was removed.

The next step is to examine these collected verbs and classify them into different textual function groups to facilitate the contrastive investigation. However, because the process of the categorisation and the related discussion of the verbs is rather complex, they are accounted for separately in Chapter 4.

3.4.2   Quantitative results of the verbs that collocate with the FPPs

Using the methodology reported above, a total number of 3,293 instances of the verbs(57 verb types) that collocate with 'I' and 'We' up to R5, and with minimum frequency of no less than 5 times with 'I' and/or no less than 10 times with 'We' were collected. This accounts for about 50% of all the instances of 'I' and 'We' which were included in the final list

Table 3.4   the extracted verbs that collocate with 'I' and 'We'

The extracted verbs that collocate with 'I' and 'We'							
SEE	747	CHOOSE	49	agree	19	arrange	9
FIND	496	conclude	48	infer	16	explore	8
KNOW	308	focus	45	quote	16	concerned	7
think	131	believe	44	present	14	test	7
DISCUSS	122	Hope	41	sense	14	cite	6
SAY	113	MEAN	38	realize	13	proposed	6
USE	90	TALK	38	act	12	apply	5
ANALYZE	87	FEEL	37	define	12	compare	5
MENTION	78	introduce	29	OBSERVE	12	divide	5
understand	70	EXAMINE	28	suppose	12	explain	5
learn	68	notice	28	worked	12		
READ	68	TELL	29	ignore	11		
look	52	consider	27	asked	10		
		hear	26	aware	10		
		argue	24	imagine	10		
		CALL	24	judge	10		
		COLLECT	21				
		study	21				

Total: 3,293

for analysis in this study. The reason why this research only covers about half of the instances of all the verbs extracted in the CEAL-CAWE is explained in the conclusion(3.5) of this chapter. Table 3.4 lists the verbs that are included for the analysis.

3.5   Conclusion

This chapter has reported the corpus, CEAL-CAWE designed for this study. It is a collection of texts of Chinese EFL learners' graduation dissertations. Within this corpus, four sub-corpora serve the purposes of comparing BM and EL, and UG and PG. I have described the methodology of using Sketch Engine to retrieve the quantitative information in this research. As mentioned earlier in this chapter, in this piece of research, I treated the learners' texts as self-contained and therefore, did not use a reference corpus in the investigations conducted in this study.

This study focuses on the phrases consisting of 'I', 'We' and the verbs collocating with them. The automatic extraction assisted by Sketch Engine (Kilgarriff et al. 2004) of the two FPPs provides quantitative information related to the different disciplines and academic levels. At the same time, based on the identification of these FPPs, it is possible to extract the verbs that collocate with them. To look at the quantitative information of 'I', 'We' and the verbs collocating with them separately would not provide much information of the phraseology and their discourse functions of the collocations. Based on the quantitative information derived from the corpus, I focus on the units of 'I', 'We' and their verb collocates. As mentioned in Chapter 1 and Chapter 2, these units are called phrases because of their comparatively fixed patterns when they collocate with the FPPs in the texts contained in this study. In the next chapter, I discuss the process of how the verbs retrieved are examined and categorised manually for further analysis.

CHAPTER 4

METHODOLOGY OF THE STUDY：
CLASSIFICATION OF THE VERBS
COLLOCATING WITH 'I' AND 'WE'

4.1 Introduction

To categorise the collected verbs reported in Chapter 3，I started with a detailed analysis of their meaning and discourse functions when they collocate with the two FPPs，'I' and 'We'. The purpose of carrying out this process is to classify them into a limited number of groups for the contrastive study that was to follow. The close examination of the verbs allows me to group them into functional categories according to their discourse meaning and functions. Based on such detailed analysis，I proposed four general functional groups of the phrases of 'I'，'We' and the verbs collocating with them，i.e. *Textual organising verbs*，*Research report verbs*，*Research interpretation verbs* and *Knowledge community construing verbs*. It should be noted that when I discuss the meaning and the pragmatic functions of the verbs，I have always considered them as part of the phrases of 'I'，'We' and their collocate verbs. In other words，it means that the meaning and the function of the verbs discussed here are dependent on the condition that they collocate with 'I' and/or 'We' in this study. In the rest of this chapter, I mostly discuss the verbs only, which is simply to avoid repetitiveness of stating a finding, for example, *when the verb* * *collocates with I and/or we*.

In this chapter and throughout the whole thesis, verbs in different forms in this study are lemmatised (e.g. *see*, *saw*, *seen* are lemmatised as *SEE*). Phrases including the two FPPs 'I', 'We', and the verbs collocating with them in texts are italicised when I discuss the actual instances and give examples.

The rest of the chapter is organised as follows. Section 2 discusses the semantics and textual function of some sample verbs that collocate with 'I' and 'We' in the corpus. In Section 3, based on the discussion of the meanings and pragmatic functions of the verbs, I categorise the verbs into four groups, as noted above, so as to provide data for comparisons to be carried out between different disciplines as well as different academic levels. To illustrate how the comparisons were carried out based on the functions proposed in this chapter, Section 4 provides a sample of contrastive analysis of the phrases of 'I', 'We' and the verb, *SEE* between BM and EL, and between UG and PG. The detailed disciplinary and academic level differences are described in Chapters 5 and 6. Section 5 concludes this chapter.

4.2   Verbs collocating with 'I' and 'We'

The aim of the examination of the verbs that collocate with 'I' and 'We' is twofold. Firstly, it is to treat it as a preliminary study to look at the phraseology of the two FPPs and the verbs collocating with them across the whole corpus. Secondly, it is to attempt to classify them into a limited number of groups. In this chapter, instead of looking at the quantitative information of 'I', 'We' and the verbs, I undertook a qualitative approach. I looked at the concordance lines of each verb to identify the phraseology, the meaning in phrases, and the textual function in discourse. At this stage, I examined all the 3,293 instances of the 57 types of verbs that were extracted from this study. On the basis of the interpretations of these verbs, functional categories are tentatively proposed in this research. Where necessary, I compare the classification of the verbs with previous research on lexical meaning and discourse functions, especially in relation to studies on the verbs used in academic discourse. The reason for this form of comparison is that if these verbs are classified without their collocates, 'I' and/or 'We', they fit well into most of the classifications proposed in previous studies (e.g. Ädel 2006; Biber et al. 2002; Fløttum et al. 2006; Hyland 1998; Kuo 1998). However, when some of the verbs are examined in context, with the two FPPs and in extended discourse, they present different meanings and discourse functions in the students' academic writings. Specifically, it is found that some of the verbs are not only frequently used with the FPPs but also used in a limited number of phrases or phrasal patterns. More importantly, these verbs vary in meaning and discourse functions when collocating with 'I' and 'We' in different phrases.

As the main purpose of this examination is to propose functional categories of the phrases, in the following subsections, instead of discussing all the verbs that are analysed at this step, I report this qualitative analysis of the following 12 high frequency verbs(with the number of occurrences shown in bracket), *SEE*(747), *FIND*(496), *KNOW*(308), *think*(131), *DISCUSS*(122), *SAY*(113), *USE*(90), *ANALYSE*(87), *MENTION*(78), *LEARN*(68), *read*(68), and *believe*(44). These verbs are discussed in groups according to their high frequency in corpus(e.g. *SEE*, *FIND*) or their semantic categories(e.g. *think*, *believe* as cognitive verbs) proposed by Biber et al. (2002).

4.2.1   *SEE*, *FIND* and *SAY*

Three of the most frequent verbs that collocate with 'I' and 'We' in the CEAL-CAWE are *SEE*, *FIND*, and *SAY*. The reason I placed them in one subsection to discuss is that they are all frequently used in the same phrasal pattern, *we can/could see/find/say (that)*. In addition, they serve the same discourse functions when collocating with the FPPs in this phrase. Other functions of these three verbs when they co-occur with 'I' and 'We' in different phraseologies are also discussed here.

The verb *SEE*

From a total of 747 instances, *SEE* collocates with 'We' 737 times. In these 737 co-occurrences of 'We' and *SEE*, the verb *SEE* is used 596 times in the frame *we * see*(' * ' indicates wildcard that represents any one single word in Sketch Engine). Even though the wildcard could be any word alternating between 'We' and *SEE*, two modal verbs *can* and *could* are the most frequent collocations with these two words. The phrase *we can/could see* occurs 529 times out of the 596 instances of *we * see*. Moreover, 51% of the instances of the expression *we can/could see* are followed by *that*-clauses, which form a longer unit, i.e. *we can/could see that*.

The verb *SEE* may be categorised into different groups according to the verb classifications provided by previous scholars. It could be a verb of *"Mental Perception"* that labels a concrete or abstract "Existence" according to Halliday(1994:148). It could also be a *Mental verb* according to Biber et al. (2002) because it indicates the mental process of processing and reception. It could also be a *Research verb* according to Fløttum et al. (2006:209) because it is considered as the 'perception verb' that relates to the research process and implies the author's role in the combination with 'I' and 'We' as a researcher. Additionally, it may also be a *Metadiscoursal verb* that functions as interpersonal markers or relational markers; that either refers to or includes or aligns the readers (cf. Ädel 2006; Hyland 1998; Kuo 1998). These classifications are derived from the analyses of different research contexts and for different types of research purposes. Biber et al. (2002) extract the verbs from a wide range of different genres, including academic text, conversations, fiction and news discourse, to achieve general reference purposes to assist the students and their teachers. The corpus used in Fløttum et al. (2006) includes only academic written texts. In that particular piece of research, they focus on the writer's roles and whether or not, the personal pronouns include the reader, namely, the exclusiveness or inclusiveness of the FPPs.

The term *metadiscourse* has been used in a number of ways. When it is defined broadly, it may cover a wide range of discourse functions. However, for the purpose of the exploration of the discourse functions in this research, it appears to be useful to adopt a much narrower definition of metadiscourse. In this chapter and throughout this thesis, metadiscourse refers to those expressions which serve text reflexive uses only (Mauranen 1993).

In many studies, it is argued that the phrase *we can / could see* is primarily a metadiscoursal expression; mainly because the phrase itself does not provide new information but directs the readership to the forthcoming content. In addition, this phrase usually co-occurs with a reference to propositions, tables, and figures in the texts, which adds weight to its function as metadiscoursal(see Ädel 2006; Crismore et al. 1993; Hyland 1998, 2004). However, in this study I would argue that this phrase performs a less obvious, but yet important function of research interpretation rather than serve as a simple signpost for information.

As an illustration, to be able to decide the discourse function of the phase *we can / could see*, one needs to put what follows this phrase in its context. In the corpus of this study, almost all the instances of *we can / could see* are followed by statements of the writers' understanding and interpretation of the previous discussions, tables or figures. These cognitive processes present the authors' judgments and evaluations on the topics or the aspects that are discussed in the texts. Figure 4.1 lists 10 random concordances extracted from the PGBM. In these 10 concordance lines, what follow the phrases *we can see* are all comments, interpretations or discussions of the previous texts. They are not mere repetition or rewording of that which has been delivered but new information coupled with understanding and evaluation of matters that the writers wish to express. This is not an assertion that this phrase does not perform the interpersonal function of directing and aligning with the readers, but that the interpersonal metadiscoursal function of including and aligning the audience is largely attributable to the plural personal pronoun 'We' instead of the verb *see*. When the verb *SEE* and 'We' collocate in the phrase *we can/ could see that* in these academic texts, arguably, the phrase is primarily used to present the writer's interpretation of the research.

down its path of several thousands years,	we can see	that "qing" have played a pivotal role
Donthu 1998). From the above discussions	we can see	that a person's perceptions are profoundly
job-related satisfaction. From the table,	we can see	differences of motivational factors between
Chinese and American cultures and motivations,	we can see	that culture plays an important role in
conflict by nature From the figure 4.1,	we can see	that Americans score much higher on the
conflict situations Through this figure,	we can see	that the differences in scores on each
counterparts, they are more direct, which	we can see	from the scores on the item B. When compared
among group members (Pizam and Jeong, 1996).	We can see	that the cross-cultural studies on tourist
individuals to comply with the group. From fig.l	we can see	that at a score of 20 China is a highly
conducted to test whether H4 was supported.	We can see	from the results of t-test (Table 8) that
reputation. In many Chinese destinations,	we can see	that some travel guides use some cheating

Figure 4.1   Sample concordances of *we can see* in PGBM

In comparison to the most frequently used phrase *we can/ could see*, Figure 4.2 lists all the other instances of 'We' and the verb *see* collocates in the Business and Management related academic texts. In most of these cases, the verb *see* in Figure 4-2 belongs to *activity verbs* according to Biber et al.'s(2002) classification. It means *to perceive with the eyes* (https://en.oxforddictionaries.com) with the '*doer*', *we* in these concordances.

create our patterns of thought; the way	we see	and experience the world; and the way we
core. The outer ring area represents what	we see	in our normal life, for example, American
societies are past oriented. Therefore,	we see	that agricultural tradition has both provided
great potential to effect positive change.	We see	opportunities to influence our own operations
closer economic and trade relationships,	we see	more Chinese using American marketing tactics
core. The outer ring area represents what	we see	in our normal life, for example, American
create our patterns of thought; the way	we see	and experience the world; and the way we
in a culture ever since we were bom. What	we see	, hear, smell, touch, feel, eat and even
. Hofstede's definition of culture that	we see	above is actually a definition of national
them with challenges. In this dimension,	we see	Chinese culture and U.S. culture as on
avoid silence and delayed responses. As	we saw	, Sanlu did not answer the calls, which
, became one. It is in this dilemma that	we see	the reasons for much of what underlies
product itself but goes much further, as	we have seen	for service. Firstly, costs are
employees did not have clear goals at work.	we have seen	the problems in the application
a very good example for other companies.	we have seen	others, and we will see more.
Dunning, 2000a). In the last two decades	we have seen	, in the more traditional economics
accumulated from international trade surplus.	we have seen	many cases of loss happening
resources it based on. In the last decade,	we saw	a trend of increasing globalization
when the last model appears on the screen,	we saw	a foreigner wearing Chinese tunic suit
a large sum of revenue. In October 2011,	we even saw	advertisements of Vancle, Yougou
lture--freely developing and releasing you; when	we saw	XYZ's logo, we understand it means

**Figure 4.2　Instances of the collocation of 'We'
and SEE other than we can/could see in BM**

The following examples are from Figure 4-2:

Example 4-1: What *we see*, hear, smell, touch, feel, eat and even think can all be traced back to the concept of culture. (PGBM 0112)

Example 4-2: To our surprises, when the last model appears on the screen, *we saw* a foreigner wearing Chinese tunic suit, which is one of Chinese own designed menswear. (UGBM 04607)

There are also a few cases in Figure 2 where the subject and verb collocation *we see* functions as a research interpretation in the form of *we can/could see* as discussed above. The extended context of one example from Figure 2 is,

Example 4-3: It is in this dilemma that *we see* the reasons for much of what underlies German culture: of the major three western European nations, Germany has suffered the most with an identity crisis, resulting in a fundamental insecurity that drives many aspects of its cultural, political, economic, and personal behavior. (PGBM 0127)

In this sense, when the verb *SEE* is used with 'We' in other sequences, other than *we can/could see*, the meaning and textual function of this phrase could vary depending on the context in which it is used.

To summarise the verb *SEE*, it is most frequently used in the phrasal pattern *we can/could see (that)* in the texts written by the Chinese novice writers. In addition, it is argued in this study that this phrase is primarily used to present interpretation of the research or the research findings in the academic texts.

The verb *FIND*

The verb *FIND* is used in two forms, *find* and *found*, in the corpus. It is found that this verb is used for two different purposes, often but not always distinguished by two different phrasal patterns in these academic texts. One function is *to present research findings* and the other is *to interpret research findings*. The former, 123 out of 267 instances, is used in the phrases *I/we find/found*, to report research findings. The latter is used most frequently in the phrase *we can/could/may/will find*, totaling 227 instances, performing a similar research interpretation function as *we can/could see* discussed in the previous section.

The difference between the two meanings of *FIND* may be observed from its surrounding context. When it is used to *present the research finding* in the phrase *I/We find/found* the content that follows this phrase is the research result derived from the investigation, the research, the reading of related literature books, or in some cases, from learning experiences. What is in common in these instances are that the contents of the instances that follows this phrase are 'hard facts' with information that withstands vigorous scrutiny of supporting evidence that was derived from the investigations that were conducted. These results cannot be questioned in the current texts, though they might be retested and proved to be false in a replicated examination. On the other hand, when the phrase *we can / could / may / will find* is used to *interpret research* the content that follows this expression is a statement of the understanding, explanation or elaboration of the entities or propositions that have been put forward or mentioned in the surrounding text, for example, *from the analysis / table / chart we can find*. When interpreting research, the employment of 'We', on the one hand, indicates the intention of alignment. On the other hand, with full awareness of the existence of the readership and their expertise in the academic community, the student writers are aware that the audience may have a very different understanding depending specifically on what has been discussed in the texts. By using the modal verb *can* in this phrase, the writers present their viewpoints for the readers to reexamine and reinterpret.

The difference between the uses of *presenting researching findings* and *interpreting research* are illustrated in the following four examples,

Example 4-4: From the interview *I found* that both Chinese also consider arriving in time for business meetings as a virtue which is promoted in the thoughts of Confucius. (PGBM 0064)

Example 4-5: These researches help us get a better understanding about the diffusion of innovations in
some particular field. Yet until now *I found* only a
few researches on the diffusion of innovation from
cultural point of view, which means diffusion of innovation in countries of different cultures. (PGBM
0073)

Example 4-6: From this figure, *we can find* that
the motivations of most Chinese companies are still in
the primary stage, such as to acquire land, to go public through buying a shell, and to diversify the business. The motivations of most companies going out are
blind. Excessive pursuit of expansion, aimless diversi-
fication and being alienated from reality create the issue that obstructing Chinese companies to close the
M&A deals. (UGBM 02208)

Example 4-7: On the other hand, *we can find* the
similarities on David Copperfield. Dickens arranged
David, a misery childhood father died before his
birth, stepfather was violent and greed, he worked as
a child labor at 9, which were quite similar to the
childhood of Dickens. (UGEL 02707)

The verb *FIND* is used to present the research findings
through an interview in Example 4-4 and by virtue of a literature review in Example 4-5. These are specific results that leave
little space for the readers to negotiate. On the other hand, in
Examples 4-6 and 4-7, the verb is used to develop the author's
point of view or understanding of the research results. In both

cases, "motivations" (Example 4-6) and "similarities" (Example 4-7) are general comments and open to debate. Again, the writer of course expects the audience to agree with him/her by using 'We' inclusively.

When serving the function of *presenting research findings*, the verb *FIND* mostly collocates with 'I'. When the function of *interpreting research* is used, this verb almost always collocates with 'We', occurring in the phrase *we can / could / may / will find*. This suggests that the meanings of this verb can be differentiated according to the different uses when it collocates with 'I' and 'We'. The difference between the two FPPs in phrase will be discussed in more detail in Chapter 7.

In general, the verb *FIND* has two main functions, *to present research findings* and *to interpret research*. Not only are the two functions used in two different phrases in most of the instances but also to collocate with, with varying frequency, 'I' and 'We' respectively.

The verb SAY

replace fantasy with bodily desires. Or	we	may *say* she does not know what she is after
respect each other' character. Therefore,	we	can *say* that their marriage is founded
forgetting them, they have their own voices. If	we	*say* that Laura's glass menagerie is the
first step towards accepting some truth,	we	may *say* , it is a kind of self-awakening
predicting future disasters and pains. Therefore,	we	may *say* that the contribution of the fourth
event in the readers' minds are aroused.	We	cannot *say* who is correct in judging some
vent for her intellectual energy. At least	we	can *say* it is not purely for other people
Collins-Charlotte's dilemma is a real one. Also	we	can *say* in Pride and Prejudice, the dilemma
study the character division of Jane Eyre.	We	d rather *say* the split character of Charlotte
make people happy and enjoy their life.	We	cannot *say* this purpose is true or not.

Figure 4.3   The verb *say* collocating with 'We' in UGEL

The verb *SAY* is, primarily, a verb of saying when it is considered on its own. However, it is observed that in all the 113 occurrences, *SAY* is used to construct an argument if it is considered in the phrase with the FPPs and in the extended discourse of this study. To be more specific, in the academic texts of this research, *SAY* is used frequently in the phrase *we / I can / cannot / may / might / should say*. Chinese novice writers use this phrase to claim or oppose propositions in their academic discourse. The modal verbs in this phrase are used either to strengthen the points of view, or as hedges to express less authoritative opinions of disagreement. The examples are given in Figures 4.3 and 4.4. These are 10 random concordance lines of *say* retrieved from the UG and PG subcorpora respectively. As illustrated, they are almost all used in the same phrase and have the same function, i.e. to argue.

as well as social ideals and philosophy.	We	can *say* that to some degree it is the high
many percents of people have this feature.	we	can *say* much more safely that compared
is a matter of learning. In this sense,	we	can *say* from the instant of birth, a child
to its subsidiaries. Through these cases,	we	can *say* that product crisis is one of the
for to communicate with the public. And	we	should *say* that Johnson and Johnson's
pnoting media and advertisement, the least	we	can *say* is that U.S. cultural industry
as well as social ideals and philosophy.	We	can *say* that to some degree it is the high
or not. Considering the grade France has,	we	can *say* that the French culture does
Web ergonomics goes along with web design;	we	can *say* that the first one dissects the
the analysis of the participant answers.	We	could *say* that the focus group will have

Figure 4.4   The verb *say* collocating with 'We' in PGBM

The following are more examples of this phrase *I / We can / cannot / may / might / should say* in the extended context in the corpus:

Example 4-8: Through these cases, **we can say** that product crisis is one of the most destructive factors to the corporations, and the corporations will become the blamed ones to all forces. Therefore, product crisis should be handled properly, which will not only affect the corporation's reputation, but also decide whether the corporation could survive, develop and expand under intense competition. (PGBM 0114)

Example 4-9: Nearly everyone in *The Forsyte Saga* is more or less influenced by social changes. So *we could say* Galsworthy is a realistic master at the turn of the century because of his success in realistic characterization. However, materialism is also reflected in the characterization of the trilogy. Galsworthy heavily depends on the description of appearance and environment in his portrait of characters. Each and every character cannot avoid some words of description of their appearance when they first appear. (PGEL 0073)

In the two examples above, both phrases, *we can say* and *we could say* are used to express the writers' judgments and viewpoints. In Example 4-8, the proposition that "product is one of the most destructive factors to the corporations" is drawn from the analyses of the cases in the texts. In Example 4-9 the evaluation of the writer Galsworthy, as a "realistic master at the turn of the century" is concluded from the analysis of the characters in his novel *The Forsyte Saga*. The verb *SAY* in both examples are not the action of *speaking* or *saying*, but the writers' evaluations and/or standpoints concerning the topics they discuss in their texts respectively.

To summarise, the verb *SAY* presents little sense of the act of *saying or speaking* in the phrase *I/we can/cannot/may/might/should say* in this study. This verb, together with the FPPs and the modal verbs, serves to expressing evaluations or viewpoints, either assertively or tentatively, in the academic texts written by Chinese students.

4.2.2   *KNOW* , *think* and *believe*

The three verbs, *KNOW* , *think* and *believe* are grouped together here for discussion because they are cognitive verbs and indicate mental processes. In this sense, writers may use these verbs to express understanding and attitude towards propositions or entities. In other words, these verbs may be used to argue for or against a particular viewpoint in an academic text. However, in this research, it is found that these verbs are not always used for this purpose. The verb *KNOW* is an exception. It shows more than one function in the text of these novice Chinese writers. In addition, each function of this verb may be found in one frequently used phrasal pattern.

The verb *KNOW*

The most frequent use of the verb *KNOW* is in the phrases (*as*) *we* (*all*) *know* and *we know* (*that*). Out of 308 total instances of *know* collocating with 'I' and 'We' in the whole corpus, 206 instances contain these two phrases. Among these 206 occurrences, 178 instances of the two phrases are used *to construe knowledge communities*, accounting for 58% of the total. In this study, it is argued that the knowledge community is construed rather than simply represented by the collocation of 'We' and *KNOW*. In other words, the writer considers the knowledge as given and in so doing construes the knowledge community. In this construed disciplinary community, it is decided by the writer that whoever encompasses the plural FPP 'We' should 'know' or 'have known' the knowledge the writer states, regardless of the fact that the asserted statement may or may not be shared intellectual property to both the writer and the readers. Further, the population of the construed knowledge community could vary in relation to what the writer tries to share. It can be rather large if the construed knowledge is the common sense that is shared by almost everyone in real life. Example 4-10 illustrates this point. The knowledge community can also be a society with a limited number of people who are equipped with knowledge specific to a certain discipline, such as the type of knowledge proposed in Examples 4-11 and 4-12.

There may be multiple pragmatic effects by adopting this assumption when construing knowledge community in academic discourse. Firstly, if the knowledge is general knowledge that requires little specific disciplinary expertise, these expressions, (*as*) *we* (*all*) *know* and *we know* (*that*), save both space and effort to explain to the readers. Secondly, if the knowledge is field-specific and is known to the readers, these expressions do not only save the space and effort, but also align the readers with the writer into one disciplinary community. This accommodation enhances the writer's credibility. At the same time, there is an implied sense of belongingness to this community, which lowers the risks of being challenged by the audience as both parties are members of a shared disciplinary society. In this sense, the writer could use *the knowledge* proposed by *as we* (*all*) *know* and *we know that* as a solid and safe stepping stone to further his/her argument.

      Example 4-10: *As we all know*, China is the largest developing country with enormous market potentials; while the United States is the largest developed country with a tremendous sum of money seeking investment opportunities elsewhere. Both countries carry a significant weight on the world stage, share important interests in maintaining world peace and stability, promoting common development of the two countries and the world as a whole. (PGBM 0099)

Example 4-11: *As we all know*, brand loyalty from customers will lower price elasticity. Starbucks is doing very well in building its brand. The brand is a recognizable voice, through which customers can get a better understanding of the company. (UGBM 07606)

Example 4-12: *We know that* as narrative develops to be textual and recorded, the narrator is abstracted to a textual voice. Under this condition, multi-level narration comes to solve the problem. (PGEL 0023)

In essence, it is unknown to the writers whether the knowledge is genuinely shared between them and their readers. Construing a knowledge community by the expressions *as we (all) know* and *we know(that)* could be the writers' deliberate employment of a writing strategy in their academic writing. It could be argued that there is a possibility that the student writers took it for granted, that the knowledge is shared due to the fact the readers would be the examiners or professionals who grade their dissertations in the same or similar fields of knowledge. Thus, it is understandable that the knowledge left unexplained by the implication of ' *we know it, therefore it is unnecessary to discuss it in detail*'.

However, even apart from this concern, it is still fairly obvious that the writer's intention is to achieve solidarity by using the two phrases, both of which suggest either an inclusion as an insider or membership of a certain disciplinary community.

The other common use of the verb *KNOW* collocating with the FPP 'We' is *we can/could know*, which functions to account for or justify new information from the analysis or discussion in the texts. In the following two examples, the interpretation of the influence of Emily's father on her life is from the reading and interpretation of the original texts in Example 4-13. In Example 4-14, the account of the meaning of the picture is from the former analysis in that thesis. Therefore, this function may be grouped into the class of *interpreting research*.

Example 4-13: He controlled and manipulated the destiny of Emily even after his death. He drove the young followers away from Miss Emily. *We know* this from the reflection of the townspeople when they thought Homer, a Yankee, broke up with Emily: "we knew that this was to be expected too; as if that quality of her father which had thwarted her woman's life so many times had been too virulent and too furious to die." (Faulkner, 1977:126) (UGEL 05606)

Example 4-14: From the analysis of this picture, *we can know* the messages in the advertisement are: Linguistic message: five big Chinese words in different sizes express the good wishes to the football game. The encoded iconic message: four classic moments of the Chinese football players in black-and-white, exalting, unforgettable. The decoded iconic or symbolic message: share all the exacting moments with the coke and enjoy the beautiful life. (UGBM 05204)

Considering the phrase *we know* serves two discourse functions in the texts. To differentiate the two functions needs the assistance of context. When the verb *KNOW* is used *to construe knowledge community* in the text, the statement is provided without further explanation, which is assumed as 'Known' to both the writer and potential readers. When *we know* is used *to interpret research* the information followed is processed or evaluated by the student on the basis of the research results or investigated material in the study, for example, an excerpt from a book or novel in the English Literature discipline.

The verbs *think* and *believe*

Both verbs, *think* (131 instances) and *believe* (44 instances), are used to express opinions. Though they are not the most frequent verbs collocating with 'I' and 'We', they are the most frequently used verbs of the mental verb class(cf. Biber et al. 2002) in this study. The research at the undergraduate and the postgraduate levels was mostly conducted by individual students. Accordingly, the verbs *think* and *believe* collocate with 'I' more frequently than with 'We' to signal the writer's individual ownership of the viewpoint. In the corpus, *think* collocates with 'I' 98 times in 131 occurrences; *believe* collocates with 'I' 42 times in 44 instances. When collocating with the singular FPP, *I think* and *I believe* are used to express the author's understanding, perspective and attitude.

Example 4-15: Many critics regard this confliction as an essential process towards Nora's maturity and awakening of her subordinate status. However, *I think* it is just her expression of disappointment of Helmer. (UGEL 00406)

Example 4-16: Since this novel covers both the

historical background of wars and the tale of personal growth, *I think* existentialism, a philosophy concerning human existence and emphasizing man's freedom of choice, is a valid approach to this novel. (PGEL 0039)

Example 4-17: For that reason, *I believe* ethics cannot be easily judged since they are rather subjective concepts. The only problem is, in this integrating world, how we can balance the ethics of different interest groups. We must note, compromises may not help us with this complication. (UGBM 10108)

In a few cases, especially in the Business and Management texts, *I believe* is used to "show commitment or contribution to the research" (Kuo 1999: 130). The examples below are instances of declaration relating to the contributions made by the theses, beliefs that the writers hold, and predictions for the future trend of the business world.

Example 4-18: Furthermore, review process is segmented into aspects of channel performance, inter-firm evaluation, and responsibility. *I believe* this exquisite segmentation can show us behavioral differences of a channel under different culture climates in a logical and clearer way. (PGBM 0062)

Example 4-19: *I believe* the study can be helpful for further studies. It is hoped that people can continue this research and provide more in-depth ideas about PSA Peugeot Citroen and then leave more meaningful thoughts for other multinational enterprises. (UGBM 04207)

4.2.3   *DISCUSS* and *MENTION*

The two verbs *DISCUSS* (122 instances) and *MENTION* (78 instances) have two forms respectively: *discuss* and *discussed* and *mention* and *mentioned*. One phrase including *MENTION* and two phrases including *DISCUSS* are frequently used when collocating with 'I' and 'We' to perform the *discourse organising* function. They are *as I/we (have) mentioned* and *I/We will discuss* and *I/We have discussed*. These phrases are used either to guide the readers as to what to expect in the following text by using *I/We will discuss*, or to remind the readers of the argument that the writer made in the previous text, as in *as I/we (have) mentioned* and *I/We have discussed*. In such instances, signposts indicate where the discussion may be found. Phrases such as *In this part* in Example 4-21 and *In this chapter* in Example 4-22, are often an indication that the information may be found in close proximity.

> Example 4-20: **As I have mentioned**, Catherine and Heathcliff are actually one person, a wild soul dwelling in two bodies, which makes them exceedingly close and intimate. (UGEGL 07708)

> Example 4-21: **In this part**, we will compare the above two case studies in such aspects as the effects of cultural differences, the evaluation and management of cultural differences, and the mode of acculturation. Then **we will discuss** and testify the two assumptions made in chapter 2. (PGBM 0113)

> Example 4-22: **In this chapter**, *I have discussed* the materialistic characterization in the trilogy. John

Galsworthy depends heavily on the description of appearance and external environment in the characterization since he regards such description as an indispensable part of character portrayal. (PGEL 0073)

4.2.4 *USE* and *ANALYSE*

The verbs *USE* (90 instances) and *ANAYLSE* (87 instances) are listed separately from the other verbs because they are used for the description of research methods and procedures in the corpus. Essentially, the verbs are used to report the tools or processes of the writers' research. In this sense, they belong to Biber et al.'s (2002) classification of *activity verb*, which are 'intentionally' performed by the writers ('doer' or 'agent') when they conduct their research (see Examples 4-23 and 4-24).

Example 4-23: First *I used* two values to describe variable IC: the mean and the standard deviation of the scores. They are important indicators of data distribution. (PBM 0068)

Example 4-24: When *I analyze* Pecola's traumatic experiences in the framework of power negotiation, the first round of bombardment is directed at the prevailing white dominance on the larger social scale. (PGEL 0018)

It is worth noting that *USE and ANALYSE* vary in frequency in different disciplines, different academic levels and collocate with 'I' and 'We' respectively, which is discussed further in Chapters 5, 6 and 8.

4.2.5 *LEARN* and *READ*

These two verbs, *LEARN* (68 instances) and *read* (68 instances), are separated from other *activity verbs*, for example, *USE* or *ANALYSE* because both verbs refer to the epistemic activities of learning and reading. However, it is observed that these two verbs are used differently in the academic texts. The verb *LEARN* is used for *argument* (16 instances) and *research interpretation* (52 instances) respectively. The verb *read* is primarily used for the reporting of the epistemic activity of reading(53 instances). This function of *read* might not present itself at all in published research papers. As mentioned in Chapter 3, the graduation dissertation is one of the most important pieces of work of the students which can determine whether or not the academic degree will be conferred. In dissertation writing, a student writer is expected to present his/ her academic achievement, including the literature he/she has read during the years of higher education. To achieve this purpose, in most of the phrases of *I/We read*, the students use the verb *read* to report their reading activities. Similar to other verbs that are discussed in this chapter, each of the two verbs shows different functions in different phrasal patterns in these texts.

The verb *LEARN*

The verb *learn* has two functions when it collocates with 'We' (there are fewer than 5 instances of *learn* collocating with 'I'). One function is to suggest what knowledge or skill 'We' can or need to acquire through the study or the findings of the study, and the other is to illustrate and interpret research findings. In all the 68 instances of *learn*, 52 instances of *learn* are used to provide suggestions, and 16 instances perform the second function, that of interpreting research findings.

In almost all the cases, this first function of providing suggestion or recommendation by the 'We' and *learn* is found in one particular phrasal structure, *we can / could / should / need to / must learn (from)*. The examples are as follows.

Example 4-25: From M's great success, *we can learn* some valuable lessons that can help a company improve the development of quality and corporate culture. (UGBM 07204)

Example 4-26: Therefore, the most basic things *we should learn from* American businesses are their focus on customer and quality. Not only for manufacturing and marketing companies, even for research institutions, they should also focus their attention on what the end user really needs so that their inventions can enter into market successfully and bring profits. (PGBM 0087)

Example 4-27: What will be discussed in part three is what *we can learn from* Walden. The writer's philosophy indicates a simple lifestyle, suggests that people nowadays should have a re-examination of our lifestyle: the ultimate goal of life should be spiritual satisfaction. The need of establishing a new type of life value should be emphasized. We should try to explore in nature independently to reach a self-realization stage. (UGEL 01505)

Example 4-28: *We need to learn* in a new way to

bring our knowledge as well as recreation to our reception of the text. Completely different readers can
be differently affected by the "reality" of It is the an-
ti-interpretation form of devaluated language and simplified stage design in this play that leads readers in
the directions of either accepting various versions inspired by allusions or interpreting in their own ways
with illusions. The uncertain, the unformulated or
even the unwritten part of the play activates our own
faculties, enabling us to recreate the world it presents.
(PGEL 0027)

The second function of the verb *LEARN* is to *interpret
findings*. This function of *LEARN* is exclusively found in English Literature texts and the interpretation is achieved by detailed reading of the literature that the writer has read. This use
is most frequently used in the phrase where 'We' and *learn* are
adjacent to each other, i.e. *we learn*. In some cases, this collocation of *we learn* is followed by a reporting clause *that* as in
we learn that. Examples 4-29 and 4-30 list this use.

Example 4-29: According to the conversation in
the final part of the story between him and the grand-
mother, *we learn* that he claimed that he had not done
that bad thing which led to this prison life. (UGEL
02408)

Example 4-30: The first thing *we learn* about him
is that he himself shortened his name, Philip Pirrip,
to the insignificant nickname Pip. (PGEL 0050)

The verb *read*

Two functions of the verb *read* are observed in this study.

One is used *to report the epistemic experience*, in which case, the verb denotes the activity of reading. The other is to talk about reflective thinking, understanding or insight from reading, especially a particular piece of literature, which is to carry out the task of *interpreting research*. With the latter use, the writers use the phrase *we can / could read* and *read something as* to perform the function of interpretation. The first two of the following five examples are of the first function, and the rest, the second function.

Example 4-31: This was exactly the description of my feeling when **I read** through Alice in Bed, when my own ideas kept flowing out and colliding with her writing. (UGEL 07104)

Example 4-32: To deeply understand these subjects, **I read** a lot of essays about case studies of specific financial firms and institutions that played crucial roles. (UGBM 10407)

Example 4-33: As illustrated before, **we can read** Dickens's "shadow" in this fiction. Although Dickens opposed people to regard it as his autobiography, many scholars who make research on Dickens still take it as one of the important resources. (UGEL 02707)

Example 4-34: From this quoted excerpt, **we could read** the respect and belief in his elders, and Stephen was in the phase of developing his own way of understanding the world and his willingness to participate, outside of school and family is strong, so familial authority will be dethroned one day: [quote]

The inner independence and doubt about the solidity
of familial authority corrupt with the changes at
home, that Stephen's father would lost his property
and his life and his family's would be thusly influenced. (PGEL 0049)

Example 4-35: Whereas ecocritics unproblemati-
cally regard Merwin's nature poems as [quote] or as
establishing [quote]. *I read it as* a testimony of structural difference or a non-adequation between man and
nature. The Moment of Green does not only establish
a bond but also dialecticizes it, pushing the love of nature to the edge of self-destruction. (PGEL 0013)

In Example 4-31, *read* indicates the act of reading of one
particular book, and in Example 4-32, *read* is the act of reading many books to fulfill the need for the completion of the essay. In the Examples of 4-33, 4-34 and 4-35, instead of referring to the act of reading, *read* actually functions as interpretation of the findings of the reading activities, which involves the
writers' understanding, evaluation and attitude. In these instances, this phrase serves the same function as *we can/could/
may/will see/find/know* (that) when the verbs *SEE*, *FIND*
and *KNOW* are examined.

I have discussed some of the most frequent verbs that collocate with the first-person pronouns 'I' and 'We' in the
CEAL-CAWE corpus. When these verbs collocate with the two
FPPs, it can be seen that they show diverse meanings and perform different functions in different phrases. This finding is in
accordance with Sinclair's argument that "[i]f a word has several senses, each sense will tend to be associated most frequent-

ly with a different set of patterns" (Sinclair 1991, cited in Hunston 2002: 139). Moreover, what is worth mentioning is that some of the functions of the phrases of 'I', 'We' and the verbs collocating with them present corresponding phrases or phrasal frames in the texts, for instance, *we have discussed*, *as we all know*, and *read * as*, whereas the functions of some verbs are dependent on their wider contexts (e. g. *we know that*).

This section has discussed a few most frequently used verbs that collocate with 'I' and 'We'. The rest of the verbs were explored in the same way as these verbs. It is observed from the analyses that, even though they are different in meanings and uses, they can be grouped into a limited number of functional categories including discourse organising verbs (e. g. *mention* and *discuss*), research reporting verbs(e.g. *use* and *analyse*), knowledge community construing verb phrase(*as we all know*) and research interpretation verbs(e.g. *see* and *think*). Therefore, in order to examine all the verbs listed in this study(see Table 3.4 in Chapter 3), I classified them into four discourse functional categories to further explore their linguistic and pragmatic features across different disciplines and academic levels. The categorisation of the verbs is explained in the next section.

4.3   Verbs classification in the CEAL-CAWE

As illustrated in the above section, the analysed verbs that collocate with 'I' and 'We' show differences in terms of phraseological patterns, meanings and discourse functions in this study. The proposed classification appears, to some extent, to be at odds with those provided by Biber et al. (2002), Fløttum et al. (2006) and Hyland(2002, 2004, 2005).

Bearing in mind the pedagogical goal of this research, I want to differentiate the evaluative and non-evaluative expressions of the FPPs, 'I' and 'We'. Therefore, I propose the following verb categories: *Textual organising verbs*, *Research report verbs*, *Research interpretation verbs*, and *Knowledge community construing verb*.

What needs to be clarified prior to the discussion of this form of categorisation is that the verbs are not classified in this study as self-contained items, as it has already been shown that they have different senses and discourse functions when they co-occur with 'I' and 'We'. To classify the verbs therefore, I focus on the phraseology and the wider context of use.

4.3.1   The Textual organising verbs

The *Textual organising verbs* category includes non-propositional and non-evaluative phrases of the verbs collocating with the FPPs that are used to develop a coherent and reader-friendly text. This verb group belongs to a part of the metadiscourse expressions found in most of the studies on this subject (cf. Cirsmore et al. 1993; Hyland 1998, 2004, 2005). In these studies, the concept of metadiscourse can be really general and inclusive. However, trying to classify the verbs and setting up a comparatively clear boundary between evaluative and non-evaluative languages, I narrowed the definition of metadiscourse expressions in this study. Briefly, the collocations of 'I' and 'We' and the *Textual organising verbs* are those verbs that are used to illustrate the organisation of a text. There is no stance or judgement involved in the uses of these phrases. Verbs have been discussed in this category in Section 3 are *DISCUSS* and *MENTION*. The rest of the extracted verbs that belong to this category are listed in Table 4.1.

Table 4.1   Textual organising verbs collocating with 'I' and 'We'

Textual organising verbs	*cite*, *DISCUSS*, *explore*, *explain*, *focus*, *introduce*, *MENTION*, *present*, *quote*, *TALK*, *study*

4.3.2   Research report verbs

Research report verbs mainly consist of the activity verbs proposed by Biber et al. (2006). These verbs describe what happened in the 'real world', and most frequently, prior to the writing of the dissertations. In this study specifically, these verbs are used to report the learning process, intern experiences, the methodology of the research, each step of an empirical study and the findings of the research. One criterion for classifying the verbs into this group is that they involve neither evaluation nor information of attitude. In other words, they are the pure facts in these texts. Examples of this functional category include some instances of *use* and some instances of *FIND* when they are used to report, as discussed in Section 3.

Further, this group can be divided into two subcategories, *Epistemic verbs* and *Research conduct verbs*. Some instances of the verb, *read*, for example, may be classified as *Epistemic verbs* when they describe the learning or reading experience of the student's years of academic education. Another two verbs of this subcategory are *live* and *WORK*. The verbs, *use* and *analyse* are classified as *research conduct verbs* because they describe the methodology of the performed research. Additional verbs on the verb list that could be put into this group are *look*, *EXAMINE*, *CALL*, *COLLECT*, etc., see Table 4.2.

Table 4.2   Research report verbs collocating with 'I' and 'We'

	Epistemic verbs	*WORK*, *read*
Research report verbs	Research conduct verbs	*act*, *ANALYZE*, *apply*, *asked*, *arrange*, *CALL*, *CHOOSE*, *COLLECT*, *compare*, *define*, *divide*, *EXAMINE*, *explore*, *FIND*, *focus*, *hear*, *infer*, *OBSERVE*, *look*, *notice*, *proposed*, *SEE*, *test*, *USE*

4.3.3   Research interpretation verbs

The *Research interpretation verbs* include verbs that express the writer's understanding, viewpoint, argument, evaluation of a certain entity as well as the representation and interpretation of the research results. Verbs like *think* and *believe* discussed in Section 3 are the examples from this group.

As stated previously, the inclusion of the verbs like *see* and *find* in the phrases *as we can see* and *as we can find* into *Research interpretation* group may be questioned. In many other studies, they are grouped into the metadiscourse category because they indicate what it is about to be presented in the following context. However, I would argue in favour of the proposed classification because of the knowledge construction function of these phrases, namely, taking into account the writer's reprocessing and reinterpretation of the research findings, that it would be more reasonable to group them into the

Research interpretation category. The phrases that these verbs are used in, suggest that a process of looking into the results and generalising the comments of the findings is taking place. The discourse contains the author's attitude and stance, either explicitly or implicitly. The writer uses the collocations of FPPs with the verbs to express their viewpoints or their evaluation in relation to their findings, good or bad, positive or negative, certain or uncertain, or the way in which it may influence the outcome of the research.

　　In this category, I also attempt to distinguish between that which implies an attitude and that which implies an agreement or difference in this group. Referring to Hunston's(1993) classification, I classified the *Research interpretation verbs* further into two subgroups(see Table 4.3).

1) Verbs of epistemological status or understanding of the research results, for example, *SEE*, *FIND*, *conclude*.

2) Verbs of arguing, which provide the attitude of the writer, including verbs presenting a writer's own point of view, and verbs indicating potential differences between a writer and original researcher or scholar. Examples of this group are *think*, *believe*, and *understand*.

Table 4.3　Research interpretation verbs collocating with 'I' and 'We'

Research interpretation verbs	Verbs of research finding interpretation	*aware*, *conclude*, *define*, *feel*, *FIND*, *imagine*, *judge*, *KNOW*, *LEARN*, *mean*, *notice*, *read*, *SAY*, *SEE*, *sense*, *suppose*, *TELL*
	Verbs of arguing	*agree*, *argue*, *believe*, *concerned*, *consider*, *hope*, *ignore*, *KNOW*, *learn*, *read*, *SAY*, *SEE*, *think*, *understand*

4.3.4   Knowledge community construing verb

The classification of *Knowledge community construing verb* group is rather tricky, partly because only one verb *know* is found to belong to this group, and partly because it is not the verb itself but the phrases *as we(all) know* and *we know(that)* perform the function of constructing the background knowledge and furthering the argument in the texts. When the verb *know* is examined in the two most frequent phrases, *as we(all) know* and *we know(that)*, both are used to construe a community who share specific or disciplinary knowledge. The use of the two phrases is to set a robust knowledge background to support latter arguments in the texts. The argument in this study is that this knowledge community is construed or created by wordings rather than in real existence in reality. The notion that the community shares knowledge is purely the writer's presumption. When writing an academic text, the potential audience may be predictable. An academic text is most probably only read by people in the same or related discipline. However, it is impossible to know exactly who the readers are. Thus, there is no ground to state that the shared knowledge is genuinely shared. Essentially, a writer does not know for sure whether the reader possesses that proposed 'shared knowledge' or not. It is the reader's assumption that it is shared by both parties, writer and reader.

4.3.5   The verbs that might be grouped into more than one category

It is important to point out that some of the verbs in the

retrieved verb list belong to more than one category when collocating with 'I' and 'We'. The verb *find*, for example, belongs to *Research report verbs* as well as *Research interpretation
verbs* class. The verb *know* is associated with *community
knowledge construing verb* and *Research interpretation*, depending on which phrase it is used in when collocating with the
FPPs. Another example is the verb *ANALYSE*. As discussed,
this verb is frequently used to report research procedures. However, it is also found that the students use *ANALYSE* in the
phrase *I/we will/be going to analyse* to organise discourse in
this study (see Section 5.3.3.2 of Chapter 5). Furthermore,
sometimes, even in the same phrase, a verb can serve more
than one function when it collocates with 'I' and/or 'We'. For
example, the verb *see* in the phrase *we can see that* can be used
for both interpretation of research findings and metadiscourse
function of text organizing. The overlap and multi-function of
these collocate verbs caused difficulties in the process of the
categorization of these discourse functions (the multi-function
of the identified phrases is discussed in more detail in Chapter
7). Even though the categorization is not without difficulties,
as Hyland(1999:8) notes that:

> " A classification scheme can therefore only
> approximate the complexity and fluidity of natural
> language use. But while it may give no firm evidence
> about author intentions or reader understandings, it is
> a useful means of revealing meanings available in the
> text and comparing the rhetorical strategies employed
> by different discourse communities and different
> genres".

This argument applies to the categorisation of the verb in this study as well. Though the boundaries of some of the categories are not clearly demarcated, the categories are purported to encompass the EFL students' linguistic and rhetorical employment of the FPPs and the verbs that collocate with them, including their phraseology, discourse functions, writer identity reflected by these means, and the principles behind the choices of 'I', 'We' and the verbs that co-occur with them.

In order to facilitate the quantitative and qualitative contrastive analysis between different disciplines and academic levels, they will be classified into their corresponding functional group(s) when the verbs are examined in the following chapters. This means that a verb may be grouped into more than one functional group if it presents multifunctional features when collocating with 'I' and 'We' at the categorisation stage. The next section presents a brief sample analysis of how the comparisons were conducted.

4.4   Sample analysis

To illustrate how the comparative analysis across the disciplines(BM vs. EL) and the academic levels(UG vs. PG) were carried out, the categories of the verbs proposed in this study may need to be highlighted again. To recapitulate, the verbs that collocate with 'I' and 'We' are classified into four classes, *Textual organising verbs*, *Research report verbs*, *Research interpretation verbs*, and *Knowledge community construing verb*. Further, the *Research report verbs* are subdivided into *Epistemic verbs* and *Research conduct verbs*. *Research interpre-*

tation verbs are subdivided into *Verbs of research finding inter-pretation* and *Verbs of arguing* (see Table 4.4). In total, 6 functional groups of the verbs that collocate with 'I' and 'We' in the corpus are identified. The verbs extracted in this study are examined as part of the phrases of 'I', 'We' and their collocating verbs, neither without the two FPPs as their subjects nor freestanding in isolation by themselves out of their disciplinary genre. There are a few places in this study where I investigate how the verbs are used without 'I' and 'We' with inanimate subjects (see, for example, the analysis of the verb *DISCUSS* in Section 6.3.1). In such cases, I mark explicitly that these verbs are examined not as part of the phrases of 'I', 'We' and their collocating verbs.

Table 4.4   Functional categories proposed in this study

Functional category	Subcategory	Example verb	Example phrase
Textual organising verbs	———	DISCUSS, MENTION, focus	*We have discussed, as I mentioned, I will focus*
Research report verbs	*Epistemic verbs*	WORK, read	*I worked, I read*
	Research conduct verbs	FIND, USE, ANALYSE	*We found, I used, I analyzed*
Research interpretation verbs	*Verbs of research finding interpretation*	SEE, FIND, KNOW	*We can see that, we can find that, we know that*
	Verbs of arguing	SAY, think, believe	*We can say that, I think, I believe*
Knowledge community construing verb	———	know	*As we know*

Take the verb *SEE* as an example (*SEE* is a lemma here

that represents the different forms of this verb, *see*, *saw* and
seen). The verb frequently collocates with the FPPs in the
CEAL-CAWE corpus. It collocates with 'I' and 'We' 747
times, which is 11% of the 6,813 instances of the two FPPs.
When collocating with 'I' and/or 'We', this verb serves the
following functions in the students' essays: *to interpret research*
in the phrase *as we can/could see(that)*. For example,

Example 4-36: From Chart 2 **we can see that** there
is also a large disparity between frequencies at which
the male and female characters are portrayed as professionals in Sino-US joint ventures ads. (PGBM 0076)

Two functions are performed by the phrase *we/I see*: one
is to *interpret research* (see Example 4-37), which is the same as
we can/could see(that), and the other is *to report research*, in
which case, the verb *SEE* is used as an *Epistemic verb* to present the student's general knowledge or experience prior to the
writing of his/her thesis, see Example 4-38.

Example 4-37: In this dimension, **we see** Chinese
culture and U.S. culture as on the two extremes. Chinese culture is typically collectivist and U.S. culture is
an outstanding example of individualist culture. (PG-
BM 0112)

Example 4-38: Pretty soon, I was friends with
many colleagues. From what **I saw**, heard and observed, people in I-TEC knew and treated each other
like sisters and brothers, especially for those who
were and had been on the same project teams. (PGBM
0117)

To compare the phrases of 'I', 'We' and the verb *SEE*

between the two disciplines, the instances of *we can / could see* (*that*) are analysed in BM and EL respectively. In all the 322 occurrences of *SEE* co-occurring with the FPPs, 81% of the instances of the verb are in this phrase in BM. In EL, 266 instances of *SEE* (63%) are used in this phrase as well. In both disciplines, the phrase functions as *Research interpretation* expression. However, due to the different epistemic knowledge construction of the two disciplines, BM as an applied social science and EL as soft and pure, the phrase can be seen as *interpreting research* through a different cognitive process. Namely, the interpretation of what *we can see* in the BM is mainly based on quantitative data, which implies objectivity in the interpretation of the results. On the other hand, the expression of *we can see* in EL is from the understanding of the details of the novel or the book the writer reads, which is more subjective by nature than issues or matters that the BM students *see*. The number of occurrences of the verb *SEE* does not show divergence when the two academic levels are compared, neither in number of occurrences nor in discourse functions. There are 323 and 321 instances of this verb used as *verbs of research finding interpretation* in the phrase *we can / could see* in UG and PG respectively.

4.5   Conclusion

In this chapter, I have discussed the meaning and the textual function of some sample verbs when they collocate with 'I' and 'We'. In this study, the methodology of identification of the phrases is to look at the instances of the verbs that collocate with 'I' and 'We' and to observe those recurrent phrases. Two elements of all the phrases observed in this study are fixed, one is either 'I' or 'We', the other is the main verb that collocates with one of the FPPs. Based on the analysis of the meaning and the textual function of the verbs, I categorised them(57 verb types) into 4 categories.

This chapter has shown that a meaningful classification of the verbs may be achieved by focusing on frequently occurring phrases rather than by considering verbs in isolation. The categorisation of the verbs needs considerable attention to detail including the examination of the collocations with 'I' and 'We', and exploration of the extended discourse when and where necessary. This means, that I have focused on a relatively small set of verbs. Despite this, the coverage I have achieved is approximately a half of all the verbs that collocate with 'I' and 'We' in the CEAL-CAWE corpus. It should thus be noted that there is still another half in the corpus left unexamined. However, while I have only examined 48% of the instances, the examination has accounted for those frequent verbs that collocate with 'I' no less than 5 times and 'We' no less than 10 times in the corpora. The verbs that are not included occur less frequently. It is also worth stressing that the verb categories proposed in this chapter are not immune from attracting critical comment challenging their veracity and may only apply to this study. As discussed in this chapter and will be further shown in the following chapters, a verb may serve more than one function depending on the phrases it is used in, whether it is 'I' or 'We' that it collocates with and in the context in which it is used.

CHAPTER 5
PHRASES OF 'I', 'WE'
AND THEIR VERB COLLOCATES
ACROSS THE TWO DISCIPLINES

5.1   Introduction

This chapter explores the disciplinary differences between Business and Management(BM) and English Literature(EL), focusing specifically on 'I' and 'We' and their verb collocates across the two disciplines.

It should be noted that when I began this research I expected to find significant differences in the range of verbs that collocate with 'I' and 'We' in the two disciplines. This is primarily due to prior research which has suggested that the language use varies according to disciplines(e.g. Charles, 2004; Groom, 2007; Hyland 2002, 2005; Swales, 1991). In this study, I did find epistemic differences between BM and EL. This being the exception, there are both similarities and differences of the phraseology and the discourse functions of the phrases including the two FPPs and the verbs that collocate with them. Indeed, for the *Research Report verbs* (RR) category and *Research Interpretation verbs* (RI) category I did find some differences between the BM and the EL disciplines. The variation may be observed from a few investigated verbs, which are used in specific phrasal patterns to convey different meanings in BM and EL respectively. Other categories are *Textual Organising verbs* (TO) and *Knowledge community construing verbs* (KC) categories. There is however, a lot less difference in relation to the meaning, phraseology and discourse functions of the FPPs and their verb collocates in these categories.

The rest of the chapter is organized as follows. Section 2 accounts for the quantitative results of 'I', 'We' and the verbs collocating with them in the different categories of BM and EL. Section 3 presents the qualitative analysis of some of the most frequently used verbs that are retrieved in both disciplines. Section 4 discusses the similarities and differences between the two investigated disciplines. The last part concludes this chapter. When the phrases are discussed in this chapter, the difference between the two FPPs 'I' and 'We' when they collocate with the verbs will be discussed only where necessary.

5.2   A quantitative overview of the verbs collocating with 'I' and 'We' between BM and EL

This section compares the quantitative results and the four verb categories across the Business and Management and English Literature texts. As mentioned earlier, with the exception of the RR and RI categories, the quantitative tests for the occurrences of 'I' and 'We', and the rest of the verb categories, TO and KC, present little statistical difference between the two disciplines.

5.2.1   Quantitative results of 'I' and 'We'

The average length of the BM subcorpus is 8,258 words per text. The average length of the EL subcorpus is 9,211 words per text. After the data was processed, there were 213 out of 241 texts and 195 out of 215 texts that contain at least one instance of 'I' or 'We' in BM and EL respectively(see Table 5. 1). One EL text presents the most frequent usage of the two FPPs with 183 instances in the whole corpus. In the BM texts, one thesis with the most frequent use of 'I' and 'We' contains 102 occurrences of these two FPPs. Despite the variation of the number of the occurrences of the two FPPs in each text between the two disciplines, the normalised frequencies of 'I' and 'We' are almost similar in BM and EL. By t-test, the mean use of 'I' and 'We' per 1,000 words for BM corpus was 1.93 (SD = 1.88). The mean use per 1,000 words for EL corpus was 2.27(SD = 2.12). This difference is not statistically significant (unpaired t-test, $t(1,407) = 1.71$, $p = 0.09$), which suggests that there is not much difference in terms of the use of FPPs between BM and EL. The difference between the instances in each text and the statistical insignificance between the two disciplines suggests that there is more intra-discipline variation than inter-discipline variation. However, the aim of this chapter is to look at disciplinary difference between the two corpora. Therefore, this chapter focuses on the instances of the FPPs of all the texts.

Table 5.1　Quantitative information of BM and EL

	Number of texts	Tokens	Types	Hits of 'I' and 'We'	Normalized frequency per 1000 words of 'I' and 'We'
BM	241	2,064,315	32,269	3,385	1.64
EL	215	2,129,098	44,783	3,468	1.63

5.2.2　Quantitative results of the verb categories

As discussed in Chapter 3, to investigate the differences of 'I' and 'We' and the verbs that collocate with them, the verbs are classified into four categories in each discipline, *Textual organizing verbs* (TO), *Knowledge community construing verb* (KC), *Research report verbs* (RR), and *Research interpretation verb* (RI). At the classification stage, it is noted that some verbs can be assigned to more than one category when they are used with 'I' and/or 'We' in different phrases or in the context of an extended discourse (see Chapter 4). Therefore, in Tables 2 to 5, one verb may appear in two or more columns according to its different discourse functions in the students' theses. For example, the verb *KNOW* is classified as *Knowledge community construing verb* (90 in BM and 88 in EL), *Research Interpretation verb* (40 in BM and 53 in EL) and *Verb of Arguing* (20 in BM and 17 in EL). Tables 5.2 to 5.5 show the verbs in each category and the number of instances of these verbs in BM and EL respectively. The percentages provided at the bottom of the tables are the proportions of the hits of the verbs from each of the columns. These account for of all the verbs assembled in the BM(1,560 times) and EL(1,733 times) respectively. A total number of 57 verb types are investigated in this study.

Figure 5.1 shows some quantitative similarities and differences of the verb categories between the two disciplines. It can be seen that the two disciplines use about the same number of KC, EP, and AG verbs. On the other hand, BM presents more instances of TO to organise text and more occurrences of RC verbs to report research than EL. EL comprises more instances of RI verbs to interpret research results than BM.

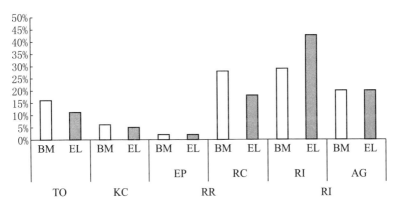

Figure 5.1   TO, KC, RR, and RI verbs in BM and EL

There is little quantitative difference in the TO and KC categories between the two disciplines, either in terms of the types of the verbs or the number of occurrences(see Tables 5.2 & 5.3). In BM and EL, the most frequently used verbs in both disciplines are almost the same, *DISCUSS*, *MENTION*, *ANALYZE*, and *focus*, etc.

Tables 5.4 and 5.5 show that BM includes more types and instances of RR than EL, and EL comprises more instances and types of the RI verbs than BM. It can be seen that some of the verbs are used uniquely in one discipline, either in BM or in

EL. For example, in the RR and the RI categories, *COL-LECT*, *arrange*, *test*, and *compare* only present themselves in BM, and *OBSERVE*, *argue*, and *infer* appear only in EL. Comparing the subcategories of RR and RI across the two disciplines, the *Research Conduct verbs* have more occurrences in BM than in EL. The *Verbs of Research Finding Interpretation* (RI) and *Verbs of Arguing* (AG) of the RI in Table 5 presents more occurrences in EL than in BM.

Table 5.2   TO verbs collocating with 'I' and 'We' in BM and EL

Textual Organising verbs			
BM		**EL**	
DISCUSS	57	DISCUSS	65
ANALYZE	37	MENTION	44
MENTION	34	ANALYZE	23
introduce	29	focus	17
focus	28	TALK	17
TALK	21	study	8
study	13	present	7
quote	11	explain	5
present	7	quote	5
cite	6		
	243		191
	16%		11%

Table 5.3   KC verbs collocating with 'I' and 'We' in BM and EL

Knowledge Community Construing verbs			
BM		**EL**	
know	90	KNOW	88
	6%		5%

The similar number of instances of TO, EP, KC and AG can only tell us that the student writers utilise almost the same number of verbs that collocate to serve these discourse functions in their academic discourse. What the tables do not tell is how these pragmatic effects are achieved in discourse and how they manifest. The quantitative difference and variation of verb types in RR and RI categories between the two disciplines are probably not unexpected taking into account the disciplinary features of BM as a Social science and EL as a Humanities discipline. BM discipline conducts more research that is empirical and stresses practical implementation, while EL focuses more on the

Table 5.4   RR verbs collocating with 'I' and 'We' in BM and EL

Research Report verbs					
Epistemic verbs				Research conduct verbs	
BM		EL		BM		EL	
worked	12	READ	35	FIND	137	FIND	130
READ	18			USE	77	look	32
				ANALYZE	22	hear	26
				CHOOSE	42	CALL	24
				COLLECT	21	notice	18
				look	20	infer	16
				EXAMINE	16	SEE	19
				SEE	12	USE	13
				act	12	examine	12
				define	12	OBSERVE	12
				asked	10	choose	7
				notice	10	apply	5
				arrange	9	ANALYZE	5
				explore	8		
				test	7		
				proposed	6		
				compare	5		
				divide	5		
	30		35		431		319
	2%		2%		28%		18%

interpretation and exploration of literary works. Hence, to better understand the similarity and differences, we need to examine the phraseology and textual function of these verbs and the FPPs collocations.

5.3   Verbs collocating with 'I' and 'We' in the Business and management and the English Literature disciplines

In this section, 3 or 4 verbs from each category, TO, KC, RR and RI of BM and EL that were used in both disciplines and on the top of the frequency lists are examined. The discussion focuses on the phraseological features, meanings and discourse functions of these verbs in academic writing across the two disciplines. In order to avoid repetition, some of the verbs are discussed under one category only, even though they may be present in more than one category in the tables listed in Section 5.2. For example, under the RR class, *FIND* is examined when it is used as a RR verb and as a RI verb, and *ANALYZE* is explored as both a RR and a TO verb in these student writers' academic texts.

Table 5.5   RI verbs of BM and EL collocating with 'I'
and 'We' in BM and EL

Research Interpretation verbs							
Verbs of research finding interpretation				Verbs of arguing			
BM		EL		BM		EL	
SEE	275	SEE	369	think	70	SAY	74
find	95	find	134	SEE	43	think	61
KNOW	40	KNOW	53	SAY	39	understand	32

continued

Research Interpretation verbs							
Verbs of research finding interpretation				Verbs of arguing			
BM		EL		BM		EL	
conclude	20	feel	32	understand	38	see	29
mean	12	conclude	28	learn	36	argue	24
tell	12	MEAN	26	believe	30	hope	23
felt	5	TELL	17	KNOW	20	consider	21
		learn	16	hope	18	KNOW	17
		read	15	agree	7	learn	16
		sense	14	consider	6	believe	14
		suppose	12			realize	13
		aware	10			agree	12
		judge	10			ignore	11
		imagine	10			concerned	7
	459		746		307		354
	29%		43%		20%		20%

5.3.1   Textual organising verbs

The two most frequent verbs, *DISCUSS* and *MENTION*, of the Textural Organising category were compared across BM and EL. Generally speaking, in this category, there is not much difference found between the two disciplines, neither in terms of their uses nor meanings when they collocate with the first personal pronouns, 'I' and 'We'.

In terms of phrases, when the two verbs collocate with 'I'/'We' and are used for metadiscoursal purpose, their general phrasal patterns in the texts can be observed. In both disciplines, the verbs *DISCUSS* and *MENTION* are used in two structural patterns *I/we will discuss/mention*, and (*as*) *I/we* (*have*) *discussed/mentioned*. These phrases serve two discourse functions.

First, they are used as pre-alert markers for the forthcoming contents. When the writers want to inform and prepare the readers for what would be discussed/mentioned in their upcoming texts, these verbs are used in the phrase *I/We + will + verbs* to function as metadiscourse organisers. Second, these phrases function as reminders of previous discussion or content in their discourse. When the writers want to remind the readers of what has been discussed or mentioned previously in their texts, these verbs are used in the pattern *I/We + present perfect of the TO verbs* to perform the retrospective function, see Figures 5.2 and 5.3.

Whilst looking at the concordances of the TO verbs, it is observed that the two phrasal frames, *I/We + will + verbs* and *I/We + present perfect of verbs* are used quite frequently in the two investigated disciplines to organise the text. Additionally, the verbs in these two frames are not restricted to *DISCUSS*, *MENTION* and the other verbs that are included in the TO section in Table 5.2. This suggests that it is the two phrasal frames and not verbs in isolation that frequently function as textual organising expressions. To test this hypothesis, by Sketch Engine, the following two query scripts, [word = "I"] [word = "will"] [tag = "VV* "]|[word = "We"] [word = "will"] [tag = "VV* "] and [word = "I"] [word = "have"] [tag = "VVN* "]|[word = "we"] [word = "have"] [tag = "VVN* "] are searched respectively. These two searching frames can be used to retrieve all instances containing the patterns *I/We + will + verbs* and *I/We + present perfect of verbs*, which allow me to examine and compare them in the whole corpus.

The search of [word = "I"] [word = "will"] [tag =

"VV* "] | [word = "We"] [word = "will"] [tag = "VV* "]
returned 264 hits containing *I/We + will + verbs*. About 78%
of these instances (207 instances) are used for metadiscourse
purposes. There are not only verbs that occur relatively frequently (which collocate with 'I' no fewer than 5 times, and
with 'we' no fewer than 10 times) but also verbs that occur in-
frequently (which collocate with 'I' fewer than 5 times, and
with 'We' fewer than 10 times). The infrequent verbs are, for
example *study*, *look into* and *make* (see Chapter 3 for the
criteria of verb extraction). Moreover, most frequently, in the
same sentence and before this phrase, endophoric markers (cf.
Crismore et al. 1998; Hyland 1999, 2002, 2004, 2005) may be
found in the contexts in close proximity. Figure 5.2 lists 20 random concordance lines of this phrase, 5 from each sub-corpus,
UGBM, PGBM, UGEL and PGEL.

The phrase *I/We + present perfect of verbs* seems particularly marked for text organisation. There are 173 instances that
are identified as TO expressions, accounting for 60% of all the
retrieved 286 instances of the [word = "I"] [word = "have"]
[tag = "VVN* "] | [word = "we"] [word = "have"] [tag =
"VVN* "] in the corpus. Figure 5.3 lists 20 sample instances,
10 from BM and 10 from EL. Like the pattern *I/We + will +
verb*, these instances include the verbs that I have identified as
TO verbs, but also other verbs that are less frequent (see Chapter 3) in the corpus, for instance, *explain* and *review* in Figure
5.3. Therefore, when this phrase serves the text organising
function, the verbs that collocate with 'I' and 'We' are not
restricted to the most frequently occurring *discussed* or *mentioned*. Some less frequent verbs may be observed in it, for

example, *explained*, *suggested* and *dealt with*. It was also observed that when this phrasal frame is used for text organising, it often co-occurs with *as*. Among the 173 instances of *I/We + present perfect of the TO verbs* function as textual organising expressions, 86 of them occur in *as I/We + present perfect of the TO verbs*. Examples are *as I have mentioned* and *as we have discussed*. Similar to the use of *I/We + will + verbs* aforementioned, the endophoric markers may be seen around this expression in the context, for example, *so far*, *above* and *in chapter three*. The rest of the 113 instances are either short quotations(see Example 5-1) or occurrences that are used for other purposes, such as reporting research procedure (see Example 5-2).

as a PR channel. In the following part,	I will discuss	some of its main advantages based on my
Hampden Tumer. They are value dimensions, and	I will focus	on some of them in the thesis. The Dutch
divided into four chapters: In Chapter One,	I will make	a preliminary introduction to my thesis
Dove gains more market share than Cadbury.	I will begin	with the comparison of the two products
higher than those of Cadbury Schweppes. Next,	I will concentrate	on the competitor's prices which I think
be further expanded. And in this section,	I will discuss	how to integrate channel strategy into
brands for middle class. In this section,	I will discuss	another means by which brands can be built
for consumers. And in the following part,	I will put	emphasis on secondary associations of companies
modes are not perfectly fit (See Figure 4).	We will study	the cultural differences of TCUs merger
The related theories are presented above.	We will discuss	the connection between theories of communication
strategies are very comprehensive. Here	I will focus	on Johnson and Johnson's communication
contemporary circumstance. In this essay,	I will focus	my reflection on the intellectual life
with cultural collision; in the third part,	I will talk	about the author's limitations of judgment
judgment as a colonist herself. Moreover,	I will discuss	the feasibility of her suggestions when
her judgment has its limitations, which	I will talk	about in the third part of the paper. Isak
interesting viewpoints to explain this question.	We will check	the two main sides viewing colonization
understand the author and her works better,	I will give	a brief introduction of American westward
psychoanalytic theories. In the first part,	I will look	into the ambivalent views expressed in
and celebrate the pre-Oedipal bond. Here	I will focus	on Luce Irigaray and Julia Kristeva. On
choose its first supermarket? In this part,	I will explore	how Wal-Mart and Carrefour locate their

Figure 5.2   Random samples of *I/We + will + TO verbs*

Example 5-1: Yet when Helmer receives Krogstad's second letter, the first reaction is "I am saved!" and he totally ignores the purpose of Nora's borrowing money, saying to Nora, "*I have forgiven you*." All these facts show that in the matrimonial relationships, Helmer never treats Nora as his equal. (UGEL 00406)

Example 5-2: In view of the analytic needs, *I have employed* sub-theories in conversation analysis like silence, as a special turn-taking to illustrate Darcy's performance and his attitudes towards Elizabeth in the process of the whole conversation, and explore his subtle mental change in between. (PGEL 0001)

technologies has lost its throne in China.	I have analyzed	Wal-Mart and Carrefour's performance in
higher than that in capitalist countries. As	we have mentioned	before, both during and after the Diaoyu
on the product's original country. As	I have explained	, some country who enjoys the identity,
are used in ways of language approach. As	I have mentioned	, all the lines said by the actors, including
Chinese. But we may go back and check what	we have discussed	in Chapter 2 and refresh our memory about
regulation System for Chinese companies: as	we have discussed	in the former chapter about the 7S model
international M &A. Based on these studies,	we have examined	and analyzed the cultural differences and
circumstances and channel performance. Now that	we have reviewed	the history of previous literature on the
communicating strategies. According to what	we have concluded	from the channel power part, there is a
also related to some channel conditions as	we have discussed	in the previous part, so I will also use
their own recipes for the problem as well as	we have discussed	in the previous chapter. This chapter will
internalized ideals and moral standards	we have acquired	from our parents and from society. The
world through personalization. From what	we have discussed	above, among all Jane Austen's novels,
producing, but still made little profit, as	we have discussed	in the previous parts of this thesis.
life by Wordsworth's concept. So far,	we have learned	about Wordsworth's subject for writing
end and Septimus at the other. Thus far	I have concentrated	on the characters at the Establishment
solidity to the intangible reality around. As	I have suggested	at the outset of this chapter, Mrs. Dalloway
myth of Noah's Ark. In Chapter Three	we have mentioned	that the motifs in Noah's Ark recur in
circumstances unavoidable. The examples	I have cited	above belong to the type of interfering
seconded by Arthur and Olney.[quote] So far	we have dealt	with that complex mode of structure of

Figure 5.3   Samples of *I/We+present perfect of the TO verbs*

When analysing the phrases and the concordances there are some challenging cases relating to expressions that may or may not be classified as TO. For example, *I will argue* in Example 5-3, could also be considered as a text organising expression in the sense that it tells the readers what to expect in the following discourse. However, in another sense, this expression could also be considered as argumentative because it expresses the writer's viewpoint or the writer's evaluation of the discourse. The verb *argue* is labeling an argument other than fact. This meaning of *argue* is more important for EFL writers than the *I + will + verb* which is used for organising texts. Given that self-intervention and personal views are expressed in phrases similar to this example, I consider *I will argue* serves the textual function of argumentation and would classify the verb *argue* into the AG of RI group. Some other expressions were ruled out from the TO category too, for example, *I will use* in Example 5-4. This is because the student writers use them to describe their research design, the terminology, the tools and the parameters of their experiments. I shall therefore attempt to draw a line between discourse organising, research procedure description and research interpretation, whilst being aware that such demarcation is not watertight and these functions may be realised by one single expression.

Example 5-3: These images, **I will argue**, are a means to construct a subdued Africa ready for imperialists' penetration. (PGEL 0007)

Example 5-4: Cause-related marketing is a more often seen term for charity marketing with more existing studies, so in my thesis **I will use** these two terms interchangeably. (UGBM 10205)

To recapitulate, the two phrase frames, *I/We + will + verbs* and *I/We + present perfect of verb* are frequently used to realise metadiscoursal functions in most of the students' texts. The phrase *I/We + will + verbs* is to inform the readers of the forthcoming content and the phrase *I/We + present perfect of the TO verb* is to remind the readers what has been discussed previously. Therefore, there are endophoric markers such as *in this section*, *next*, *in the following chapter*, are frequently found preceding or following this phrase. In addition, when these two patterns are used, the verbs are not restricted to the TO class collected for the purpose of this investigation. The reason that some verbs found in these two phrases were not included in the verb list is due to the fact they are below the threshold that was set for this study, or alternatively, they are delexical verbs, such as *make* and *begin* in Figure 5.2.

5.3.2   Knowledge community construing verb

In this study, the only verb that serves the KC function is the verb *KNOW*. In both disciplines, BM and EL, *KNOW* is used frequently(no less than 5 times) only with 'We' in novice writers' theses. When it co-occurs with 'We', *KNOW* has two main functions. One is to construe a knowledge community to achieve multiple objectives. These objectives include the setting up of a community of limited members to introduce background information and general knowledge, and also to achieve solidarity with the readers by suggesting that the knowledge is shared by both the writer and the readers. When it is used to achieve this function, *KNOW* occurs in sequences *as we all know*, *we all know that*, *as we all know that*, *as we know*, *we know that*, and *we know*, which can be formalised as: *(as) we (all) know (that)*. As discussed in Chapter 4, this phrase frame is employed to present the shared knowledge as known to a limited number of people within that discipline. The writer uses it as the stepping-stone for his/her further argument without further explanation or interpretation of that "known" statement. Essentially, when using this phrase, the writer includes the potential readers into a community, in which the members share the provided knowledge. Therefore, this knowledge that (*as*) *we* (*all*) *know* (*that*) is recognised and needs no further explanation or illustration. In the texts that are investigated in this study, the knowledge comes from either familiarity with BM(see Example 5-5) as a field or familiarity with English Literary works(see Example 5-6).

Example 5-5: *As we all know*, the U.S. Federal Reserve committee is a 'private' central bank that represents the Wall Street's interests. In 2009, in response to the financial crisis, Ben S. Bernanke, who is the current US Federal Reserve Chairman, decided to reduce interest rate with markets' applauses. (UGBM 10407)

Example 5-6: *We know* he is no stranger to the sea. But to feel the morning coming in the darkness of the open sea calls for a closeness with nature that most of us don't have. This closeness to nature is reinforced when we listen to Santiago's thoughts about the sea itself and its creatures. (PGEL 0038)

In general, there is no difference between BM and EL of the phrases of 'We' and *KNOW* in relation to the meaning conveyed and the function they serve in the student writers' academic texts. One observable difference, however, is the number of occurrences of the phrase *as we all know* in the two disciplines. 38 instances in BM as opposed to 6 instances in EL. It was also found that of the 38 occurrences of *as we all know* in BM, 28 instances were in the undergraduate BM subcorpus, and 10 in the postgraduate BM subcorpus. Of all the 6 instances of this expression in EL, 5 were found in the undergraduate EL subcorpus and only 1 occurrence in the postgraduate EL subcorpus. Thus, this expression appears to be overused by undergraduate student writers of BM.

Another function of *KNOW* is to interpret the student's own research results. This function is frequently found in the phrase *we can/could know (that)* in the student's academic texts. Among all the collocations of 'We' and *KNOW* in this corpus, namely 40 instances, about 25% in BM, and 53 instances, about 33% in EL pertain to this form of usage. This use is, in a way, contradicting with the function of KC. Specifically, when used as KC, the phrase(*as*) *we*(*all*) *know*(*that*) is to introduce what is 'Known' to both the writer and the readers. Conversely, when used as RI verb, this phrase *we can/could know*(*that*) is followed by new information that the readers do not know until the writer informs them. This point may be seen from the expressions of "*from the above analysis*" in Example 5-7 and "[*t*] *hus*" in Example 5-8 the writers are interpreting something new in their texts. It seems that the purpose of using the plural FPP 'We' to collocate with *KNOW* is an attempt to mitigate the subjectivity or authority of the statements. To illustrate this point, in Examples 5-7 and 5-8, both the phrases are, in fact, strong statements. The writers claim that what they argued is true; because the usage takes the form of 'we' *know* it. On the other hand, because it is the knowledge that 'We', both 'you' the reader and 'I' the writer, *know*, and not 'I', the writer herself/himself *know*. In Example 5-7, it could be described as *I argue that* instead of *we know that*. 'We' is used to express understanding or a particular viewpoint, to obscure any form of subjectivity. This use of inclusive 'We' to avoid the singular FPP 'I' may also be seen from the phrase *we can/could see*, which is discussed shortly in this chapter and will be explained further in greater detail in Chapter 7.

Example 5-7: **From the above analysis, *we know that*** in need recognition period there are two types: the actual state type and the desired state type. And we know that the Chinese consumers are more of the actual state type. Americans probably belong to the desired state type. (PGBM 0063)

Example 5-8: Claudio seems well-mannered in the first place, however, when misunderstanding emerges; he tends to believe in delusion and takes impulsive movement without second thought. **Thus, *we know that*** Claudio seems to be a decent gentleman, but he is an immature young man with vindictive psychology. (UGEL 06009)

The disciplinary difference of the verb *KNOW* of the RI function may be explained in terms of the epistemic difference between the two disciplines. In Business and Management, the phrase *we can/could know(that)* is usually used to present an interpretation of the empirical analyses. In EL, it presents assessment, interpretation or enlightenment drawn from the writer's understanding of literature work. In the discipline of English Literature, knowledge is mainly gained by reading in depth of the original work. The disciplinary difference is due to the different subjects of the disciplinary studies. The meaning and the function of the collocation of 'We' and *KNOW* in this phrase are the same. In other words, the writers of different disciplines *know* different things, knowledge of Business and Management and English Literature respectively. This difference may also be observed from the RR verbs discussed in the following subsection.

5.3.3   Research report verbs

The *Research report verbs* are further divided into *Epistemic verbs*(EP) and *Research conduct verbs*. In the RR category, the meaning and the textual function of the verbs do not vary much between the two disciplines. However, they do present an epistemic difference, namely, where and how their disciplinary specific knowledge is acquired.

5.3.3.1   Epistemic Verbs

The two verbs, *worked* and *read* that belong to the EP subclass were found. All the instances of *worked* and 29 instances out of 68 of *read* collocate with 'I'. When collocating with the FPPs, all the instances of *worked* are found in BM, and there are more *read* in EL than BM(35 vs. 18 instances). In the subcorpus of BM, the writers use *I * worked* to report their work experiences as interns in business enterprises (see Figure 5.4). The students of both disciplines use the phrase, *I * read* to report what books, the number of times and the volume of literature they have read before the composition of their theses.

	I	
Methods of Interpersonal Conflict Management,	I	*worked* out a simple table to represent
management result. As pre-employment internship,	I	have *worked* for Sales Department, Volkswagen
Hangzhou while assisting the German Consultant.	I	have *worked* deeply into the real life of
I also brought them to the company where	I	*worked* as an intern and asked my male colleagues
have enough time to travel around. For me,	I	*worked* there only about two months, but
government or big institutions. Furthermore,	I	*worked* in Disney for six month, so I could
).According to the survey data received,	I	*worked* out an overall picture (see figure
other party. I had such experience when	I	*worked* as an intern in a state organ and
solution to any problems arisen between us. If	I	still *worked* for the SOE, it would be quite
Assumed name for the organization at which	I	*worked* and collected data from) came to
it had compared with the other companies	I	had *worked* in. People had to swipe a card

Figure 5.4   All the instances of *I* * *worked* in BM

	I	
me very much. After returning to China,	I	*read* some reports about Hong Kong Disneyland
ceaselessly carry out new ideas and strategies.	I	*read* many books on public relations, in
brands. During my preparation for the thesis,	I	*read* a lot of books and find that different
research capability on this topic. Besides,	I	have also *read* some relevant books on brand
management. To deeply understand these subjects,	I	*read* a lot of essays about case studies
much older wealthy doctor in Paris. When	I	first *read* F. R. Leavis's The Great Tradition
standpoints of the authors on the readers.	I	have *read* the novel for several times and
gave me quite different impression when	I	*read* the novel Gone with the Wind. In this
by ourselves. Take myself as an example,	I	have *read* the novel Gone with the Wind
exactly the description of my feeling when	I	*read* through Alice in Bed, when my own

**Figure 5.5   Examples of *I* * *read* in BM and EL,
5 instances from each subcorpus**

Figure 5.5 lists some examples of *I* * *read*, namely, 5 instances from each of the disciplines. The disciplinary difference could explain this variation. As a social science discipline, BM focuses on on-site practice as almost all the students undertake some intern work during their higher education years. Whereas, with English Literature being a pure humanities discipline, academic research mainly means reading primary texts (e.g. *Pride and Prejudice*) and secondary texts(e.g. books about *Pride and Prejudice*).

5.3.3.2   Research Conduct verbs

In the *Research Conduct verbs* category, the disciplinary difference between BM and EL is marked. As mentioned in Section 2, the two disciplines use different verbs to describe

their research procedures. Some of the verbs are present only in
BM(e.g. *collect*, *asked*, *arrange*, *compare*) or in EL (e.g.
hear, *CALL*, *infer*, *OBSERVE*), with others occurring in
both with varying frequency. For example, there are 22
instances of *ANALYZE* in BM and 5 instances in EL; 42
instances of *CHOOSE* in BM, and only 7 instances of this verb
in EL. One exception is the verb *FIND*, which occurs about the
same number of times in the two disciplines; 137 in BM and
130 in EL. Furthermore, variations of the meaning and textual
function of the verbs may also be observed when they collocate
with the two FPPs, 'I' and 'We' between the two disciplines.
Two verbs, *FIND* and *ANALYZE*, in RC category are examined in detail.

The verb *FIND*

As discussed in Chapter 4, a verb might be multi-function-
al and have multi-meanings when it collocates with the FPPs.
The verb *FIND* is a good example. In the students' texts, when
it collocates with 'I' in *I find/found* it is used to state what
the writers' findings were. In BM, the writers report two different kinds of findings. One finding is what they found
through observation during their apprentice experiences,
which is only observed in the undergraduate BM texts (see
Example 5-9). The other is the finding that is obtained by
carrying out research(see Example 5-10). In EL, the finding
is gained through reading books on that subject or topic (see
Example 5-11). In other words, when reporting the research
findings, the expression *I find/found* in the two disciplines is
obtained through different means. BM from internship,
epistemic research or case study and EL mostly from literary

reading.

Example 5-9: During the daily PR work, *I found* that press release (which is also called news release) plays a very important role in Public Relations work. It is a basic vehicle that makes the clients' information reach media and gets publicity for a company or product. (UGBM 01506)

Example 5-10: From the interview *I found* that both Chinese also consider arriving in time for business meetings as a virtue which is promoted in the thoughts of Confucius. Chinese consider time is valuable in a holistic view and it is repeated. (PGBM 0064)

Example 5-11: Through comprehensive analysis on his art of satire composing, *I found* that vivid and clear language is a quite desirable pattern for satiric works. (UGEL 00905)

When *FIND* collocates with 'We', it is most frequently found in the phrase frame *we can/could/will find*. As discussed in Chapter 4, in this study this phrase is considered as an expression to interpret research findings instead of reporting them. In other words, *we can/could/will find* does not serve to recount research procedure, but to interpret research findings, which involves the writer's assessment, understanding and viewpoints. Comparing the two disciplines, the phrase *we can/could/will find* interprets different subjects of the two disciplines, showing similarity with the expression *I find/found*. In BM, the phrase is always about business cases, figures, and comparisons (see Figure 5.6).

level. In the Chinese Spring Festival case,	we	can *find* that the commercial is full of
motivation are needed. From this figure,	we	can *find* that the motivations of most Chinese
discussion in part four of this thesis,	we	can *find* several differences between western
of Warcraft with domestic network games,	we	can *find* that there are many disadvantages
even live with people from another region.	We	can *find* scholars are making efforts at
societies in the world. From the chart below,	we	could *find* Chinese culture is more collectivism-oriented
model of dynamic comfort. From the above,	we	could *find* that C5 has made a great deal
to the core of these two advertisements,	we	can *find* that the two products are foreign-invented
developing system, but after making a comparison,	we	can *find* that the employees in lenovo pay
this sort. Therefore, through the figure,	we	can *find* out that, even if disobedience

Figure 5.6   Samples of the phrase *we can find* in BM

In the English Literature subcorpus, the phrase *we can/ could/will find* is used to present interpretations of the writer's reading and thinking, either of the details or of the whole original book that the author wrote about(see Figure 5.7). In these EL texts, the interpreted findings are not figures or facts, but the writers' understanding, evaluation, and judgement. It could be about the investigated book and it could also be about ideological thinking stimulated by the book. Examples 5-12 to 5-13 demonstrate this point.

Example 5-12: However, if we examine the details about the relationship between Evie and Sergeant Babbacombe, *we can find* it is not a surprise at all that Evie behaved like that. Sergeant Babbacombe was a cruel and domineering father, treating his daughter as a despot treated his slave. Without the true solicitude for Evie's heart and mind, he took Evie as his private property and confined her to his strict control, denying her the freedom to make her own decisions and punishing her with ruthlessness for the smallest mistakes. (PGEL 0060)

Example 5-13: If we consider McEwan own comment on his *Atonement* as his "Jane Austen novel" during one interview with Jeff Giles in Newsweek, *we will find* that as far as the moral focus is concerned, McEwan shares similarity with Leavis in that both uphold "the great tradition" of English novels in moral thinking, thus making the appreciation of the novel from the perspective of literary ethical criticism a meaningful endeavour. (PGEL 0059)

Indeed, after reading the whole novel,	we	can *find* that the development of the clues
in the whole story, but after analysis,	we	can *find* that it was just Jude, who was
happens to anyone who breaks the rules.	We	may *find* the fact that he believes in the
as a Protestant. By analyzing Villette,	we	can also *find* Lucy Snowe's extreme self-respect
process of history. With detailed inspection,	we	can *find* that these images are the formulated
literary work, but through careful review,	we	could *find* out many useful messages, which
harmony and integrity of all in nature,	we	can *find* the most advanced ecological philosophies
too many handsome men and beautiful women.	We	can easily *find* that a perfect match between
what Jane favours and what she detests,	We	will *find* that she is critical to Mr. Brocklehurst
restriction and without pretence. Still,	we	can *find* some traces of Charlotte Bronte

Figure 5.7   Samples of the phrase *we can find* in EL

In general, in the expression *I find/found*, the verb *FIND* in both BM and EL is used to report the research findings that are obtained from practice in the real word, experimental investigation, and an extensive and in-depth reading of the investigated novels, dramas, or poems.

Turning to the phrase *we can/could/will find*, in both BM and EL, "findings" of what *we can/could/will find* are not findings in numbers or in any concrete form but viewpoints or stances held by the writers. With regard to disciplinary difference, in BM, the expression *I can/could/will find* is used to interpret the quantitative results of the research, whereas in EL, this phrase is used to express what the writer observes by reading and thinking. Therefore, the pragmatic effect of this phrase may vary in degree in these two disciplines respectively. In BM, *we can find* implies that the writer and the reader can extrapolate the same things, and consequently draw the same conclusion. The phrase is used to seek alignment and support as the interpretation is proposed with confidence and supported by the experimental results. In EL, the alignment of this phrase *we can / could / will find* is also established. However, this alignment is not guaranteed. The choice of inclusive 'We' can be regarded as a way to avoid being too subjective. It is deemed being too authoritative when writers of English Literature state that the understanding is of their own. Therefore, using 'We' to collocate with *FIND* in EL is a strategy of seeking alignment as well as being modest (cf. Harwood 2005, 2007).

The verb *ANALYZE*

The verb *ANALYZE* is discussed in this category because we often intuitively consider the verb *ANALYZE* as an *activity verb* (Biber et al., 2002) and, consequently, may classify it belonging to the RC category if the co-text was not looked at. In fact, in this research, as shown in Table 5.2 and Table 5.4, this verb is classified into two categories, *Textual organising verb* (for example, *I / we will / attempt / am (are) going to ana-lyze*) and *Research conduct* verb(for example, *I / we analyzed*) when it collocates with 'I' and/or 'We'. As shown in the two tables, this verb shows more instances as a TO verb than as a RC in the texts of both disciplines. In other words, in these Chinese EFL students' theses, when *ANALYZE* collocates with 'I' and 'We', it is usually not used to describe research proce-dure. Rather, it is frequently used for text organising function in both BM and EL. This is evidenced by the phrase pattern of

I / WE will / be going to / want to analyze. It is also most likely that endophoric expressions will be found immediately before or after this phrase(see Figure 5.8).

The other phrase of *ANALYZE* when collocating with the FPP, *I / We have analyzed*, is of a similar form of usage(see Figure 5.9). The phrase is not used to state what had been done before the dissertation. It is more about what has been discussed in the texts. This phrase, together with *I / We will / be going to / want to analyze*, could be regarded primarily as a metadiscoursal phrase, which is to remind or summarise the content of the discussion up to that point in those texts. Therefore, in both phrases, the original meaning of *ANALYZE*, examine methodically and in detail the constitution or structure of(something, especially information), typically for purposes of explanation and interpretation (https://en. oxforddictionaries. com/definition/us/analyze) is marginalised. Instead, the phrases flag directions of what may be found in the thereafter(e.g. *I will analyze*) or previous(e.g. *I have analyzed*) discourse.

In all the 59 instances of *ANALYZE* found in BM, 37 instances are classified as TO verbs and 22 of them are in the RC category. In EL, there are 23 instances of TO and 5 instances of RC. Examples 5-14 and 5-15 are longer texts to illustrate the categorisations of this verb in TO category.

Example 5-14: In this section, **I will analyze** the differences in employee motivational mechanism from both side of the M&A cases dealt by the companies between China and American. (UGBM 05404)

scope. In chapter three and chapter four, | I | will *analyze* cross-cultural management
venture capital in China and the USA, then | I | *analyze* this topic both in theory and practice
cultural aspect and the individual aspect. Here | I | will mainly *analyze* the influence on the
long-term orientation. In this section, | I | will *analyze* the differences in employee
according to what I get in the last part, | I | will *analyze* what the problems will be
studied in China at present. In my thesis, | I | will *analyze* charity marketing from western
the cultural factors. In the next chapter, | we | will specifically *analyze* the case of Hongkong
decision-making process. In this chapter, | we | will *analyze* deeply how culture influences
consumer behavior will be discussed. Then | we | will *analyze* a case to understand cultural
studies. In the third part of the paper, | we | proceed to compare and *analyze* the differences
are mainly about the strategies. Before | we | *analyze* the cases, it will be helpful to
continuous development. In this chapter, | we | will *analyze* three cases reflecting corporate
to reconciliation. Thus in this thesis, | I | will probe and *analyze* the mother-daughter
to praise the good parts. In my thesis, | I | will *analyze* both good and bad sides of
together and make a comparison, and then | I | will *analyze* Bilbo and Sam respectively
important part of this thesis. First of all, | I | will *analyze* the text, especially the parts
or turn-final. In the following sections, | I | attempt to *analyze* the functions of turn-taking
transgresses gender boundaries. In this paper, | I | am going to *analyze* Shakespeare's crossdressing
the role she should play by society. Now | I | would like to *analyze* George Eliot's concern
admired. In the main body of my thesis, | I | will *analyze* the Jane Austen's feminist

Figure 5.8   Examples of *I/We will/be going to/want to analyze* in BM and EL

technologies has lost its throne in China. | I | have *analyzed* W-M and C's
companies between China and the west. | I | have *analyzed* the problems and solutions
and business fields. As to the reasons, | I | have *analyzed* from the aspect of M. Y.
media create are the second kind, who, as | I | have *analyzed* in section 3, represent a
short-haul flights and 'no frills' service. | We | have *analyzed* that AirA has abolished the agent costs
preserve a long-term relationship. So far, | we | have *analyzed* marketing suggestions in
products, services and fame of brands. As | we | have *analyzed* above, China's auto enterprises
the above corporate cultural differences, | we | have *analyzed* Geely and V's corporate
objectives and social responsibility. As | we | *analyzed* in the 3.2, there are a lot of
international M &A. Based on these studies, | we | have examined and *analyzed* the cultural

Figure 5.9   The phrase *I /We have analyzed* in BM and EL

Example 5-15: *As we have analyzed* above, China's auto enterprises mostly acquire the cross-border companies with famous brands, for example, MG Rover, Volvo and SAAB. So how to retain the famous brand image and improve the fame of their brands is of great significance for the success of M&A. (PGBM 0093)

When the verb *ANALYZE* does mean *examine* or *investigate* in the texts, the collocations of the FPPs and this verb serve different pragmatic purposes. The students use expressions that collocate to restate what they have done prior to the writing of the paper (see Example 5-16), and to discuss the methodology or possible methodology options of conducting the research (see Examples 5-17 and 5-18). Figure 5.10 presents all the instances of *ANALYZE* that are categorised in RC group in BM and Figure 5.11 illustrates all the 5 instances of this verb classified as RC in EL.

venture capital in China and the USA, then	I	*analyze* this topic both in theory and practice
current situation. From those materials	I	tried to *analyze* the law of the development
through a case study of Mengniu Dairy Group,	I	*analyze* how it combined itself with the
the most prominent findings I found that	I	*analyzed* the motivation mechanism both
In order to succeed finishing this paper,	I	have carefully searched and *analyzed* many
and business fields. As to the reasons,	I	have *analyzed* from the aspect of Ma Yun
purchasing to selling to the final customers.	I	collected and *analyzed* IK's feature
conditions of the historical background.	I	*analyzed* typical M&A cases the various
news coverage on RMB appreciation issues,	we	could *analyze* misperception existing in
between west-Sino cultures clear. After this	we	can *analyze* the difference and convergences
survey probably cannot be applied. Above all	we	*analyze* how the cultural elements affect
Their culture guarantees their success. When	we	*analyze* their way to find why they are
motives and effects of both stages M&A,	we	could *analyze* whether the M&A did or did
and helping with the disaster relief. If	we	*analyze* HC's CSR initiatives with the
industry. Based on the theory and work,	we	*analyze* the features of traditional industrial
phase of preparing to promote new artist,	we	have completely *analyzed* the market we are going to enter
the Engel-Blackwell-Miniard Model which	we	use to *analyze* the cultural influence,
conflicts between Geely and Volvo, firstly	we	*analyze* the national culture differences
differences between China and Sweden, and lastly	we	*analyze* the corporate cultural differences
(2007)s division of corporate culture,	we	can *analyze* the corporate culture differences
safety. Speaking of institutional culture,	we	can *analyze* from the aspects of structure
international M &A. Based on these studies,	we	have examined and *analyzed* the cultural

Figure 5.10   The collocations of *ANALYZE*
and 'I'/'We' that are classified as RC in BM

as representative characters of that era.	I	want to *analyze* the way how the two heroines
and reflection on A Room of One's Own,	I	would like to *analyze* the three main factors
which I think is beyond any doubt. However,	I	want to *analyze* this novel in the other
I focus on the ambivalence in the story.	I	attempt to *analyze* three modes of ambivalence
warring ideals in one dark body (5). When	I	*analyze* Pecola's traumatic experiences

Figure 5.11   The collocations of *ANALYZE*
and 'I'/'We' that are classified as RC in EL

Example 5-16: The scope of my research concerns

the whole business process of IK, from purchasing to selling to the final customers. *I* collected and *analyzed* IK's feature contributed to its success. (UGBM 09707)

Example 5-17: Speaking of institutional culture, *we can analyze* from the aspects of structure, style and systems. And the style includes decision-making and information flow style. (PGBM 0093)

Example 5-18: However, *I want to analyze* this novel in the other way round—how people's social values help shape the contemporary social circum- stances. And in my thesis, I would like to narrow down the social values to a more specific aspect—Vic- torian notion of property, that's to say, what Victori- an notion of property is like, how Victorian notion of property comes into being and in what kind of way it influences the Victorian society.

Considering the functions of the verb *ANALYZE* when it collocates with the two FPPs, there is barely any difference found between Business and Management and English Litera- ture, either as TO or as RC. The usage of *ANALYZE* as TO when it collocates with the FPP, 'I' and 'We' implies that the students consider the research can be "undertaken within the text" (Fløttum et al. 2006:209). In both disciplines, the novice writers treat their interpretation of the research results or their understanding of the investigated material as in-text research process. They consider the discussion or negotiation of the meaning of the contents as part of the conduct of the research. In hard science, for instance, Chemistry or Physics, *analyses* are usually conducted before the research is reported and discussed. In this study, students from both applied social science BM and pure humanities EL, show a clear preference for choosing the verb *ANALYZE*, a verb which is usually used in hard discipline subjects coupled with more quantitative data and empirical studies. This choice may be explained as the students' intention of making their research papers sound more reliable and convincing. To them, *analyze* implies doing proper research and is less authoritative than presenting their own interpretation plainly in their texts.

There is however, a divergence between the disciplines on how knowledge is processed or obtained by using *ANALYZE*. It is *analyzing* real business cases in BM, and reading literary work in EL. The relationship between the verb *ANALYZE* and also verbs such as *KNOW*, *FIND* and *SEE* to the nature of the respective disciplines is an interesting one. I shall come back to this in Section 5.4 of this chapter.

It is acknowledged that the boundaries of these functions are not without grey areas. Taking Example 5-14 as an example, the expression *I will analyze* informs the readers what follows, the analysis of "*the differences in employee motivational mechanism*" between Chinese and US companies. At the same time, it also informs the reader of the contrastive methodology that the writer chose to address the research question. In this case, *I will analyze* may be considered as a metadiscoursal expression as well as a research report phrase. The multifunctional feature of the verbs when collocating with the two FPPs leaves the researcher to determine which group it belongs to when categorising them. By looking at the extended discourse of these phrases and those frequent endophoric markers around them, as well as the fact that these expressions do not involve any person's opinion, I concluded that the expressions, *I/We will/be going to/want to analyze* and *I/We have analyzed* are primarily used for metadiscourse purposes in this study.

5.3.4   Research interpretation verbs

The two subgroups of the *Research interpretation verbs*, *Verbs of research finding interpretation* and *Verbs of arguing*, occur more frequently in English Literature than Business and Management. Most verbs in the two subcategories in BM may also be found in EL. The question is whether or not they have the same meaning and/or function in the two disciplines. To address this question, six verbs, *SEE* and *read* of the RI group and *think*, *SAY*, *LEARN* and *understand* from the AG group are investigated in detail.

The verb *SEE*

In both BM and EL, *SEE* is most frequently used in the phrase *we can/could see*: 262 instances out of 322, accounting for 81% in BM, and 266 instances out of 425, accounting for 63% in EL. When used in this phrase, its function is mainly to present research interpretation. In both disciplines, the verb *SEE* and the FPP collocation *we can see* serves the function of interpreting the data or being more explicit about the understanding or appreciation of the literature work that is under investigation. In one sense, there is not much disciplinary difference because it is used to present interpretation in both disciplines. When looking at it in another way, the function of the phrase *we can see* does differ across the two disciplines. The difference between the disciplines is the difference relating to where and how the knowledge is constructed or how the new information is processed. In BM, what follows this phrase is a detailed discussion of actual statistics, for example, tables and figures. Things are "seen" from a qualitative data perspective, which suggests objectivity. In EL, this phrase is used frequently to probe into the details of the plots or dialogues that the writer quoted from the original book. "Seeing" is interpretation or viewpoint or argument. Considering the readership in BM, the proposed stance is likely to be echoed by the audience of the texts because it draws upon the same concrete figures. Whereas, as noted above, in EL, as the interpretation or explanation mainly relies on the writer's own understanding, the audiences may or may not "see" things in the same way as the writers do. The following two examples are taken from BM and EL respectively to illustrate this point.

Example 5-19: From the above statistics *we can see that* American interviewees evaluate experiential needs higher than social needs. They look for brands that can fulfill their desire for change. Newness or emotional expressions are valued most for the demonstration of their personalities. (PGBM 0059)

Example 5-20: "He had come in his own car, which he had the day before bought from the American Consul, and he did not want to get out of it till I had seen him in it." From this, *we can see* that the chief is in favor of his new cars. However, it is his son that drives the car for him. In fact, he has no idea of the new car, and he just shows his superiority as a Kikuyu chief. For the drink, he had it, but then fainted like a dead man. (UGEL 00606)

In Example 5-19, basing his/her argument on the quantitative data provided in the text, the writer may have a good chance of getting the endorsement of the reader. In Example 5-20 however, as it is the writer's personal interpretation of the extracts from that literature, the audience may or may not agree with the writer.

One way to explore this verb further in these students' essays is to see how this phrase functions with an impersonal subject. The passive form of *I/We can see* can demonstrate how the verb *SEE* is used without 'I' and 'We'. To achieve this, the phrase *can be seen* is searched by Sketch Engine. This search returns 151 instances and 113 instances of *can be seen* in BM and EL respectively(see Table 5.7). It is found that this expression is more frequently used in two longer phrasal patterns, *can be seen as* and *It can be seen (from ...) (that)* in these students' dissertations. These two phrases account for about half of all the instances of *can be seen* in the whole corpus. In addition, there are more instances of *It can be seen (from ...) (that)* in BM than EL, whereas the other phrase *can be seen as* occurs more frequently in EL than in BM. The difference in frequency is due to the different discourse functions of the phrases. The expression *it can be seen (from ...) (that)* is more frequently used in BM to describe the data or the results of the research. It has the same function as *we can see* but in the passive voice. Without the personal pronoun 'We', the expression may not be marred by any personal subjectivity. Therefore, this suggests both impartiality and unbiasedness. The *can be seen as* phrase can be further generalised into the pattern *can be seen as* + abstract noun/noun phrases in EL to express the writer's understanding or viewpoint in the texts. Examples 5-21 and 5-22 are listed below to show the difference.

Example 5-21: From Figure 6, *it can be seen that* more than a half of the micro blogs on broadcast information are used for marketing the show including broadcast and live show, which is a direct marketing for the Voice of China. (UGBM 01609)

Example 5-22: While the structure *can be seen as* a Darwinian metaphor, the depictions of the Africans are totally devoid of metaphoric pretension. Racism is at times applied head-on onto the image of the Africans. (PGEL 0007)

Table 5.6   Phrases of *can be seen* in BM and EL

	can be seen	*can be seen as*	*It can be seen* (*from* ...) (*that*)
BM	151	30	44
EL	113	47	24

What follows *it can be seen* (*from* ...) (*that*) in BM (Example 5-21) is a more detailed explanation of the quantitative results, which presents the writer's understanding of the numbers, tables, and figures illustrated in their essays, whereas *can be seen as* (Example 5-22) is more of an interpretation or elaboration, which negates the concrete facts or details and elevates the proposition to an abstract or theoretical level. Therefore, when it does not collocate with 'I' and 'We', *can be seen* needs to be considered in longer expressions as two different phrases, *can be seen that* and *can be seen as*. This is because the function of each phrase is specific to the phrase when they are used with an impersonal pronoun.

In general, it is found in this study that the verb *SEE* is most frequently used in phrasal frames to present research interpretation. Whether the subject of the verb *SEE* is a personal pronoun or not, the function of this verb in *we can see* or *can be seen* stays the same. The difference between these two uses is the suggestion that there is personal intervention in the interpretation of the research findings. It is interesting to see that both groups of writers select the same verb, *SEE*, almost as if the research process was the same in BM and EL. Further discussion on this point will be presented in Section 5.4.

The verb *read*

The verb, *read*, has two meanings when it collocates with the two FPPs 'I' and 'We'. One meaning is the actual act of *reading*. All the instances in BM allude to this meaning, and it is mostly used in the undergraduate texts of BM. The writers use this verb to present their experiences of reading the book(s) that inspired them or used as the resource books for their research or analyses. In these cases, the phrasal pattern *I/we + read + concrete object* (e.g. book) is used. As shown in most of the instances in Figure 5.12, the instances of *read* collocate with 'I' in Business and Management discipline. There are a few instances of the same function in EL as well, although not as many as those in BM. They are mostly used to describe the writers' reading experiences, whether they be novels, documents, or any other materials that the students have read.

The other meaning of *read*, not the real act of reading,

but *to illustrate or present the understanding of the meaning or implication of a book or an artwork*, can be found in two phrases in postgraduate texts, particularly in postgraduate English Literature texts. In the phrase *we + can/could + read + abstract Noun/Noun phrases*, *read* means the conceptual interpretation or understanding of some description of the literature attained through the activity of reading. For instance, *read* in Example 5-23 indicates the understanding of the excerpt of the original work, and in Example 5-24 *read* means the two alternative interpretations of the sentences. In *we + read + linguistic Object(it) + as + abstract noun*, the verb *read* expresses the writer's understanding and evaluation of the content that he/she read(see Figure 5.13).

much older wealthy doctor in Paris. When	I	first *read* F. R. Leavis's The
standpoints of the authors on the readers.	I	have *read* the novel for several times and
confirmed my impression. In most documents	I	*read* , Lincoln and the Northern states
gave me quite different impression when	I	*read* the novel Gone with the Wind. In this
strong implications on the readers. When	I	*read* this, I had a confused thought because
because implications on the readers. When	I	*read* this, I had a confused thought because
description was totally different with what	I	*read* in the novel. Also, in many sources
by ourselves. Take myself as an example,	I	have *read* the novel Gone with the Wind
ideologies, so no one can be totally objective.	I	should *read* more and absorb different sourc
firmness and desperate impavidity, when	I	*read* her talking to Elizabeth
exactly the description of my feeling when	I	*read* through Alice In Bed, when my own
destroyed by him likewise? In this approach	I	*read* the novel and make inquiries. Then
explain their underlying messages. When	I	first *read* Jane Austen's Pride and

Figure 5.12   The verb *read* collocates with 'I' in BM

Example 5-23: From this quoted excerpt, *we could read the respect and belief* in his elders, and Stephen was in the phase of developing his own way of understanding the world and his willingness to participate, outside of school and family. (PGEL 0049)

Example 5-24: We do not know for certain

whether the pronoun, which refers to Lemuel or the wolf; *we can read it either way*: the wolf is a dog without a master, or, Lemuel is a dog without a master. (PGEL 0013)

this, she cannot change this habit. She wants to	read books as	men do, which is prohibited by her father. She
in Merwin' poetry of the 1960s, I tend to	read it as	a Derridean supplement, a substitutive
we may divest it of any Christian intention and	read it as	a manifesto of man's metaphysical aspiration
poems as[quote] or as establishing [quote] . I	read it as	a testimony of structural difference or a
human relationships, they are still as widely	read today as	they have ever been (Austen, Persuasion
the journey to India and the resolution to read continuously as before. Eventually, he combined knowledge,		
of rape striking and disturbing would rather	read it as	seduction instead of 'rape. Others

Figure 5.13   Instances of *read* * *as* in the PGEL

It may be seen that the meaning of the verb *read* becomes specific when it is used in specific phrasal patterns. In fact, this may apply to most of the verbs that have been investigated in this study. Therefore, the meaning of a verb depends on the specific pattern or phrase it occurs in, and different connotations of a verb may be distinguished by identifying different patterns. This observation is in accordance with that has been discussed in Hunston and Francis(2000).

The verbs *think*, *SAY*, *learn* and *understand*

As shown in Table 5.5, student writers of EL use more types of AG verbs than the BM students. In this subcategory, to investigate the disciplinary similarity and difference, the top four most frequently used verbs, *think*, *SAY*, *learn*, and *understand* from the two disciplines were examined. Except the verb *understand*, little semantic or phrasal difference is found in relation to the other three frequent verbs. In both BM and EL, these four verbs are all used for the delivery of the writers' opinions and viewpoints. In almost all the instances, the verb *think* collocates with the singular first-person pronoun, 'I' as in *I think*; the verbs *say* and *learn* most frequently collocate with the plural first-person pronoun, 'We', as in *we can / cannot / may / might / should say* and *we must / can / should / need to learn* (see Chapter 4). The differences of the verbs *think*, *say* and *learn* mainly exist between the two academic levels, and between the features that collocate with 'I' and 'We', which will be discussed in Chapters 6 and 7.

support. Under this kind of circumstances	we	can easily *understand* why she would be
Lancelot's lover and a fallen woman,	we	can *understand* Tennyson characterization
universe. If we accept Parke's analysis,	we	can readily *understand* why there are so
The writer does not share the same ideas.	We	could *understand* from the novel that, in
do. But he is providing us with a vision.	We	could well *understand* the concern of the
characteristics when James created Peter Pan,	we	will *understand* his writing intention better
To sum up, the symbolic use of rose helps	we	readers better *understand* the story and
capitalist values. By analyzing this short story,	we	can *understand* and appreciate the feelings
logic. Following his stream of thoughts,	we	can easily *understand* the development of
knowledge about the author and Alice James,	we	can *understand* the reason why Sontag chose
the history of English literature. Thus	we	could better *understand* the symbolic meanings
demonstrates the evil side of human nature.	We	may better *understand* this proposition
analyzing the reason of the misinterpretation,	we	can *understand* the anxiety of cultural
pretentiousness and cynical truth which	we	*understand* . More examples can be found
contrast things, you show their differences.	We	can really *understand* only those things
are familiar to us or similar to things	we	already *understand* , so comparing and contrasting
daughter: so far we are equal.(1991: 316)	We	can clearly *understand* Elizabeth, who goes
the relationship between mother and us.	We	should *understand* their different caring
symbol of falsehood. Only in this light can	we	*understand* why Gregers asks Hedvig to kill
linguistics with literary critical views,	we	can further *understand* the essence of literature
cause Pecola's trauma. In which way shall	we	*understand* her misery as concluded by Morrison
support of this. By adopting this definition,	we	can better *understand* feminist literary
father to son. And from the four words,	we	*understand* that Lena's mother is a traditional
employing feminist theory in this paper,	we	*understand* that both worship and critique
existentialism and novels of black humor so that	we	can *understand* the black humor in The End
natioral inclination to protect non-human life.	We	*understand* that other beings, ranging from
discrimination should be well grasped before	we	could better *understand* the present identity
underscores the difference between what	we	*understand* as readers and what David sees
himself. The more we read his poems, the more	we	*understand* himself. The more we read his
himself. The more we read his poems, the more	we	*understand* this giant poet. He won a lot
attitudes to achieve social stability. Meanwhile	we	can also *understand* George Eliot's deep
dependence on her: [quote] With this in mind,	we	may *understand* why almost all of O'Neill

Figure 5.14   All the instances of 'We' collocating with *understand* in EL

In comparison with the three other most frequently used verbs in this category, the verb *understand* is used more frequently with 'We' than 'I' in both disciplines. In EL, it is almost exclusively used in *we can understand* to express the writer's understanding of the original literature(see Figure 5.14 for all the instances of *understand* collocating with 'We' in EL). In these texts, 'We' is used as an exclusive personal pronoun, which actually means 'I', referring to the writer himself/herself. The inclusive and exclusive usages of the plural FPP 'We' will be revisited in detail in Chapter 7.

In BM, apart from some instances of *we can understand*, the verb *understand* also collocates with 'We' and obligatory modals, as in *we must / should / need to / have to understand*. In these sentences, 'We' is used as inclusive pronoun including both the writer and the readers; and the verb *understand* itself means the cognitive process of *knowing the meaning or importance of something*. The phrasal expressions are used to stress the necessity and importance of understanding the propositions that the writers proposed. Examples 5-25 and 5-26 exemplify this function.

Example 5-25: In considering what motivates people, *we have to understand* their needs, goals, value systems, and expectations. It is important to understand first what work means to people from different backgrounds. (PGBM 0072)

Example 5-26: To fully understand resale price maintenance, *we must* first *understand* the vertical monopoly. Vertical, opposite to horizontal, is a vertical relationship between enterprises in different economic levels, such as manufacturers and distributors, wholesalers and retailers. (UGBM 01709)

In general, the verbs of *Research Interpretation* show a diverse and complicated picture when co-occurring with 'I' and 'We' between BM and EL. Some of the verbs in the RI category present meaning and phraseological difference between the two disciplines, as illustrated by *read*. Some verbs do not present disciplinary difference but vary when collocating with 'I' and 'We', and of different academic levels, for example, *think* and *SAY*. Moreover, there are verbs differing in meaning and function when co-occurring with the inclusiveness and exclusiveness of the plural first-person pronoun 'We', such as *understand*.

5.4 Discussion

Though it is predicted that there would be disciplinary differences across the two disciplines, it is found in this study that some of the verbs present little difference when they collocate with the FPPs, 'I' and 'We'. The finding of similar uses of the phrases of 'I', 'We' and their verb collocates, as well as the same discourse functions of these expressions is in itself worthy of further discussion.

One observation is that the student writers use the same phrases to describe the divergent research processes of their respective discipline. Taking the verb *ANALYZE* as an example, as noted in the analysis, it is one verb, being used to convey a myriad of meanings in the two disciplines respectively. In Business and Management discipline, analysis is at the heart of what they are doing, the analysis of data or experimental results. In English Literature however, in most cases, *analyze* is the synonym of explanation or interpretation. The writers of the two disciplines also use the same verbs to refer to different types of academic work. The students of BM acquire knowledge from real world case studies, statistics and interviews. The students of EL observe or 'see' things through in-depth reading or interpret the meaning of literature made up of novels, poems and short stories. As discussed above, additional examples of the verbs that are used to serve the same discourse functions across the two disciplines are *KNOW*, *SEE* and *READ* in the BM and EL disciplines.

Considering the different epistemology of the two disciplines, the students who write about English Literature use the same vocabulary as people who write about Business and Management might be a bit odd. English Literature is a discipline that mostly relies on personal interpretation or interpretation from a secondary source, for instance, critics. On the other hand, Business and Management is a discipline that hinges on experimental numbers, hard facts and real-world application. In other words, what the EL students discussed in their texts are ideas, and/or evaluation of the characters, the words, the plots, the conflicts and the impact created by the literary pieces they worked on. By using the verbs such as *ANALYZE* and *FIND* to collocate with the FPPs, English Literature writers express their interpretations as their own, and at the same time, attempt to achieve persuasive effects in their dissertations. It is an open question as to whether the English Literature students are correct in using the vocabulary. A comparative study exploring the types of verbs used by expert writers of English Literature, in their published discourse course would be a worthwhile academic pursuit. This is one possible direction for future research. This difference also raises the more general question of how aware the two groups of the students are of their disciplinary conventions in relation to other disciplines. This corpus based study cannot answer this question. However, it does signpost the importance of raising the students' awareness of disciplinary writing. This issue is discussed in Chapter 7 in greater detail.

5.5　Conclusion

In general, the contrastive investigation of the phrases of 'I', 'We' and their verb collocates reveals textual and pragmatic similarities as well as differences in the two disciplines in this study. The similarities between the two disciplines are that in many cases, the verbs are used in identical phrases and serve the same discourse functions. The disciplinary difference is mainly in the semantic and functional differences of those verbs collocating with the first-person pronouns between BM and EL. When the meaning of a verb differs in the two disciplines, the phraseological behaviour of that verb differs, too. The epistemic difference discovered through the verbs in all four categories can be ascribed to the different knowledge acquisition approaches adopted within the two disciplines. That very similarity and the divergence casts light on how EFL student writers conceptualise their research processes, their writing processes and ultimately, the outcome of their academic writing, which may also assist to shed some light on the teaching of EFL academic writing.

CHAPTER 6
PHRASES OF 'I', 'WE' AND THEIR
VERB COLLOCATES ACROSS
THE TWO ACADEMIC LEVELS

6.1　Introduction

In this chapter I shall be comparing the academic texts produced by the students from two different academic levels, namely, undergraduate (UG) and postgraduate (PG). The hypothesis of this chapter is that there are differences in the forms of usage of the two FPPs, 'I', 'We', and their verb collocates in the dissertations between students at UG and PG levels. This difference would be made apparent by manner in which the students use of the verbs collocating with 'I' and 'We'. It is my contention that the students from different academic levels may use different sets of verbs or use the same verbs but with varying frequencies. It is also my contention that some of the phrases of 'I', 'We' and their verb collocates could be used for different pragmatic functions in the texts.

The methodology employed in this chapter is similar to the methodology that was used to compare the disciplinary differences in Chapter 5. The investigation of the differences occurring between the two academic levels starts with the quantitative examination of the four classes of verbs, *Textual organising verbs* (TO), *Knowledge community construing verb* (KC), *Research reporting verbs* (RR), and *Research interpretation verbs* (RI). Further, the RR verbs are subdivided into *Epistemic verbs* (EP) *and Research conduct verbs* (RC). The RI verbs are subdivided into *Verbs research finding interpretation* (RI) and *Verbs of arguing* (AG) (see Chapter 4 for the categorisation of the verbs). After grouping the verbs into these different categories, some of the frequent verbs that collocate with 'I' and/or 'We' in each category of the UG and the PG levels are examined in more detail, both quantitatively and qualitatively.

In this contrastive study, it is found that the postgraduate students use less personal expressions and undertake more retrospective textual organisation in their theses than do the undergraduates. They tend to use more 'We' rather than 'I'; and in some cases, they tend to use more impersonal constructions rather than expressions with 'I' and 'We'. In general, the postgraduate students present themselves to be more impersonal in their academic texts than the undergraduate students. This difference is made all the more manifest as a direct result of an increasing awareness of the disciplinary conventions governing academic style and conformity to the same.

It is important to note that the difference between 'I' and 'We' is only discussed when necessary in this chapter. Particularly, when the verbs present different meanings in different phrases while collocating with 'I' and 'We', they will be brought to discussion. Otherwise, 'I' and 'We' and their roles when collocating with the verbs in these Chinese students' academic texts will be discussed later in Chapter 7.

The organisation of this chapter is as follows. After this introductory section, Section 2 consists of the quantitative results of the FPPs and the four function categories pertaining to the two academic levels, UG and PG. In Section 3, I look at some frequently used verbs that collocate with 'I' and 'We' in each category, TO, KC, RR, and RI. Section 4 concludes this chapter.

6.2   Quantitative overview of the verbs collocating with 'I' and 'We' across the undergraduate and postgraduate levels

Overall, the quantitative result of the FFPs 'I' and 'We' shows a notable difference between students at the UG level and at PG level. The postgraduate students use fewer FPPs in their academic texts than the undergraduate students. The calculation of the verbs in the textual function categories found that the UG students use more verbs to organise text, construe knowledge community, report their study and internship, and to argue than the PG students. On the other hand, the PG students tend to use the FPPs and their verb collocates more frequently to report research methodology, procedure and interpret the research results than do the UG students.

6.2.1   Quantitative results of 'I' and 'We'

Table 6.1 lists the quantitative information of the UG and PG corpora. The average length per text is 4,398 words in the UG corpus and 15,165 words in the PG corpus. The number of occurrences of 'I' and 'We' varies greatly from text to text, ranging from 186 instances in one of the postgraduate texts to no instances at all in 7 PG dissertations after the data was pro-

cessed. In UG level, the text with the most occurrences of the
FPPs contains 80 instances of 'I' and 'We'. There are 266 out
of 305 dissertations that contain at least one instance of 'I'
and/or 'We'. The mean of 'I' and 'We' uses per 1,000 words
for the UG corpus was 2.40(SD = 2.11). The mean of the two
FPPs uses per 1,000 words for the PG corpus was 1.51(SD =
1.63). The unpaired t-test revealed that this difference is statistically significant, $t(1, 407) = 4.42$, p<.0001. Thus, the number of occurrences between UG and PG shows a statistically
reliable difference.

Table 6.1   Quantitative information of UG and PG

	Number of texts	Tokens	Types	Hits of 'I' and 'We'	Normalised frequency per 1000 words of 'I' and 'We'
UG	305	1,758,833	35,519	3,520	2.00
PG	151	2,434,580	46,135	3,293	1.35

From the statistics, it is apparent that the PG writers use
fewer instances of 'I' and 'We' than the undergraduate
students. Table 6.2 shows that there are fewer occurrences of
the singular FFP 'I' in the postgraduates' texts than the
undergraduates'. The normalised frequency of 'I' of the PG
corpus is about half of that of the UG corpus.

Table 6.2   Quantitative information of 'I'
and 'We' respectively in UG and PG

	Hits of 'I'	Normalised frequency per 1000 words of 'I'	Hits of 'We'	Normalised frequency per 1000 words of 'We'
UG	1,030	0.58	2,489	1.41
PG	699	0.29	2,591	1.06

6.2.2   Quantitative results of the verb categories

Figure 6.1 illustrates the proportional difference of the four general discourse functions, TO, KC, RR and AG. The subcategories of the functions, EP, RC, RI, and AG are also listed. As the figure shows, the undergraduates use more instances of TO, KC, EP, and AG. The postgraduates use more instance of 'I', 'We' and their verb collocates to serve the RC and RI functions.

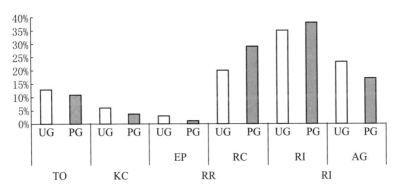

Figure 6.1   Verbs collocating with 'I' and 'We' in UG and PG

Tables 6.3 to 6.6 show the 4 groups of the verb collocates of 'I' and 'We' in the undergraduate and the postgraduate students' texts. The percentages provided at the bottom of the tables are proportional to the total of the verb instances in each column and they account for of all the verbs identified in the undergraduate level(1,738 times) and postgraduate level(1,555 times) respectively.

Table 6.3 shows that the students of both levels use almost the same types of TO verbs. The undergraduate students use 'I', 'We' and the verb collocates to organise the text slightly

Table 6.3   Textual organising verbs in UG and PG

Textual organizing verbs			
UG		PG	
DICUSS	63	DISCUSS	59
MENTION	53	mentioned	25
ANALYZE	33	ANALYZE	25
introduce	20	quote	16
TALK	26	TALK	12
present	14	study	21
cite	6	introduce	9
explain	5		
	220		167
	13%		11%

Table 6.4   Knowledge community construing verb in UG and PG

Knowledge Community Construing verb			
UG		PG	
KNOW	111	KNOW	68
	6%		4%

Table 6.5   Research reporting verbs in UG and PG

Research Report verb							
Epistemic verbs				Research conduct verbs			
UG		PG		UG		PG	
read	37	read	16	FIND	120	FIND	147
worked	9	worked	3	use	41	USE	49
				CHOOSE	29	look	52
				focus	23	focus	22
				ANALYZE	22	CHOOSE	20
				infer	16	notice	18
				SEE	16	EXAMINE	16
				COLLECT	14	SEE	15
				hear	14	call	13
				define	12	act	12

continued

Research Report verb			
Epistemic verbs		Research conduct verbs	
UG	PG	UG	PG
		examine 12	hear 12
		CALL 11	OBSERVE 12
		notice 10	asked 10
		explore 8	arrange 9
		compare 5	ANALYZE 7
			collected 7
			test 7
			proposed 6
			apply 5
			divide 5
46	19	353	444
3%	1%	20%	29%

more frequently, specifically 2% more than the PG students. The KC verb(see Table 6.4) displays a similar pattern. UG has more instances of the verb *KNOW* than PG. In relation to the EP verbs, the PG students use fewer instances of these in their theses than the UG writers. However, they use more RC(see Table 6.3) and RI verbs(see Table 6.6) than the UG students. Compared to UG, it is also seen from Table 6.6 that there is a less frequent use of AG verbs in the PG corpus. These differences are of interest and warrant closer scrutiny. In order to further explore the differences between UG and PG students, Section 6.3 examines some of the most frequently used verbs in each verb group and their discourse functions when collocating with the two FPPs in the UG and PG texts.

Table 6.6   Research interpretation verbs in UG and PG

Research interpretation verb							
Verbs of research finding interpretation				verbs of arguing			
UG		PG		UG		PG	
SEE	323	SEE	321	think	83	SAY	49
FIND	136	FIND	93	SAY	64	think	48
KNOW	40	KNOW	52	understand	37	SEE	35
conclude	30	MEAN	31	learn	32	understand	33
TELL	24	FEEL	18	SEE	37	argue	24
feel	19	conclude	18	hope	36	learn	20
imagine	10	sense	14	believe	28	believe	16
suppose	7	learn	11	KNOW	23	KNOW	14
mean	7	judge	10	consider	21	ignore	11
read	6	aware	10	agree	19	consider	6
learn	5	read	9	realize	13	hope	5
		suppose	5	concerned	7		
		tell	5				
	607		597		400		261
	35%		38%		23%		17%

6.3   Verbs collocating with 'I' and 'We' across the undergraduate and the post-graduate levels

In this section, I shall firstly discuss some of the most frequent verbs that are used with 'I' and 'We' in both UG and PG. Then, I look into some of the alternative expressions of the phrases of 'I', 'We' and their verb collocates. In so doing, I aim to find those impersonal expressions that the PG students use to disguise their personal presence in the texts.

6.3.1   Textual organising verbs

From Table 6.3, it is evident that the undergraduate students use marginally more *Textual Organizing verbs* than their postgraduate counterparts. The following discussion focuses on two verbs, *DISCUSS* and *MENTION*, which are the most frequently used TO verbs by both undergraduate and postgraduate students.

The verb DISCUSS

In this study, the verb *DISCUSS* serves two purposes as a metadiscourse organising verb. One function is to introduce what is about to be discussed. When using this function, the undergraduate students almost always(11 out of all the 12 instances), collocate *DISCUSS* with 'I' in the phrase *I will / want to / would like to discuss* (see Figure 6.2). In the postgraduate texts, there are 7 instances of *I will / want to / would like to discuss* (Figure 6.3), and 12 instances of *we will / shall / tend to discuss* (Figure 6.4) to serve the same function. This suggests that at UG level, the student writers frequently use the singular FFP 'I' to collocate with *DISCUSS* to inform the readers of the content of their following discourse. In PG, it may be seen that in some instances the students choose 'We' in the phrase *we will / shall / tend to discuss* to organise the texts.

The second function of the verb *DISCUSS* is to remind readers what has been discussed in the text. There are 18 instances and 36 instances of (*as*) *We have (already) discussed* in the undergraduate and the postgraduate theses respectively. Only 3 instances of *I have discussed* are found in the whole corpus. This choice between 'I' and 'We' when collocating with

as a PR channel. In the following part,	I will discuss	some of its main advantages based on my
new opinions about this failure. Moreover,	I will also discuss	about the conflicts facing international
new opinions about this failure. Moreover,	I will also discuss	about the conflicts facing international
theories in the future. In this thesis,	I want to discuss	the relationship between culture and brand
control the risk simultaneously. So secondly	I want to discuss	the perfect legislation. Though we have
in Jude and Sue's life happened, which	I will discuss	later. The scenery of the distant Christminister
judgment as a colonist herself. Moreover,	I will discuss	the feasibility of her suggestions when
the result of the previous two chapters,	I will discuss	Rice's depiction of Louis and Lestat in
recreated her life with imagination. And	I will discuss	more about the play and characters in the
novels an example to illustrate, What	I am discussing	here is novel. I think novel is very important
unjust and greedy; and the third one is what	I would like to discuss	more here, Walden, the book of simple life
escape the temptation. In this Chapter,	I will try to discuss	the reason that why they have different

Figure 6.2   *I will/want to/would like to discuss* in UG

status and their choice of power strategies,	I will first discuss	how channel power impact conflicts management
be further expanded. And in this section,	I will discuss	how to integrate channel strategy into
brands for middle class. In this section,	I will discuss	another means by which brands can be built
the process of deduction and, whafs more,	I will discuss	the identical plot structure in ME.Then
in descriptive translation studies. Then	I shall discuss	how various historical dynamics (ideology
more infallible guide. In this chapter	I will discuss	how the materialistic tendency is reflected
range of the first literary movement. What	I am going to discuss	in the following sections shall fall into

Figure 6.3   *I will/want to/would like to discuss* in PG

incorporating function of consciousness,	we will also discuss	the transcendence attribute of consciousness
strategies and its cultural differences,	we intend to discuss	cross cultural communication strategies
flow from alternative evaluation processes.	We will discuss	some significant aspects. Though Chinese
recommendations for their cultural integration as	we will discuss	in the next part. Geely, which was founded
based on the dimensions of culture, which	we will discuss	in the next section. Individualism is proven
differences, and the mode of acculturation. Then	we will discuss	and testify the two assumptions made in
The related theories are presented above.	We will discuss	the connection between theories of communication
effects to the development of the crisis, and	we will discuss	this in Sanlu's case. This can be seen
is a natural result of the narration, but	we should discuss	the flood scene into the context of literary
acceptable to its audience.In this part,	we will discuss	the flood myth in the novel. We will make
character knows. In the part on narrative voice,	we will discuss	first the time of narrating and meet the
of the spatialization of clock time that	we will discuss	here, is the repetition of images and motifs

Figure 6.4   *We will/shall/tend to discuss* in PG

the verb *DISCUSS* is further discussed at the end of this subsection(Section 6.3.1). I shall now focus on the TO function of the phrases of 'I', 'We' and *DISCUSS*.

The other observation of the verb *DISCUSS* is that this expression(*as*) *I/We have (already) discussed* is often used with what Hyland(1998: 442) called endophoric markers, the reference to "the information in the other parts of the texts" in the discourse. Taking *"in the former chapter"* in the following sentence as an example,

> Example 6-1: The main problems can be divided into the following categories: The stubborn regulation System for Chinese companies: *as we have discussed in the former chapter* about the 7S model of NAC's, the system of the company formal and informal procedures that support the strategy and structure is a very important part of the company culture. (PGBM 0060)

To find out how the students avoid being visible while using *DISCUSS* to organise text, is to find how the verb *DISCUSS* is used for textual organising function without collocating with 'I' and 'We'. To do this, I searched the lemma *DISCUSS* in Sketch Engine(Kilgarriff et al. 2004). It returned 501 occurrences of this verb in UG and 682 instances in PG. The investigation of all the instances of *DISCUSS* aims at finding out how this verb is used when organising text. It also aims to discover how the two expressions discussed above, *will discuss* and *have discussed*, are used with other personal pronouns, for example, *they*, *he*, *she*, or the impersonal pronoun *it* as their subjects. By manual examination of the retrieved concordances, 148 in UG and 234 in PG refer to other people's work, i.e. it is referring to someone else's work, which has nothing to do with 'I' and 'We'. For instance, in Example 6-2, *have discussed* is used to introduce the criteria of newsworthiness which text books on reporting stress on. Such instances are not discussed in this research.

> Example 6-2: For decades, *text books on reporting have discussed* the classic elements of news. Crite-

ria considered as determining newsworthiness include these: Timeliness. Is it a recent development, or is it old news? Proximity. Is the story relevant to local readers? Conflict. Is the issue developing, has it been resolved or does anybody care? (UGBM 01506)

There are 316 instances at the UG level and 422 instances at the PG level of the verb *DISCUSS* being used for TO without 'I' and 'We' as their subjects. Among these TO instances, 143 occurrences in UG and 240 in PG, which account for 45% and 56% of this verb, is in the form of *discussed*. When the verb *DISCUSS* is used in the form *discussed* to organise text, it performs both functions of *introducing what is going to be discussed* and *reminding the readers what has been discussed*. In such instances, *DISCUSS* is frequently used in the following four phrases, *will be discussed*, *as discussed*, *is/are discussed*, *has/have been discussed*. See Examples 6-3 to 6-6.

Example 6-3: In this part, three women characters **will be discussed**, Joanna Burden, the dietitian, and Bobbie Allen. Unlike the above-discussed traditional women, none of the three are married. Their life is already ruined before they step into the tomb of marriage. (PGEL 0020)

Example 6-4: **As discussed** in previous chapter, there are totally 6 different interest groups in a company which can classified as internal groups like owners and employees, and external ones including consumers, suppliers, creditors, distributors, dealers, government and the society. (PGBM 0123)

Example 6-5: The elements constituting this mix

are discussed below. Visual image or corporate symbol is an important element within the corporate identity mix. It is that aspect of the mix which communicates a company's corporate identity through visual means to the public. (PGBM 0061)

Example 6-6: As *has been discussed* in the previous two sectors of this chapter, love offers possibility for the three female protagonists to gain redemption after confronting their individual Gothic image of Medusa and more importantly salvages the serial killer Paul Whitmore from his heinous crime, the redemption of violence can be possibly fulfilled through altruistic love and kindness, leading finally towards positive freedom. (PGEL 0058)

With regard to the instances of *will discuss* and *have* ∗ *discussed*, it can be seen from Table 6.7 that the UG and the PG students use about the same proportion of *I*/*we will discuss* to refer to what is going to be discussed in their texts. On the other hand, the PG writers use proportionally more instances of *I*/*we have* ∗ *discussed* to remind the readers what has been said previously in their texts.

Table 6.7 The instance of *will discuss* and *HAVE discussed* in UG and PG

	will discuss	*I*/*we will discuss* (% of *will discuss*)		*HAVE* ∗ *discussed*	*I*/*we HAVE* ∗ *discussed* (% of *HAVE* ∗ *discussed*)	
UG	43	5	12%	37	18	49%
PG	31	4	13%	51	36	71%

Frequently, when *will discuss* and *HAVE* ∗ *discussed* do

not collocate with the FPPs, the inanimate endophoric markers are used as the subjects. For example,

Example 6-7: ***Chapter 5 will discuss*** the implications of Sbk' success for Chinese multinational companies. (UGBM 07606)

Example 6-8: ***The First Chapter of this paper has discussed*** the numerous parallels and connections between the past and present in Ackroydian narrative, mainly focusing on the resemblances between the characters. (PGEL 0016)

To recapitulate, when collocating with the FPPS, the verb *DISCUSS* is frequently used in the phrases *I/We will discuss* and (*as*) *We have (already) discussed* to perform the metadiscourse function of discourse organisation in the students' academic discourse. There are more instances of the passive voice or the past participle of this verb, *discussed* in the postgraduate students' texts. The postgraduate students also prefer both 'We' and other subjects, like, *this chapter*, *in the previous chapter* to collocate with *DISCUSS* in their academic texts. As a result, there is less self-presentation in the postgraduate texts than in the undergraduate texts.

The verb *MENTION*

When collocating with 'I' and 'We', the verb *MENTION* shows a significant difference between the undergraduate and the postgraduate students' writing. The undergraduate students use this verb, collocating with the FPPs, about twice as often as the postgraduate students do.

In both UG and PG texts, *MENTION* is almost exclusively used in the phrase (*as*) *I/we (have) mentioned*, 78 instances in total. The differences between the two academic levels may be observed by their frequency of collocation with 'I' and 'We'. At the UG level, there are 37 instances of (*as*) *I* (*have*) *mentioned*, 10 instances of *as we mentioned*, and 6 instances of *I will* (*have to*) *mention*. Comparatively, there are 19 instances in which 'We' collocate with *mentioned* in the postgraduates' texts, and only 6 instances of (*as*) *I* (*have*) *mentioned*. In other words, the verb *MENTION* is used, most frequently, in the phrase (*as*) *I*/*We* (*have*) *mentioned*. It collocates with 'I' more frequently than with 'We' in the undergraduate texts. Conversely, in the postgraduate texts, this verb collocates more frequently with 'We' than 'I'.

Apart from the fact that the number of occurrences tells us that the PG students tend to use *MENTION* with the plural FPP, 'We', like the verb *DISCUSS*, it could be of interest to find out how *MENTION* is used without 'I' and 'We' in the UG and PG texts. The exploration of the impersonalisation of this verb would tell us how this verb is used without an agent, or more precisely, without the writer referring to himself/herself as 'I' and 'We'. I then, searched the lemma *MENTION* in the students' academic texts of both academic levels respectively. This search returned 524 instances *MENTION* in UG and 603 instances in PG. It is found that there are 288 instances (54%) at the UG level and 268 instances (44%) at the PG level that serve the TO function after conducting a manual examination of the retrieved concordances. These instances include those 78 occurrences that *MENTION* collocates with 'I' and 'We'. Comparing the TO instances of PG with those of UG, it is observed that all the 268 occurrences of *MENTION* in the PG

are used in the form of *mentioned*, which could be considered
as anaphoric use as it refers to what has been discussed in the
text. Twenty concordances are listed in Figure 6.5.

corporate culture construction process. As is mentioned earlier, new Lenovo is facing with serious
service before consumption. Based on the above mentioned principles, the athletic shoes, laptops and
brand perception is obvious. As previously mentioned , Keller established the brand knowledge
. Separation: separation is just like the one mentioned before, but with the national culture taken
that corporate identity may have. The mentioned four components have covered the necessary
Europe and the United States towards China. As mentioned above, an increasing number of Swedish
to distinctive national cultures. The above mentioned cognitive, affective and behavioral
variables which are likely to relate with the mentioned personal traits concerning adaptation. They
for Future Efforts Despite the above mentioned significance, the thesis is far from complete
take IC and PD into consideration because as I mentioned above, the studies of most scholars in this
, 2001: 46). The relationship between the above mentioned variables is as the following hypotheses: H3:
are distributed and collected among the above mentioned three groups of employees to test the four
future generations. Hypothesis 3: [Quote] As mentioned in the Chapter Two, the relationship of
China and tJie western societies. As just mentioned above, few scholars have delved into CSR from
entering an era of social responsibility. As mentioned above, there are tremendous definitions of CSR
of research convenience, the corporations mentioned in this thesis are all big ones and the small and
to employees, etc. The existence of all these mentioned above could be attributed to the attitudes of
. A survey conducted by that Committee mentioned above shows that the 100 odds charitable
of research convenience, the corporations mentioned in this thesis are all big ones and the small and
, six from Sweden and eight from Finland. As mentioned in a previous session, that's 3.2.2.1, the

Figure 6.5   The verb *mentioned* uses as TO in PG

At the UG level on the other hand, except those instances
of *mentioned* that are used to refer to what has been said,
there are 15 instances of TO that refer to what is going to be
said, which may be considered as cataphoric use of this verb.
These instances are illustrated in Figure 6.6.

Turning to the phrase *as mentioned*, it is a popular expression used to organise discourse in academic papers and used liberally across a variety of academic disciplines. It transpired that
there were 63 and 102 instances of this phrase in the UG and
PG levels respectively. The verb *MENTION* functions as a TO
verb in the postgraduate texts and doubled in the undergraduate
texts. The more frequently used phrase *as mentioned* in the PG

carefully. In Hofstede's theory that I will	mention	in next chapter, the cultural dimension of
work they are doing. The power distance I will	mention	in next part has a great relationship with
the leader and staff. One thing that needs to	mention	is that the relationship between employer and
. It was the first but not the last. We can also	mention	the participation of Lal in the festival
brand carefully and culturally. Thirdly, I	mention	how to use your culture to become a world famous
like uniform people and also the same brand. As I	mention	above, brand is just like a person and has his
for the consumer before and after sale. When	mentioning	of the direct distribution model, DI is an
computer the consumer wants. What the author	mentions	above are the four main direct distribution
Lenovo, we will see an opposite situation. When	mentioning	the success of DI, the success of Levo is an
eyes. To start with, it is necessary to	mention	first the famous statement by Wordsworth that
of a single part means nothing. Here I'd like to	mention	a kind of things which are similar with human
groups. Including the two dramas we are about to	mention	. Originated in France, comparative
The following discussion will not only	mention	this type of children's fantasy fiction, but
the value of Emily's opinions, we should	mention	the features of Victorian literature.
power and his mother. Another thing I want to	mention	which is also talked by Lawrence in his letter to

Figure 6.6   The verb *MENTION* of cataphoric use in UG

text could be attributed to the purposes of avoiding subjectivity in the texts. Being more experienced in writing academic prose, the postgraduates acquired more rhetorical devices for organising discourse. Using *as mentioned* helps the writer to distance himself/herself from the discussion. Therefore, these theses sound more impersonalised and objective than(*as*) *I* / *we* (*have*) *mentioned*. In general, in comparison with the undergraduate students, the investigation of the lemmas of the verbs, *DISCUSS* and *MENTION* suggest that the postgraduate students' texts are more impersonal when these two verbs are used to organise their texts.

I now turn to the discussion of the finding that the PG students use the plural FPP 'We' to collocate with *DISCUSS* and *MENTION* more frequently than the undergraduates. This replacement of 'We' with 'I' may suggest that the plural FPP is more of an alignment device to establish solidarity in these postgraduate students' texts. It may also imply that the avoidance of the singular FFP 'I' is to disguise the student writers themselves behind the collectiveness of the plural FPP 'We'.

This choice between 'I' and 'We' will be discussed in Chapter 7 in greater detail.

6.3.2   The knowledge community construing verb *KNOW*

In Chapters 4 and 5, *KNOW* was found to be used most frequently in two expressions(*as*) *we*(*all*) *know* and *we know that*. The first phrase(*as*) *we*(*all*) *know* is to introduce background knowledge by construing an academic community; the latter one *we know that* is to either construe knowledge community or to interpret research findings. As discussed in previous chapters, when the verb *KNOW* is used to introduce general knowledge, it is found that this function is most frequently realised in the phrase(*as*) *we*(*all*) *know*. This phrase serves as the stepping stone for knowledge acquisition and knowledge sharing for the purposes of further discussion. By proclaiming a common background of their disciplinary knowledge, the student writers attempt to appeal to a select number of members from an academic community that include themselves and potential readers of their academic texts.

Comparing the academic level difference, there are more instances of *KNOW* as KC in the texts produced by undergraduates than those produced by postgraduates(111 as opposed to 68 instances). Although both of the phrases, (*as*) *we*(*all*) *know* and *we know that*, are found to be used for this function, (*as*) *we*(*all*) *know* is more frequently used by both UG and PG students. Figure 6.7 illustrates 20 random examples of *KNOW* as KC from both undergraduate texts of Business and Management and English Literature disciplines.

the eastern and western cultures are. As	we	*know* social cultural background and values
market comes into being and becomes what	we	*know* today after decades of developments
differences, but it is not true. For instance,	we	all *know* that there is a Chinese instant
represent the reunion of the family. As	we	*know* , collectivism is very important to
consumption pattern and living style. As	we	all *know* , China as the fastest growing
since 2005. These efforts didn't work. As	we	*know* , Eb, Dd and QW all have good
in market share of this social market. As	we	*know* eBay is the biggest e-commerce vendor
Character is more important than intellect. As	we	all *know* , America is one of the countries
Fans, leading a kind of new culture. As	we	all *know* , product is the most important
strong competitor rather than a poor copycat.	We	all *know* that there is a group of loyal
history, laws are the center of regulation. As	we	*know* , the economic and financial laws
weak points of the Chinese institutions. As	we	*know* , the non-performing asset rate has
his concept of 'God' and 'Man'. As	we	all *know* , God plays an extremely significant
will again till she's as he is now! As	we	*know* , the major setting of Jude the Obscure
husband freely. At the end of the novel,	we	*know* that Charlotte is pregnant. The story
following advantages: At the end of the novel,	we	*know* that Jane and Bingley come to enjoy
Carver is very close to his protagonists:	we	*know* that several of the stories have biographical
to be truly in love. From the beginning,	we	*know* that the story of Romeo and Juliet
relate with well-educated lady. And also,	we	*know* that Estella is educated by Miss Havisham
Mile End Terrace, Landport, Portsmouth. As	we	all *know* , David Copperfield was also born

Figure 6.7   Examples of *know* as KC in the phrases (*as*)
we (all) know* and *we know that

The quantitative difference of the occurrences of *KNOW* used as KC when it collocates with the FPPs between the two academic levels suggests that there is less self-presentation on making claims in the postgraduate texts than in the texts of the undergraduate students. This is especially so when the claims made are of common knowledge which is shared between the student writers and the audience. In the postgraduate texts, KC expressions such as (*as*) *we (all) know* and *we know that* are discarded when interacting with the academic community due to their informality.

The other function of *we know that*, is used to interpret research. This function is more apparent when it is used with some endophoric expressions. Examples 6-9 and 6-10 illustrate this use.

Example 6-9: From the interview, *we know that*

advertising is the most influential channel to inform Chinese consumers of the brands. (PGBM 0059)

Example 6-10: From the short presence of Janaa's mother, *we know that* they have never had a good relationship. (PGEL 0043)

Indeed, the verb *KNOW* is unique in these students' discourse. The collective belongingness suggested by the phrases *(as) we (all) know* and *we know that* will probably find empathy with the readers, who would then probably go on to agree with the writer's point of view. This function could also be attributed to the avoidance of redundancy. In this case, the background knowledge needs no elaboration as it is either plainly self-evident or considered as basic disciplinary knowledge and shared jointly by both the writer and the reader. However, I have to admit that as a third party who studies these instances, not in the capacity of being an affiliated member of a particular academic community but as a linguistic researcher, it is hard to determine whether it is part and parcel of the writers' rhetorical strategy, or if the common knowledge is genuinely shared by both the writer and the reader.

6.3.3　Research report verbs

The *Research report verbs* are divided into *Epistemic verbs* and *Research conduct verbs*. Not much proportional difference in the use of the *Research conduct verbs* has been detected in the texts written by the undergraduate and postgraduate students; even including the most popularly used verbs *FIND*, *ANALYZE* and *USE*. However, there are some noticeable disciplinary differences and some differences in the manner that these verbs are used when they collocate with 'I' and 'We' respectively. These findings have been discussed in Chapter 5.

This subsection focuses on one verb from the *epistemic verb* category, *read*. Some instances of this verb are used quite differently between the two academic levels when it collocates with 'I' and 'We'. Two distinct meanings of the verb *read* may be observed when it collocates with the two FFPs. One meaning is the actual activity of *reading*. It is most frequently used in undergraduate texts. The undergraduate writers use this verb to present their experience of reading the books that inspired them or used as their resource books for the purposes of analysis. Figure 6.8 lists 15 random instances from the undergraduate texts, both in Business and Management and English Literature disciplines. These 15 instances are mostly used to describe the writers' reading experience, whether they are novels, documents, or any other materials that the students have read. This *read* refers to the act of reading.

confirmed my impression. In most documents	*I*	*read*, Lincoln and the Northern states
gave me quite different impression when	*I*	*read* the novel Gone with the Wind. In this
strong implications on the readers. When	*I*	*read* this, I had a confused thought because
description was totally different with what	*I*	*read* in the novel. Also, in many sources
by ourselves. Take myself as an example,	*I*	*have* read the novel Gone with the Wind
According to Rousseau, if there is one book	we	must *read*, it is Roubinson Crusoei*supplies
consider the historical background when	we	*read* the novel. Only in this way can we
today? In my opinion, it is because when	we	*read* her novels, behind her irony, we can
about her attitude on that question, but as	we	*read* more carefully the book, we surprisingly
sympathy that has already been forged.What	we	could *read* in the lines of A Passage to
me very much. After returning to China,	*I*	*read* some reports about Hong Kong Disneyland
which arose my strong interest. Then, after	*I*	collected and *read* various materials related
countries as shown by those above. So here	*I*	have *read* those relevant books Horst Siebert
rules in PR, but with all the materials	*I*	*read* and the experiences I had in PR companies
would bring marvelous results. All the books	*I*	*read* hold one same view that Public Relations

Figure 6.8   The verb *read* used as EP verb at UG level

The other meaning of *read*, not the actual act of reading, but to *illustrate or interpret the understanding of the meaning or implication of the book or the art*, can be found in a few cases in postgraduate texts, particularly in the postgraduate English Literature texts. When *read* is used to interpret research findings or to express the writer's understanding, it is almost always used in the phrase *we (can, could) read*. In the two examples listed below, *read* is used to interpret the writers' understanding of different objects, for example, the pattern *read + it +* a particular way (*either way*) in Example 6-11 and the phrase *read +* abstract noun (*respect and believe*) in Example 6-12. The interpretation function may also be found in the phrasal pattern *read * as*, see Figure 6.9. In these cases, the objects of *read* are more frequently, the third person singular pronoun *it* to refer to the things mentioned previously in the texts.

she cannot change this habit. She wants to	read books as	men do, which is prohibited by her father
in Merwin^ poetry of the 1960s, I tend to	read it as	a Derridean supplement, a substitutive
divest it of any Christian intention and	read it as	a manifesto of man's metaphysical aspiration
as[quote] or as establishing [quote] I	read it as	a testimony of structural difference or
relationships, they are still as widely	read today as	they have ever been (Austen, Persuasion
rape striking and disturbing would rather	read it as	"seduction" instead of "rape". Others

Figure 6.9   Instances of *read * as* in the PGEL

Example 6-11: We do not know for certain whether the pronoun, which refers to Lemuel or the wolf; *we can read* it either way: the wolf is a dog without a master, or, Lemuel is a dog without a master. (PGEL 0013)

Example 6-12: From this quoted excerpt, *we could read* the respect and belief in his elders, and Stephen was in the phase of developing his own way

of understanding the world and his willingness to participate, outside of school and family. (PGEL 0049)

To summarise, the verb *read* has multiple meanings in
these students' academic texts. Moreover, it has its own phrasal
structures when used to express different meanings, namely, *I*
(we)(have) read to express the act of reading, and *we can/*
could read to interpret the research finding or express the
understanding of the original work. Further, when the verb
read is used to interpret, it is used in some other phrases as
well, for instance, *read* + *it* + a particular way, *read* + abstract
noun, and *read * as*, to express the writers' understanding of
the literature work.

6.3.4   Research interpretation verbs

The *Research interpretation verbs* are divided into two subcategories, *Verbs of research finding interpretations* (RI) and
Verbs of arguing (AG). As no differences were found in RI
category, the main discussion of this subsection focuses on the
Verbs of arguing category.

As mentioned in the previous chapters, AG verbs may be
regarded as the indicators of the writer's stance when they
collocate with the FPPs, which is an authorial presentation in
the academic texts. Undoubtedly, verbs of mental process(see
Biber et al. 2002), for example, *think* or *believe*, belong to
this category. This is because these verbs describe active mental
or emotional activity. They can differentiate writer from author, which in essence, suggests that a writer is a discoursal
constructor and an author is a view point owner(Ivanič 1998;
Tang & John 1999). When collocating with 'I' and 'We', AG

verbs are of importance. It is through this group of verbs that the writers' own opinions are voiced, their evaluation of certain matters made apparent and the writers' stance becoming visible. Interestingly, in this study, it is found that some activity verbs of verbal process in Biber's(2002) classification, e.g. *SAY* and *learn*, are also used for arguments in the student writers' texts. Here, I compare the 4 most frequent verbs from the two academic level texts, *think*, *believe*, *SAY*, and *learn*.

The verb *think* and *believe*

There are 47 usages of *think* used with 'I' in UG texts and 29 usages with 'I' in PG texts. When *think* collocates with 'I', it is often used to express the writer's own viewpoint. On the other hand, when it collocates with 'We', it means the activity of thinking, which expresses little indication of understanding or judgement. These differences in the meaning of the verbs when collocating between 'I' and 'We' will be accounted for in Chapter 7.

The verb *believe* is used 14 times in the UGBM and 16 times in PGBM. No difference in the number of occurrences or in the meaning is observed between the two academic levels of this discipline. In the undergraduate English Literature texts, 14 instances of *I believe* were found. There is no instance of *believe* found collocating with either 'I' or 'We' in the postgraduate English Literature subcorpus. The interpretation of the difference in occurrences of *I think* and *I believe* between the two academic levels, is as follows.

One possible account for why there are more instances of *I think* and *I believe* in the undergraduate subcorpora could possibly be due to postgraduate students becoming more careful or

self-restrained in their use of the most obvious personal pronouns to collocate with AG verbs. The singular FPP 'I' is considered as a blatant intrusion in the text. This high degree of
visibility makes the writer stand at the front line and becomes
subject to both challenge and criticism. Therefore, the collocations *I think* and *I believe* are much more threatening than the
expressions without the FPP, for example *it is believed (that)*.
In order to avoid being visible, other forms of expressions that
express the student writers' opinions might be used, for example, *it is ... that*, *it is ... to*, as in the next two examples.

Example 6-13: A reaction is perceived proper
may appear arrogant, even an insult by another. ***It is
essential to*** respect the different values of the other
cultures. (PGBM 0086)

Example 6-14: ***It is believed that*** the long-lasting
love between them inspires many of Galsworthy's stories and that Ada is the prototype of Irene in The Forsyte Saga. We can sense the author's particular sympa-
thy over Irene throughout the trilogy. (PGEL 0073)

The Examples 6-13 and 6-14 above illustrate the writers'
points of views by using the inanimate *it* as the subject of sentences and disguises the writers' presence. It is observed that
the postgraduates use these structures more frequently than the
undergraduates. In the whole corpus, 545(PG) as opposed to
341(UG) times of *it is* * *that* and 592(PG) as opposed to 437
(UG) times of *it is ... to* were retrieved. However, it is noted
that in these occurrences, there may be some expressions like *it
is reported that*, which has no evaluative value or point of view
involved. I did not look at these instances any further as I

focused on the academic level differences of the FPPs in this chapter. However, the examination of the extent to which these two structures are used for evaluative purposes in the EFL students' academic texts might be a task to be undertaken after this study.

When looking at the instances of *believe*, it is found that there are instances of other expressions to replace 'I' and 'We'. For instance, "[*t*] *his thesis*" in Example 6-15 and "[*t*] *he author of this thesis*" in example 6-16.

Example 6-15: This thesis *believes* that domestic network games should improve its quality, creativity and development capabilities. (UGBM 03909)

Example 6-16: The author of this thesis *believes* that Orsino fails to demand the two men's respect(the Second Officer and Antonio) because of his impotence in the sea war against Antonio. (PGEL 0003)

Another possible explanation is that, other than 'I' and 'We', the postgraduate students use adverbs in their academic writing. For example, words such as *importantly*, *obviously*, *necessarily*, and *apparently* all seem to express evaluation and offer viewpoints. These adverbs are pervasive in the texts. Using Sketch Engine, I searched [tag = "RB* "][tag = ", * "], which searches sequences where an adverb is followed by a comma. This search was conducted to find those adverbs that are put at the front of the sentences and used to frame opinions or stances. Some examples are given below.

Example 6-17: My study is consistent with Aaker's perspective that studying consumption sym-bols such as commercial brand is a useful approach for understanding how cultural beliefs and values are presented and institutionalized. Also, the empirical research testifies previous research (Roth 1995) but more ***importantly***, makes some adjustments in accordance with China's specific cultural features. (PGBM 0059)

Example 6-18: ***Apparently***, utterance (31) is an assertion but the illocutionary force is that Darcy frequently breaks the conversation by making no answer and to indicate that Darcy must have done something wrong to Wickham and has guilty conscience for he tries to evade topic about Wickham by silence, so it is also an indirect speech act. (PGEL 0001)

Both of these two examples state explicitly the writers' opinions. The first claims that his/her study is important because it focuses on Chinese culture. Therefore, it is culture specific. In Example 6-18, the writer expresses his/her understanding that 'utterance (31)' is an indirect speech act by explaining the implication of the same.

Due to the fact that adverbs are widespread in the texts, it would be difficult to decide how many instances are evaluative expressions. I shall end my discussion on this point at this juncture for the time being. By illustrating the two alternative rhetorical strategies of *I think* and *I believe*, the point I want to make is that the verbs *think* and *believe* are fewer in postgraduate theses in comparison to the undergraduates' and could possibly be so, due to more advanced writers finding other ways to substitute these two expressions.

The verb *SAY*

The verb *SAY* is, primarily, an activity verb (Biber et al.

2002). It is probably impossible to include it into the *Verb of arguing* group when it is considered out of context, and not in a phrase or in an expanding context. However, I would argue that in most cases, it is used for argument in this study. To be more specific, in the texts of both academic levels, *SAY* is used almost always in the phrase *I/we can/cannot/may/might/ should say*. The novice writers use it to claim or refute a proposition. The modal verbs are used either to strengthen the points of view, or as hedges to express less authoritative opinions of disagreement. The examples are given in Figures 6.10 and 6.11. These are random examples of *say* in the UG and PG subcorpora. As illustrated, they are almost uniformly used in the same phrase and for the same function, i.e. to argue.

replace fantasy with bodily desires. Or	we	may *say* she does not know what she is after
respect each other' character. Therefore,	we	can *say* that their marriage is founded
forgetting them, they have their own voices. If	we	*say* that Laura's glass menagerie is the
first step towards accepting some truth,	we	may *say* , it is a kind of self-awakening
predicting future disasters and pains. Therefore,	we	may *say* that the contribution of the fourth
event in the readers' minds are aroused.	We	cannot *say* who is correct in judging some
vent for her intellectual energy. At least	we	can *say* it is not purely for other people
Collins-Charlotte's dilemma is a real one. Also	we	can *say* in Pride and Prejudice, the dilemma
study the character division of Jane Eyre.	We	d rather *say* the split character of Charlotte
make people happy and enjoy their life.	We	cannot *say* this purpose is true or not.

Figure 6.10   The verb *say* that collocate with 'We' in UGEL

as well as social ideals and philosophy.	We	can *say* that to some degree it is the high
many percents of people have this feature.	we	can *say* much more safely that compared
is a matter of learning. In this sense,	we	can *say* from the instant of birth, a child
to its subsidiaries. Through these cases,	we	can *say* that product crisis is one of the
for to communicate with the public. And	we	should *say* that Johnson and Johnson's
pnoting media and advertisement, the least	we	can *say* is that U.S. cultural industry
as well as social ideals and philosophy.	We	can *say* that to some degree it is the high
or not. Considering the grade France has,	we	can *say* that the French culture does
Web ergonomics goes along with web design;	we	can *say* that the first one dissects the
the analysis of the participant answers.	We	could *say* that the focus group will have

Figure 6.11   The verb *say* that collocates with 'We' in PGBM

In reference to the function of *SAY*, the difference between the undergraduate and postgraduate texts is not apparent. The main difference is the different choice of 'I' and 'We' by the students at different academic levels. The undergraduate students on 17 occasions use *SAY* with 'I'. Conversely, in the postgraduate students' theses, no occurrence of this verb collocates with 'I' is found.

The verb *learn*

The verb *learn* has two discourse functions in the UG and PG students' texts. They are *to interpret research* and *to argue*. In the postgraduate texts and primarily in the postgraduate English Literature texts, the verb *learn* functions to report the interpretation of the research finding(RI), in which case, it presents itself in the phrase *we(can) learn(that)*. Figure 6.12 lists all the 11 instances of *learn* used as RI verb in PG. This phrase is similar to verbs like *find*, *see*, and *know*. This phrasal pattern is further discussed in Chapter 7.

definitions: [Quote] From the above definition,	we	*learn* that 1) Culture determines one's
can make more efforts in these aspects. As	we	have *learned* in the case, when making promotion
'the death car' to Gatsby's house and	we	*learn* later from Tom's words that Wilson
story. In the chapter on narrative duration	we	*learn* that the story was set in 1922. And
thoroughly identified with their husbands that	we	never *learn* their first names while they
loyalty and love for one's mate. In this case	we	*learn* that Santiago certainly doesn't
mothering"(2). Even in psychoanalytic studies,	we	*learn* less about what mother-daughter relationship
Fathers who know their own daughters best.	We	could *learn* that Mr. Bennet, Elizabeth
wisdom. Her development to individuality,	we	could *learn* in the novel where Anne and
Bath because of the financial problems.	We	*learn* that Anne arrived in Bath finally
seem to have a real name. The first thing	we	*learn* about him is that he himself shortened

Figure 6.12   All the instances of *learn* used as RI verb in PG

To illustrate this point in longer sentences, in the Examples 6-19 and 6-20, it is noted that *we(can) learn (that)* serves the RI function as the two '[*f*] *rom*' phrases are key indicators that the research is being interpreted in the texts.

Example 6-19: From Austen's works, *we could learn* that female happiness life is merely a drop in the ocean and the most important is that we may know by a handful the whole sack. (PGEL 0046)

Example 6-20: From the above definition, *we learn that* 1) Culture determines one's perception of the world and shapes one's words and behaviors. 2) 'Culture is learned' not inherited. (PGBM 0128)

Like the categorisation of the AG verb *SAY*, it is equally interesting to find that some instances of the verb *learn* belong to the *Verbs of arguing* category. From the lexical meaning of this verb, it may seem unlikely to put *learn* into AG group. However, the concordances suggest otherwise when it is examined with 'We' and the modal verbs, as in the phrase *we must/can/should/need to learn from/about (that)*. The following is the discussion of it collocating with 'We' across the two academic levels. There is no instance of *learn* collocating with 'I' in the corpus.

As mentioned above, the verb *learn* is almost exclusively used in the phrase *we must/can/should/need to learn from/about (that)*, 32 out of 37 instances at the UG level and 18 out of 31 instances at the PG level. These phrases are mostly used to proffer advice in a real world scenario (see Figure 6.13). There are 26 instances found in the undergraduate Business and Management subcorpus. It might be argued that *learn* itself means 'gaining knowledge or acquiring skill'. However, in the case of novice writers' texts, it is not the act of learning that *we must/can/should/need to learn from/about (that)* is stressed, but the writers' intention of providing suggestions and recommendation for future practice. In other words, lessons or experiences should be learnt from the failure or success of the business. With the collocation of 'We' to express authoritativeness, modal verb to express the modality, and the verb *learn*, the phrase *we must/can/should/need to learn from/about (that)* attempts to establish the writer's authorial status in these dissertations. This intention is shown clearly in the following examples.

Example 6-21: From Motor's great success, *we can learn* some valuable lessons that can help a company improve the development of quality and corporate culture. Motor's tough goal setting should be concerned. Without a clear and appropriate goal, a company cannot be successful. (UGBM 07204)

Example 6-22: Because of this many local drink companies are losing ground to TOC in our own market turf. We know that this situation poses a grave threat to our local industry, and *we need to learn* from this world beverage giant in order to be stronger. (UGBM 05204)

In the students' academic writings, when the verb *learn* collocates with 'We', it is not used to describe the act of learning, but more likely to argue for the importance or necessity of gaining or acquiring disciplinary specific knowledge. The phrase *we must/can/should/need to learn from/about (that)* emphasises the function of arguing instead of describing the action itself.

directions. This is another way of arguing that	we	must *learn* to think in circles. (Betina
especially in dealing with foreign cultures.	We	can *learn* lots of useful experiences from
how to handle these problems. This is what	we	can *learn* from the study of Coca Cola¡⁻
analyzing China economic threats theory,	we	can *learn* from fundamental perspective
many of them going to bankrupt. From this	we	can *learn* that how dagerous it would be
should be subject to antitrust law. What	we	should do is to *learn* from the United States
China does not have its own luxury brand. If	we	can *learn* from this luxury giant and adopt
are the rivals in this severe competition.	We	can *learn* how they improve themselves from
the ample capital to make the M&A deals.	We	can *learn* from the following figure that
such as: Fresca, Mr.Pibb, Mello Yelllo. So	we	can *learn* from that case. Brand extensions
of the leading FMCG companies from whom	we	could *learn* how to launch a successful
here in China. There are numerous things	we	could *learn* from its success such as the
typical of Chinese firms at that time. From it	we	can also *learn* the significance of work
grave threat to our local industry, and	we	need to *learn* from this world beverage
McD is so popular in China? And what can	we	*learn* from its successful experience to
gap is wide, the Chinese will not give in.	We	can *learn* from the most advanced enterprises
order to eliminate miscommunication, first	we	must *learn* about our own culture, through
and cognition about other cultures; then	we	also need to *learn* about the basic theory
different cultures, and at the same time	we	can *learn* others' expectation to us. So
changes. From Motorola's great success,	we	can *learn* some valuable lessons that can

Figure 6.13   The verb *learn* that collocates with 'We' in UG

6.4   Discussion and conclusion

This chapter has discussed the differences of the phrases of 'I', 'We' and their verb collocates between the undergraduate and postgraduate academic levels. In general, there is statistically, a significant difference in the occurrences of the two FPPs between the UG level's and PG level's corpora. The undergraduates use more FPPs than the postgraduates. When taking into account the most frequently used verbs from the four verb categories, *TO*, *KC*, *RR*, and *RI*, for example, *DISCUSS*, *KNOW*, *FIND*, *SAY*, and *think*, the research shows that there is no significant proportional difference between the two academic levels. However, the qualitative analyses do suggest that some of verbs differ in meaning and also differ in discourse function. For example, *read* means the act of *reading* in most cases for the UG writers, while it means the *understanding of reading* a certain piece of literary work in some instances for PG writers. Qualitative analysis also found that the postgraduate students have a greater range of rhetorical choices at their disposal, while the undergraduate students keep the basic meanings or uses of the verbs to collocate with 'I' and 'We'.

The comparison of UG and PG students' written work indicates the development of writing skills from undergraduate to postgraduate. The findings of this chapter indicate that the postgraduate students show greater conformity to a more academic style of writing. Firstly, this is evident from the quantitative results, in that the postgraduates use fewer FPPs and have a greater range of verbs to collocate with 'I' and 'We' than the undergraduates. Further, when the verbs were examined in cases where they did not collocate with the FPPs, a wider range of expressions of the investigated discourse functions are found in the texts of postgraduates. This suggests to a degree that the postgraduate students are being more objective. It would seem that the postgraduate writers tend to avoid using 'I' and 'We' in their academic texts to a greater degree than undergraduates. It could be that the employment of 'I' and 'We' is regarded as informal(Hyland & Jiang 2017). Therefore, they use a wider range alternatives to distance themselves and to maintain a degree of objectivity, for example, frequent use of the phrase *as mentioned*. This is clearly evidenced when comparing undergraduate texts with postgraduate texts. It is also found that the postgraduate writers use more instances of 'We' in comparison to 'I', for example, (as) *we have* (*already*) *discussed* / *mentioned* , which might suggest that 'We' is considered as a self-presentation expression but with less visibility than 'I' in their academic discourse. This point has been briefly discussed in Section 6.3.1 and will be revisited in Chapter 7.

CHAPTER 7
DISCUSSION

7.1 Introduction

I undertook this piece of research with the following hypotheses. Firstly, that there would be a greater number of FPPs in English Literature texts in comparison to texts from the discipline of Business and Management. Secondly, that there would be a greater usage of the FPP 'I' than of the FPP 'We' in English Literature than in Business and Management. Thirdly, I held the view that the texts of postgraduates would be more conformed to academic conventions than those written by undergraduates and that accordingly, there would be lesser use of the FPPs by postgraduate students in comparison to undergraduate students.

However, the results indicate that these hypotheses were only partially correct. Firstly, the results of my research show that both the Business and Management and English Literature students use approximately the same number of the two FPPs, 'I' and 'We' in their texts. Secondly, the usage of the FPP 'We' was greater than the usage of the FPP 'I' in English Literature in comparison to Business and Management. Thirdly, in comparison with the undergraduates, the postgraduate writers utilise a greater number of conventional expressions of the FPPs in their academic discourse. I would propose that this increased usage as an enhanced conformity to academic conventions and hence view this as an improvement. Whilst such improvement may be seen from the change in the quantity of the FPPs used and the range of the discourse functions of the investigated phrases, it was noted that the postgraduates tended to replace 'I' with 'We' in their texts, which is considered as an inappropriate use of the FPPs in this study. Generally, this study on the FPPs, 'I' and 'We' and the verbs that collocate with them in Chinese EFL learners' dissertations has presented the following results:

1) Four general discourse functions of the phrases of 'I' and 'We' and the verbs are identified. They are used to *organise discourse* (TO), *construe knowledge community* (KC), *report research* (including *report study or internship* (RS) and *recount research procedure* (RR)), and *interpret research* (including *interpret research result* (RI), and *argue for or against viewpoints* (AG)).

2) This study identifies some frequently occurring phrases of 'I', 'We' and their verb collocates that are associated with discourse functions.

3) There are more similarities than differences in relation to the phrases and the discourse functions of 'I' and 'We' between the two disciplines, Business and Management and English Literature.

4) In comparison with the undergraduates, the postgraduate writers tend to be less personal in their academic

writing. They use more impersonal expressions and utilise more retrospective textual organisation expressions to organise and develop their dissertations.

These results are discussed in the following sections in detail. The rest of this chapter is organised as follows. Section 2 is the discussion of the discourse functions proposed and identified in this study. In this section, I also discuss the writer identity of these EFL students made manifest in their academic discourse. A correlation between discourse functions and writer identity is proposed. Section 3 discusses the phrases of 'I' and 'We' and the verbs that collocate with them. Section 4 focuses on the disciplinary and academic level differences that are observed in this study. Section 5 discusses the choice between personal pronouns and impersonal expressions; between the singular FPP, 'I' and the plural FPP, 'We'. It also discusses the inclusive and exclusive 'We'. A set of principles that may influence the student's choice of the FPPs is proposed in this section. Section 6 is the conclusion of this chapter.

7.2 Discourse functions of the phrases of 'I', 'We' and their verb collocates

In this section, I shall discuss the four categories of the discourse functions that have been identified in the students' academic writings across the whole corpus. I shall also relate these discourse functions to writer identity. Three writer identities are proposed and discussed in accordance with the discourse functions proposed in this research.

7.2.1   The discourse functions of the phrases

As discussed in Chapter 4, 5 and 6, the phrases including the FPPs and their verb collocates are used to *organise the texts* (e.g. *as we have mentioned*), *construe knowledge community* (e.g. *as we all know*), *epistemic knowledge report* (e.g. *I worked*), *recount research procedure* (e.g. *I collected*), *interpret research results* (e.g. *we can see that*), or *argue for/against viewpoints* (e.g. *I argue*).

The distribution of the four discourse functions across the whole corpus is as follows. About 32% of the instances are used for RI, 30% for RR, 18% for AG, and 11% for TO and 9% for KC. The function of EP accounts for a very small proportion of all the functions identified. This difference in frequency may be accounted for by drawing on the concepts related to face-threateningness and assertiveness(cf. Hyland 2002; Tang & John 1999). It is found that the functions that are less face-threatening, i.e. TO, RR, and KC, account for half of all the usages of 'I' and 'We'. The more personal RI and the most authorial function of AG accounts for the other half of all the instances. This means that about half of the total instances of 'I' and 'We' are used for expressing the writers' evaluation and viewpoints. However, the different degree of authoritativeness should be noted here. In these essays, RI accounts for 32% and AG function accounts for 18% of all the identified discourse functions. Between these two functions, RI is less face threatening than AG. As mentioned in the previous chapters, when the phrases are used to interpret research, the interpretation is usually based on the quantitative or experimental results presented in the students' texts. These 'hard facts' lower the probability of being challenged by readers. With regard to RI phrases, the modal verbs of possibility *can* and *could* lower the authoritative tone of the authorial presence in the theses. Therefore, even though the students use 50% of the investigated instances of 'I' and 'We' to express their viewpoints, they tend to use moderate expressions, for instance, *we can see* and *I think*, *personally*. The findings of this study is in line with Tang & John (1998), Hyland (2002) and Charles (2005) that student writers use the personal pronouns to perform less important rhetorical purposes in their academic writings. In this study, the student writers choose the FPPs to represent themselves where there is little likelihood of being questioned or criticised. This is further discussed in the Principle of using 'I' and 'We' in Section 5.

The study also found that different phrases of 'I' and 'We' serve different discourse functions in the texts. The functions of EP and RR are frequently realised by the phrases including the singular FPP 'I' and the verb collocates. The functions of TO, KC and RI are frequently seen from the phrases including the plural FPP 'We'. The AG function is observed from the phrases of both 'I' and 'We'. However, except for the function of EP, which is almost exclusively served by 'I', the plural FPP 'We' may be found in all the rest of the functions identified in this study.

7.2.2 The discourse functions and writer identity

The work of this thesis inevitably raises the question of writer identity. As discussed in Chapter 2, there is considerable research on writer identity, some of which is related to personal pronouns. Writer identity is not the theme or the focus throughout this thesis, but at this point, it would seem relevant to inquire what the relationship between the study of the FPPs and the concept of writer identity is. As stated by Ivanič and Camps(2001, p. 3), "writing always conveys a representation of the self of the writer". In this study, I would argue that the most direct way to examine writer identity is probably through the functions of the phrases including the FPPs and the verbs in these students' texts. Looking at the functions that I have identified, I would like to propose three distinct identities: Self as Reporter, Self as Text Organiser and Self as Evaluator. What should be noted is that writer identities and discourse functions are all based on the findings of the phrases of 'I', 'We' and the verbs that collocate with them in the students' texts. There could be other writer identities or discourse functions that are presented by expressions other than the two FPPs, which is beyond the scope of this study.

The TO function of the phrases of 'I' and 'We' represents the Self as Text Organiser identity because the student writer focuses on the readability of his/her discourse. The RR function matches the Self as Reporter identity because the student writer recounts what he/she did prior to writing the dissertation. The KC and RI functions correspond to the Self as Evaluator identity because he/she is trying to persuade, to claim authority and to establish his/her status in the academic community. Table 7.1 illustrates the mapping of the discourse functions and their corresponding writer identities.

7.3 Phrases of 'I', 'We' and their verb collocates

In this section, I discuss the findings of the phrases including the two FPPs and their verb collocates across the whole corpus. Based on the analyses of the phrases in the previous chapters(Chapters 5 & 6), three types of frequent phrases or phrasal forms of 'I' and 'We' are observed in this study and discussed below. The phrases identified are a mixture of colligation(a pronoun and a particular tense), collocation(a pronoun

Table 7.1 The textual function and the writer identities

Writer identity	Discourse functions	Examples
Self as Text Organizer	*organize discourse*	*As **I mentioned** in the previous part* ... (PGEL 0005)
Self as Reporter	*report research*	*with all the materials **I read** and the experiences I had in PR companies* (UGBM 05906)
		*For interviews **I used** both a list of questions based on the questionnaire.* (PGBM 0064)
	construe knowledge community	*As **we know**, Joyce's Dubliners, though is realistic to some degree, is full of the penetration into the mind of characters as well.*(PGEL 0076)
Self as Evaluator	*interpret research*	*From the numbers listed above, **we can see that** Christianity in general was the predominant religion in colonial America.* (UGEL 00107)
		*Contrary to his argument **I argue** that Coleman Silk regains his black identity through white Other Faunia Farley.*(PGEL 0077)
		*First, **we should understand** our cultures in an all-round way, and then we begin to know other cultures based on cultural empathy.*(PGBM 0096)

and particular verbs) and some longer phrases based on these colligations and collocations(e.g. *as we have discussed*, *as we all know that*).

7.3.1 The collocation *I + verb*

Two patterns of *I + Verb* in these academic texts were found in this research. One is the collocation of the singular FPP 'I' and past tense of some action verbs. The other is 'I' followed by the base form of cognitive verbs or verbs of arguing(see Chapter 3 for the categorisation of such verbs in this study).

● *I read / learnt / worked / collected / analysed / found*

In the students' academic texts, the bigram of *I + V-ed* describes what had been done before writing the dissertations, including their learning experiences and research procedures. The writers choose 'I' to claim their studentship and state their research practice. Two pragmatic effects could be achieved by this self-representativeness. Firstly to present the students epistemic background(e.g. *I read Pride and Prejudice a few times*) and secondly to recount research(e.g. *I found*). In this collocation, the verbs are not limited to the most frequent verbs that are discussed in the previous chapters, Chapters 4, 5 and 6. There are a number of other types of verbs in past tense co-occurring with 'I' that are used for the descriptive purposes in these academic texts. Figure 1 illustrates 20 instances that were randomly selected from the PGBM. Almost all of the concordances here serve to depict what had been done prior to the writing of the dissertations. Many of the verbs(e.g. *borrowed*, *conducted*, *investigated*, *designed*, etc.) in Figure 7.1 were not included in the analyses in the previous chapters because of their infrequent occurrences in the corpus(see Chapter 3 for the threshold of the verb identification).

- *I think / believe / argue / hope*

The verbs in the bigram of *I + base form of the verbs* are mostly mental verbs(e.g. *think*) or verbs or saying(e.g. *argue*). The students use this phrase to express their personal viewpoints and claim authoritativeness. If the students express assertiveness about what they are saying in the text, they would use expression like *I believe*, *I argue* and *I hope*. If they are less certain, but also want to claim the opinions as their own, they would use *I think*, implying a lesser degree of certainty.

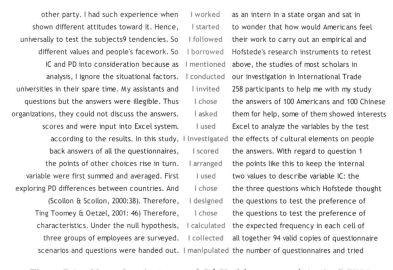

other party. I had such experience when	I worked	as an intern in a state organ and sat in
shown different attitudes toward it. Hence,	I started	to wonder that how would Americans feel
universally to test the subjects9 tendencies. So	I followed	their work to carry out an empirical and
different values and people's facework. So	I borrowed	Hofstede's research instruments to retest
IC and PD into consideration because as	I mentioned	above, the studies of most scholars in
analysis, I ignore the situational factors.	I conducted	our investigation in International Trade
universities in their spare time. My assistants and	I invited	258 participants to help me with my study
questions but the answers were illegible. Thus	I chose	the answers of 100 Americans and 100 Chinese
organizations, they could not discuss the answers.	I asked	them for help, some of them showed interests
scores and were input into Excel system.	I used	Excel to analyze the variables by the test
according to the results. In this study,	I investigated	the effects of cultural elements on people
back answers of all the questionnaires,	I scored	the answers. With regard to question 1
the points of other choices rise in turn.	I arranged	the points like this to keep the internal
variable were first summed and averaged. First	I used	two values to describe variable IC: the
exploring PD differences between countries. And	I chose	the three questions which Hofstede thought
(Scollon & Scollon, 2000:38). Therefore,	I designed	the questions to test the preference of
Ting Toomey & Oetzel, 2001: 46) Therefore,	I chose	the questions to test the preference of
characteristics. Under the null hypothesis,	I calculated	the expected frequency in each cell of
three groups of employees are surveyed.	I collected	all together 94 valid copies of questionnaire
scenarios and questions were handed out.	I manipulated	the number of questionnaires and tried

Figure 7.1   20 random instances of *I+Verb(past tense)* in the PGBM

7.3.2   The phrases I/We+have+past participle and I/We+will+base form of a verb

- *I / We have discussed / mentioned / said / talked / explained*

The phrases of *I/We have done* and *I/We will do* are most

frequently used for metadiscoursal purposes in the students' academic texts.

The first expression, *I / We + have + past participle* organises text by indicating what has been discussed in previous discourse. It generalises information and introduces new viewpoints or proposition simultaneously on the basis of the previous information. With respect to this function, it may be called "recapitulation" as it recalls information from earlier text and predicts the contrast, elaboration or explanation in the following text(Tadros 1994). This phrase may also belong to "*Reminder*" metadiscoursal class of metadiscourse categories proposed by Crismore et al. (1993). When this phrase is used, the most frequent verbs that collocate with the two FPPs are *I / We have discussed / mentioned / said / talked / explained*, and other less frequent verbs include *shown*, *presented*, *dealt with*, *looked at*, etc.

- *I / We will discuss / mention / talk / explain*

The phrase *I / We will do* as in *I / We will discuss / mention / talk / explain* serves the metadiscoursal function of informing the readers what will be discussed in the student's essays. The most frequent verbs that collocate with the FPPs are *Verbs of saying*. Examples are *discuss*, *mention*, *talk* and *explain* as listed above. Like other phrasal frames discussed, there are more types of verbs observed in this phrase in the students' texts, for example, *focus*, *look into*, and *analyse*, which are also used for metadiscoursal purposes(see Chapter 4).

7.3.3　The phrase we + modal verb + verb

The modal verbs are mostly used with the plural FPP 'We'

to serve different functions, for example, to interpret study, or express personal opinion in the text, and to give advice or suggestion. These functions are mostly realised by the collocation of 'We' and the *possibility and ability modal verbs* and *obligation and necessity modal verbs*(Biber et al. 2002, p. 485).

● the phrase *we* + *possibility and ability modal verbs* + *verbs*

The phrasal frame of the *we* + *possibility and ability modal verbs* + *verbs* is mostly presented in the students' academic discourse in those frequently used expressions like *we can/could/ will see/find/know/learn/say*. These expressions are categorised to serve as metadiscoursal functions of attitude and/or as commentary makers (e.g. Crismore et al. 1993; Hyland, 2005). It is worth mentioning that the minimum meaning and function unit is the phrase. In these academic texts, neither *we*, nor the modal verbs *can*, *could*, *will*, nor the verbs *see*, *find*, *know* , etc., represent the writers and serve the evaluative purposes independently. It is the phrasal patterns that express these meaning and perform the discourse functions.

● the phrase *we* + *obligation and necessity modal verbs* + *verbs*

In the students' texts, the phrase of *we* + *obligation and necessity modal verbs* + *verbs* is mostly presented in expressions such as *we should/must/have to learn/know/focus*. This phrase is most frequently used to give suggestions in real life situations, especially in the Business and Management discipline. The student writers only use 'We' to collocate with the obligation and necessity modal verb. The purposes of using the plural FPP, 'We' are twofold. One is to claim membership and authority in a specific academic community; the other is to specify the practical contribution of the research.

In general, the bigram *I* + *verb in past tense* can be used either to recount the student's educational experience or to express personal point of view; the phrasal patterns *I/We* + *have* + *past participle* and *I/We* + *will* + *base form of a verb* are mainly used for metadiscoursal purposes; and the phrasal pattern *we* + *possibility and ability modal verbs* + *verbs* is mostly used for interpretation and argument, in which a number of personal stances are adopted.

7.4　Comparisons across the disciplines and the academic levels

Much research on disciplinary discourse to date has investigated linguistic variations in different disciplines(e.g. Charles 2004; Hyland 2002, 2004; Hyland & Jiang 2017). Differing from most of the reported studies, the present study found that the difference of the two FPPs, 'I' and 'We' is more notable across academic levels than across the disciplines of Business and Management and English Literature. It is found that, as the students' progress from undergraduate to postgraduate level, some of their uses of the FPPs become more in line with the academic conventions. This is especially true for the singular FPP, 'I'. However, it was also found that as a consequence of being tentative about the usages of the FPPs, the postgraduate students seemed to use the plural FPP 'We' to replace 'I' at the expense of weakening their authorial voice in the discourse. The following two subsections look into the similarities and differences in more detail.

7.4.1 Comparison between the disciplines

It has been reported that language uses differ in different disciplines (e.g. Groom 2007; Harwood 2005; Hyland 2002, 2005, 2005; Kuo 1999; Swales 1991). The differences may be seen resulting from varying disciplinary conventions, rhetorical strategies and phraseological choices. In this research, however, both similarities and differences are found between the disciplines of Business and Management and English Literature. As demonstrated in Chapter 5, both the types and the frequency of the TO and KC verbs that collocate with 'I' and 'We' are about the same in BM and EL. The discourse functions of these phrases of 'I', 'We' and their verb collocates are also similar. In the RR and RI categories, variation between the two disciplines may be seen from the different types of the verbs used as well as the discourse functions of the phrases including the FPPs and the verbs. Where differences are apparent, they are consistent with the findings reported in most of the disciplinary studies on academic texts. The variations are largely due to the disciplinary divergence in that Business and Management is a discipline of Applied Social Sciences and English Literature is a discipline of Pure Humanities. Since disciplinary differences have been extensively discussed in previous studies, I shall now focus on the interpretation of the similarities between these two disciplines hereinafter.

The unexpected level of similarities between the two disciplines of BM and EL may be explained by examining the educational background of the students. These Chinese EFL writers from both disciplines were taught academic writing as a singular concept rather than as a separate disciplinary discourse. Secondly, the models the students follow are essentially research papers or PhD dissertations. These genres could be highly quantitative, which may explain why they use verbs like *FIND* and *ANALYZE*.

7.4.2 Comparison between the academic levels

The hypothesis relating to the different levels of proficiency between academic levels seems uncontroversial. With three additional years of academic training in universities, the postgraduate students are likely to become better writers in comparison to the undergraduates. Their academic texts tend to be more conventionalised because of engagement to a greater extent in reading and writing exercises and deeper immersion in the academic community. However, as mentioned earlier, this hypothesis is shown to be only partially true in this study. It is found that in the case of the FPPs, 'I' and 'We' in academic writing, the postgraduate writers become more cautious in their use of 'I'. At this level, the singular FPP is used frequently with verbs of argument, for example, *I argue*. This improvement is more obvious in English Literature, in which discipline reading and writing are two common learning practices frequently engaged in. However, some changes of the uses of the FPPs do not necessarily represent improvement, particularly, the replacement of 'I' by 'We'. This observation applies to both BM and EL texts. The postgraduate students seem to increasingly prefer the usage of 'We' to 'I'. It is possible they do so in order to avoid challenge and criticism whilst at the same time, retaining subjectivity. They are therefore following the Alignment Principle and Modesty Principle at the expense of the Authority Principle, which will be discussed below in terms of principles and conflicts in Section 7.5.2.1. It seems that in order to be more subjective and avoid face-threatening challenge to their argument, the students substitute the obvious self-representative pronoun 'I' with the less obvious and collective 'We'. It is as if they could safeguard their research from being criticised by using 'We', by which they include the reader to disguise the viewpoints or interpretation put forward as shared between both parties. The improper substitution of 'I' by 'We' leads to the loss of the students' own voices in their academic discourse. In other words, this weakens the authorship in their writings. Meanwhile, it is doubtful that this exchange of the FPPs would make their texts sound more objective.

The reasons for the lack of improvement in the use of the FPPs may be firstly, the students' own assumption that using 'We' is better than 'I'. The plural FPP has more advantages than the singular 'I'. For example, it establishes solidarity with the readers and avoids critical remarks. Secondly, avoiding the use of the FPPs in academic texts is widely taught in the Chinese EFL academic writing classrooms. Consequently, students at the more advanced postgraduate level, who choose to express their own points of view by the means of FPPs, opt for the less authoritative 'We' and discard the proscribed 'I'. This influence of choosing 'I' and 'We' is discussed in more detail in Section 7.5, in which a set of principles and restrictions on the choice of the FPPs is proposed.

7.5   The rhetorical choices between personal pronouns and impersonal pronouns in academic texts

One of the goals of academic writing is to stress the newsworthiness of the research and to seek consensus with the readers. In this respect, "[w]riters have to select their words so that readers are drawn in, influenced and persuaded"(Hyland 2002, p.1093). In the genre of dissertations, two more objectives need to be achieved through the texts. It needs to report the student writers' academic achievement and prove their research and academic writing ability. To achieve these interactive writer-reader goals, the writers always face a number of choices. Firstly, whether to include self-representation pronouns or non-self-representation expressions. As an example, the student needs to decide if he/she wishes to write, *as I have mentioned* as opposed to as *mentioned*. He/she also has to decide between the singular FPP 'I' and the plural FPP 'We'. The writer needs to decide which FPP is more appropriate to achieve the pragmatic goals that he/she seeks to achieve. For example, he/she needs to decide whether to write, *I can see* as opposed to *we can see*. Additionally, the writer needs to decide between the inclusive and exclusive 'We'. He/she needs to decide whether or not include the readers or simply use 'We' to replace 'I' to avoid being singled out or be obvious in the discourse, for example, the uses of *as we all know* and *we conduct the research* in a singly authored thesis. In this section, the choices that these student writers face are discussed. A set of principles influencing the usage of the two FPPs and also the constraints of using 'I' and 'We' are proposed. Before doing so, I have to admit that these discussions are highly subjective and are reliant on my interpretation. However, I would argue that the discussion on the choices and the principles are based on the analyses of students' uses of the FPPs, the phrases of 'I', 'We' and their verb collocates, and the discourse functions in their dissertations. The research may therefore serve as a useful reference in EFL academic writing or training practice.

7.5.1 The choice between 'I', 'We' and other impersonal expressions

If a writer of an academic text wants to present himself/herself and display commitment in the texts, one common linguistic choice is the employment of the FPPs. On the other hand, if a writer wants to maintain distance from the proposition and to sound objective, or to assert general truth, or to be more conventional to the academic style he/she may choose various impersonal expressions. For instance, he/she could use the passive voice or utilise reporting sentence structures.

In fact, the phrases or the phrasal patterns discussed in Section 7.3 can all be substituted by other impersonal expressions if the students wish to avoid using the two FPPs, 'I' and 'We'. The rhetorical devices could be the employment of passive voice (for example, use *it is found that* to replace *I found*), or some conventionalised academic expressions(for example, use *as mentioned* to replace *as I have mentioned*), or report structures of *it ... that* or *it is ... to*. In Chapters 4 and

5, a few verbs are searched in their passive form to determine how they are used without 'I' or 'We'. For example, *believe* was tested in the form *it is believed that*. Comparatively, the postgraduate writers use more instances of *it is ... that* and *it is ... to* than the undergraduate students to adopt and maintain a stance or express personal points of view. This more frequent use of impersonal expressions may suggest that the postgraduate writers prefer to express personal viewpoints by impersonal expressions to sound objective in their theses. The reason for this could possibly be due to postgraduate student writers undergoing 3 additional years of academic education in comparison to the undergraduates. This exposure to the academic community and academic training helps to raise their awareness of the conventionalised style of academic text.

In his study on the use of 'I' in the methodology section of the Computer Science discipline, Harwood(2005, p.263) argues that the students use 'I' in their project reports than those in the expert RA "because of the unique demands of the students' genre of the computing project report". In this study too, the specific genre of EFL students' dissertation requires the students to report their achievement after their year of higher education. This is more so of undergraduate students, at which level, both academic and practical knowledge are required. This could be the reason why in some of the dissertations, the students use 'I' to report on their intern work and their epistemic improvement.

On the one hand, the choice of using the FPPs suggests the students' awareness of the functions of the FPPs in academic discourse and their willingness to present themselves in their academic writings. On the other hand, as EFL learners, the choice of the FPPs may also indicate that they tend to use those oft-used expressions in their academic texts such as expressions *as we all know*, *we can see that*, and *as we have mentioned / discussed*. As shown in Chapter 6, these expressions are particularly common in the undergraduate learners' texts because of their limited vocabulary as well as the inflexibility of using other expressions to replace the FPPs phrases to achieve the designated discourse functions in their academic texts.

7.5.2   The choice between 'I' and 'We': the principles and the constrains

In terms of the choice between 'I' and 'We', although the two FPPs are both obvious self-representation expressions and are subjective, these two words differ in immensely for the Chinese EFL student. In the students' texts, in comparison to 'We', the singular FPP 'I' is considered as more personal and egocentric because it refers to the writer himself/herself in the texts. It is threatening because the novice writer may consider 'I' as an expression of being authorial and may feel that he/she would lack the support of his/her peers. The plural FPP 'We', on the other hand, could be the writer himself/herself, the writer and the reader, and the writer and the whole academic community. Therefore, the concept of singularity and collectiveness leads to the choice between the singular 'I' and the plural 'We'. Based on the discourse functions discussed in the previous chapters, in this section I would propose and discuss a set of principles that guide the student writers to choose either 'I' or 'We' or other impersonal expressions.

7.5.2.1 The principles

The principles discussed in this study are the influences and motivations that encourage the student writers to choose 'I' and/or 'We' in their academic discourse. They are the reasons or triggers leading to the usage of the FPPs in the dissertations. More specifically, the novice writers are guided by the principles to choose 'I' and/or 'We' purposefully in their dissertations. The word 'principle' is used in line of Leech (1983) when he talks about the difference between rules and principles. The difference between these two is that rules are essentially a question of either a yes or a no. The notion of principles is more flexible than rules in that it can be "applied to a certain extent"(Leech, 1983, p.21). In this respect, principle seems to be the right word that applies to this study because, as will be discussed in the following, the student writers apply these principles flexibly and strategically in their writing.

Before introducing the principles, the correlation between the writer identities, the discourse functions and the principles of the two first-person pronouns should be addressed here. These three notions are interrelated. They can be interpreted from the different chronological points of the writing process. When facing a choice between the two FPPs during the writing process, prior to the actual act of writing at certain point of the academic text, the proposed principles influence the student writers in making a choice of either 'I' or 'We', or other impersonal pronouns. The writer identities are reflected throughout the writing process. The student writer is a *Writer* when he/she is constructing a cohesive and logical discourse. The student is a *Reporter* when he/she states his/her learning experience, internship and the research procedure prior to the writing up of the thesis. The student writer is an *Evaluator* when he/she expresses personal opinion or embarks on a process of evaluation of certain entity. In essence, what a writer does in the writing determines writer's identity (cf. John 2005). The discourse functions are the effects that the writers set out to achieve through the texts. It is a post-writing concept because the text has to be read by someone. Until then, the writer would not know whether his/her rhetorical choice is appropriate or not. Therefore, the effectiveness of the discourse functions depends on the choice that the student writer makes and these choices are influenced by the principles mentioned thereafter. It also depends on how successfully the writer is playing his/her role in the text, which impacts his/her writer identity. In a nutshell, the principles are pre-writing influence. The writer identity is what is constructed during the process of writing. The discourse functions are post-writing interactive effects the writers aim to achieve. Following Leech (1983), in discussing the principles proposed below, I also illustrate what these principles suggest.

1) Reader Friendly Principle('I' and 'We')

The Reader Friendly Principle may be expressed as 'Make your organisation of the text clear'. Academic writing is inherently interactive. With the knowledge of who the potential readers of the academic text may be, the student writers use rhetorical strategies accordingly. One of these rhetorical strategies is the usage of 'I' and 'We' to show awareness of the readership when a writer engages in the construction of his/her discourse. Specifically, being reader friendly means to present the readers a well-organised and readable text.

This principle is most obviously presented by expressions of metadiscoursal organisers (e. g. *I have discussed*), which were discussed in detail in Chapters 4, 5 and 6. Recognising the existence of the potential readers, the novice writers frequently include the reader and 'guide' (Tang & John, 1999) them through the text. By using the metadiscourse expressions with the FPPs, the writers explicitly present the outline of their texts. For example, they could prepare and guide the readers by expressions such as *I/we will discuss*; and remind and restate what has been discussed or mentioned, for example, *I/we have discussed/mentioned*. From the writers' point of view, the use of the FPPs is seen as an effective means of signalling directly to the readers of their essays. It is a tacit way to show their awareness of the potential readers and extend their friendliness to them by explicitly displaying the organisation of the text and the information that needs to be recounted and emphasised in the essays. It is expected that the readers would appreciate the well-organised discourse with identifiable clues and clear statements about the layout and the thread of the texts.

Influenced by the Reader Friendly Principle, the writers' effort of discourse organisation may be appreciated when the readers are able to follow the text easily. Nonetheless, as there is no personal opinion involved and the use of 'I' and 'We' is not face-threatening, there is a propensity for this choice to lead to the overuse of some expressions like *I/we will discuss* or *I/we have discussed/mentioned* in the undergraduates' texts. Comparatively, it is found in this study that with more academic training, the postgraduate students use fewer instances of 'I' and 'We' and more impersonal expressions to organise the text to ensure the readability of their texts. Meanwhile, in some cases, the Reader Friendly Principle overlaps with the Alignment Principle, especially when the word 'We' is chosen.

2) Alignment Principle('We')

The Alignment Principle is to 'Present yourself as a member of the community and be persuasive'. This principle influences two discoursal functions in the students' academic writing, the *knowledge community construing* function and *research interpretation* function. In both cases, the writers choose 'We' to solicit solidarity(Hyland 2002, 2004) and avoid confrontation. This principle includes the following two aspects.

● Writers include themselves and the readers as members of a community

Effective communication between an addresser and an addressee in academic writing means both of them share background knowledge of that field, preferably, in the same academic community. For instance, it would be difficult to ask a Business and Management expert to examine a dissertation on Shakespeare, or to ask an English Literature professor to decide how good an article on the cross-cultural aspects of the international soft drinks trade between China and UK is. Knowing that the reader of their dissertations would be someone with expertise in that discipline, the student writers use 'We' to include themselves into that academic community so that they can converse with the examiners, i.e. the readers of their theses. Briefly, one aspect of the Alignment Principle is that the writers purposefully include themselves into the disciplinary community with shared disciplinary knowledge.

This aspect of the Alignment Principle is best illustrated by KC expressions such as *as we(all) know* and *we know that*. In this case, the writer includes the readers into a community. This community can be general. In these cases, 'We' can be anyone who shares the common knowledge that is known to almost everyone, for example, the common knowledge of *"different countries have their own advantages and disadvantages"*(UGBM 05704). The community construed by the writer may also be restricted. It may be restricted to an academic community of a certain discipline. Bearing in mind that the readers of the dissertations are experts of the related disciplines, the student writers use 'We' to include people, by their own assumption, who know or should have known the disciplinary knowledge. This 'We' in *as we * know* and *we know that* are limited to the members of a specific community with whom the writers align. When motivated by this Alignment Principle, either the writers take it for granted that the proposition is known to the audience that reads the article, or the writers deliberately do so because they harbour a pre-conceived impression that whoever reads the text should have known the propositions and that there is no need to argue or question those propositions further. This knowledge community in a sense, is marked off by the writer. However, the knowledge is field specific, which may or may not be accepted as known by those involuntarily included as readers. There are chances that they would question the proposition because they are compulsorily taken into a community that they may or may not belong to, or be familiar with. Therefore, this principle can be a double-edged sword. If the readers acknowledge the shared knowledge, it is likely that they will agree with the writer. If they do not think that the proposed knowledge should be presented as "*as we ∗ know*" but needs further explanation, the writers put themselves in the firing-line to be criticised by choosing 'We'.

To summarise, when student writers include themselves as members of a community, there are two types of knowledge common to those in these academic circles. One is that the knowledge is common information, which is probably shared by a very large section of society. The other is field-specific knowledge that is construed by the writers and passively sub-scribed to by the reader. In this context, the knowledge is used as a launching platform for later discussion but will not be dis-cussed in detail, as it is deemed as known by the writer.

● Writers align with the readers to seek agreement and avoid negation

A thesis needs to be convincing, which is another aspect of the Alignment Principle. To prove the credibility of their inter-pretation, viewpoints or understanding of the text, the writers deliberately draw in their readers. According to Hyland(2001), the employment of 'We' is to realise the rhetorical purposes of seeking solidarity and crafting reader agreement in the text. The interaction between the writer and the readers in academic discourse occurs as the writer acknowledges the presence of the readers and tries to seek alignment and avoid self-predicted ne-gation from the reader. This aspect of alignment can be illus-trated by the phrase frame *we can / could / may / will see (that)*, which is frequently presented in this study. By using 'We', the writer is strategically saying that "the conclusion or the inter-pretation is not my own postulation". Regarding this choice of

'We' instead of 'I', it has been argued that the researcher only uses this phrase when "they are confident enough that the
readers would agree with them"(Harwood, 2005). Although it
is doubtful in this study if the student writers used this expression with the same confidence, it is likely that they would have
at the very least, sought to secure their arguments and/or viewpoints so as not to be challenged by the experts who grade their
dissertations.

3) Modesty Principle('I' and 'We')

This Modesty Principle is indeed, 'Be modest'. It encoura-
ges the writer not to be too assertive and not claim too much
authority and originality. It is motivated by two concerns on
the writers' side. One is to avoid being too assertive or arrogant
when they express opinions or deliver propositions. The other is
to foster a special relationship or affinity between the student
writers and the expert readers. In these texts, the student writers want to present their personal opinions in their theses but,
at the same time, do not want to sound overtly authoritative to
warrant disapproval or criticism.

This principle marks the proposition as belonging to the
writer themselves, but in a humble manner. One example of
the Modesty Principle is the expression *I think*. There has been
some research about how the verb *think* and the expression *I
think* in academic settings could mean humble, tentative, un-
sure, and polite in academic settings(Biber et al. 2002; Flottum
et al. 2006; Gómez 2004; Harwood 2005; Hyland 2001, 2003,
2005; Quirk 1985). However, just by looking at the bigram *I
think*, it is hard to decide whether the writer is being modest or
authoritative. I will show later in the Authority Principle sec-

tion that this expression may also be indicative of the writers' self-confidence. Looking at the extended discourse is probably the only way to decide what the writers are aiming for, being modest or being authorial. In this study, when modesty is needed, *I think* is often found paired with expressions such as *personally*, *for me* (see Examples 7-1, 7-2 and 7-3). By adding these adverbial expressions in the sentences, the writers attempt to state that the proposals are personal, which may or may not be true and could be disagreed with if the readers think otherwise.

Example 7-1: **Personally**, *I think* that issuing a film is the same as issuing a commercial product in the market. The market investigation and analysis could not be omitted, as well as the mature schedule and plan. (UGBM 04407)

Example 7-2: **For me**, *I think* there is still a long way to go before MNCs eventually achieve the objective of being globalized and utilize global resources with little costs. For businesses operating in China especially, staff localization will remain the optimal choice for a while. (UGBM 05507)

Example 7-3: But after attentively reading those three novels mentioned above, **personally speaking**, *I think* Jude the Obscure deserves more attention than it receives. (UGLi 00307)

In these texts, by saying it is his/her personal opinion with the modest aspect of *I think*, the writer of each example tries to find a balance between the justification of their personal view and also concurrently avoids being too self-assured to be criticised by the examiners.

The employment of the plural FPP 'We' could possibly be due to the influence of the Modesty Principle as well. There are many instances of 'We' co-occurring with modal verbs, *can* and *may*, and some research interpretation verbs, e.g. *find*, *see*, *say*, *learn* in the phrase *we can / may find / see / say / learn*. The modal verbs in these expressions are used to soften the assertiveness of the interpretation or the arguments in the texts, which leaves room for the writers to have their ideas put forward, and at the same time, give the readers flexibility to agree or disagree. This is also the reason why the writers choose the collective personal pronoun, 'We' instead of 'I'. By using the expressions such as *we can say that*, the writers are saying: "this (proposition) may or may not be true, however, ' *we* ' worked it out together". In short, the writers try to be modest and persuasive with the expression, *we can / may find / see / say / learn*.

The expressions chosen for the Modesty and Alignment Principles somehow overlap. Similar expressions may illustrate both the Modesty and the Alignment Principles. This indicates that a single expression may be influenced by one or more than one principle. This multi-faceted feature of the principles will be discussed further later.

4) The Authority Principle('I' and 'We')

The Authority Principle can be interpreted as 'Be authoritative, or be assertive strongly'. One of the most important uses of the two FPPs 'I' and 'We' is to present authorial voices in academic writing. These writers seek to claim these understandings or perspectives as their original property or contribution(Tang & John 1999, p.29). This is the principle that contrasts with the Modesty Principle in the sense that one allows one to proudly claim authorship, whilst the other allows one to remain less conspicuous.

- The choice of 'I'

To claim authority in the texts is one of the motives that influences the writers to choose 'I' in their dissertation. By using 'I', the writers show their confidence and commitment to their understanding or propositions. The verbs collocating with 'I' could be the verbs of cognitive act, for example, *think* and *believe*. The verb, *argue*, which implies saying with confidence, is also included in this group. When the writers want to show confidence on the proposed entity they choose 'I'. With the intention of establishing their authority in the texts, the writers choose 'I' to collocate with verbs of strong assertive connotations, for example, *I argue* and *I believe*. The expression, *I think*, which is chosen because of Modesty Principle, can also be chosen for the Authority Principle. In such circumstances, it can be quite authoritative when it is looked at in wider context of the students' theses. For example, a student writer(UGEL 04006) paired *I think* with the assertive expression *beyond any doubt* to stress the point. The single FPP 'I' is also used to present academic achievement in the corpus. This only applies to the dissertation genre, which is in accordance with Harwood(2005). Being possibly the most important piece of writing in the student writers' education, the students are expected to present their learnt disciplinary knowledge. This includes not only the intention to impress the examiners with their ability to conduct research, with their skills in academic writing but also what they have learnt, read and done during their years of study. This attempt to influence may be found in the expressions, for example, *I used/analysed/saw/found* when the students recount their research procedures.

The Authority Principle is partly influenced by the assessment in academia that research should have a theoretical and/or practical implication. With this expectation in the forefront, the choice of the first-person pronoun 'I' is usually used to specify the writer's disciplinary contribution. For undergraduate and the postgraduate student writers, it may be challenging for them to claim what they found to be of any significant importance. Nonetheless, the students face the dilemma that if they were to claim the contribution as those of the authors. It would be too bold, particularly by using 'I'. Conversely, if there was no theoretical or practical implication stated, it may suggest that the research was of little importance. Under this pressure, some students choose 'I' to emphasis the significance of the originality of their research. From this perspective, the Authority Principle may or may not be a positive influence on the student writers.

● The choice of 'We'

Being authorial in an academic text requires one to be original to a large extent. In those single authored dissertations, the choice of 'We' could indicate the dilemma that the student writers are facing. The apprentice writers position themselves to claim ownership and credit by using the FPP when they present their points of view in their written work. Meanwhile, being aware that they are communicating with professionals via the dissertation, they may also attempt to avoid the criticism of being over confident. Consequently, they tend to choose the plural first-person pronoun 'We' instead of 'I', even though the interpretation or viewpoint is generated completely by the writers themselves. Therefore, there is a conflict between the Authority Principle and the Modesty Principle here, such as the phrase *we can/cannot say* when it is used to express an opinion.

In addition, the Authority Principle is also reflected from the choice of 'We' when it is used to provide suggestions or recommendations in the students' dissertations. These examples could be the phrase *we should/need/can learn(from)*. By using these expressions, the novice writers give advices on, for example, how to run a business in the Business and Management discipline, and on how to live a decent or happy life in the English Literature discipline. As discussed in the previous chapters(Chapters 5 and 6), in the texts where suggestions or advice are provided by using 'We', the writers present themselves as experts of the discussed field. By the choice of 'We', they claim their own authorship by self-initiated viewpoints as members of the community.

5) Passivation Principle

This Passivation Principle is in essence, 'Avoid 'I' and 'We' in the academic text'. Differing from the above principles that choose both of the two FPPs or either one of 'I' or 'We', this is the principle of not using 'I' or 'We' in academic writing practice(e.g. *it is believed that*). This principle is most likely asserted by the EAP instructors in the EFL classrooms. Out of a pre-conceived notion that that academic discourse needs to be objective and avoid personal intrusion, the employment of the FPPs is consequently restricted. Thus, instances of

'I' and 'We' are encouraged to be replaced by the passive voice to avoid personal representation in the discourse. This is the case that I cited at the beginning of Chapter 1. A student was asked to remove all the 'I' in her dissertation by her supervisor. This PhD student is from the Computer Science department, a discipline where empirical findings are highly valued. A disciplinary requirement could possibly be the reason to avoid the FPPs. However, the usage of these two FPPs is not prohibited in expert discourse. Harwood(2005) found 0.2 per 1,000 words of 'I' and 7.30 per 1,000 words of 'We' that are used for self-mention in ten published papers from two of the most prestigious journals of the Computer Science discipline. As argued by Harwood(ibid), these instances are used for the assertion of newsworthiness and originality in the experts' papers. The clear instruction of not using the FPPs in the students' dissertations and the purposeful uses of 'I' and 'We' in the published papers show gaps between EAP classroom instruction and real practice in academia.

6) The multi-faceted nature of the principles

The multi-faceted nature of the principles refers to the fact that obeying one principle also means conforming to the other principle(s). For example, the Reader Friendly Principle and the Alignment Principle coincide to a large extent. Being reader friendly not only provides an uninterrupted reading experience but also helps with interacting with the readership positively to build solidarity, and to align oneself with the readers. Likewise, the alignment with the readers is likely to happen if the writer and the readers belong to a same disciplinary community. Being reader friendly is more probable with a readable and cohesive text than a text that is poorly organised. Both principles could lead to the choice of the FPP, 'We'. One example could be the expression *as we have discussed*. One purpose of using 'We' in this phrase is to remind the readers of the previous discussion. An additional purpose would be to highlight the joint effort of the writer and the reader. If the writer chooses one principle, he/she is also likely to choose the other. In some expressions, the Reader Friendly, Alignment and Modesty Principles overlap in the choice of 'We', too. For instance, the expression *as we can see* is when the writer directs the reader to the forthcoming content, which is reader friendly. This expression also includes the reader in interpreting research results by using 'we', which is alignment. At the same time, 'we' and the possibility modal verb, *can* in this expression, *we can see* suggest some element of modesty.

The principles might also come into conflict with each other(cf. Leech 1983). For instance, there is an obvious paradox between the Modesty Principle and the Authority Principle. Following the Modesty Principle, the choices can be 'I', 'We' or other impersonal expressions. When the FPP, 'I' is chosen, it is used with other expressions to present modesty, for example, *personally speaking* in Example 7-5. Being modest may result in using 'We', which implies a collectiveness and joint effort(e.g. *as we can see* discussed in the previous paragraph). The Modesty Principle may also lead to not using the FPPs. The expression *it may be interpreted that* in Example 7-4 illustrates this point. The interpretation is made by the writer himself/herself; however, with the impersonal expression, the understanding is presented in a humble manner.

Example 7-4: To a certain extent, *it may be interpreted* that Doctor Reefy would rather isolate himself and let himself become a grotesque than break the barriers, fearing those inevitable misunderstanding, because he cannot find a successful means of communication. (PGEL 0053)

Influenced by the Authority Principle, the use of 'I' could help the writer to claim sole responsibility to his/her viewpoint. Alternatively, the students can also assert an opinion without the employment of 'I' and 'We'. One of the choices is to use evaluative structure, like *it is ... that/to*, and cleft sentences. The choice between being modest and being authorial depends on what impression the writers want to impress their readers. It could be either a humble community member or a confident author. Between the two, choice of one almost always tends to overrule the other. Being modest means being humble and not boasting, while being an author and asserting achievement and contribution could suggest quite the opposite.

To illustrate this paradox, I shall present one example from the corpus and shall attempt to rewrite it to illustrate the range of choices at the writer's disposal. In Example 8-5, the expression '[p]ersonally speaking, I think', can be considered as following the Modesty Principle. In this sentence, the writer expresses humbly that his/her suggestion may or may not be considered as the right choice. The Rewritten A, could be a claim to authority. In rewriting it, I removed the expression '[p]ersonally speaking' from the original sentence. The expression *I think* and the modal verb *should* imply an authorial voice without staking a claim for the opinion held. The writer can present assertiveness that the proposal is his/her under-standing, and not anybody else's. The Rewritten B also projects authority to a certain degree. Even though I deleted the whole '[*p*]*ersonally speaking*', *I think*, and changed the sentence to an impersonal statement, the modal verb of obligation *should* still imply authoritativeness. The difference is that the writer is less visible in B than the original sentence and A. In giving this example, I aim to illustrate the conflict between the Modesty Principle and the Authority Principle. In this example, even with the same expression, *I think*, it can suggest either modes-ty or authority. The pragmatic effect has to be one or the oth-er. With respect to the authoritativeness between the rewritten versions of A and the rewritten versions of B, I would argue that A is more authoritative than B. In A, the FPP, 'I' clearly projects the writer and prioritises the personal ownership, whereas in B, the writer is less visible. Consequently, the state-ment is still authoritative but weaker than A because of the in-visibility. In short, whether it is appropriate to use the original sentence, the rewritten A or B, depends on the wider context and also depends on which principle the writer decides to fol-low. The writer could be modest(Examples 7-4 and 7-5), or au-thoritative(Rewritten A), or less visible and less authoritative (Rewritten B).

Example 7-5: Personally speaking, *I think* the company should hold a press conference at this point to show a concern attitude to the public. The theory of equivocal communication strategy advocated by Susan may take some effect at the beginning of the crisis. To sum up, J & J took massive actions to restore the company's image. All of the actions taken can be referred to the theories of crisis communication. (PG-BM 0114). (The Modesty Principle)

- Rewritten A: *I think* the company should hold a press conference at this point to show a concern attitude to the public. (The Authority Principle)
- Rewritten B: At this point, the company *should* hold a press conference to show a concern attitude to the public. (The Authority Principle)

The principles are guidelines and not restrictions. The dissertation writers who choose 'I' and 'We' purposefully and strategically not only meet the requirements of the theses but also impress their potential examiners. In essence, the writer-reader relationship in this study is not expert to expert as in research articles, but rather, student to teacher. This unbalanced writer-reader relationship affects the principles of choosing the FPPs in the students' theses. Even if a writer follows these principles, the readers may or may not be similarly minded as what the writers had envisaged. For example, if a writer chooses 'I' to be modest, the reader may interpret it as an authoritative expression to claim authority. As noted above, the principles are guidelines that the writers appear to be following. Whether these guidelines are working or not may depend on how the writers express themselves in an expanding context or even across the whole texts. Apart from these principles that motivate the students to use 'I', 'We' and other impersonal expressions in their academic discourse, there are a few other factors which may also influence the students' use of the two FPPs. These are discussed below.

7.5.2.2 Other factors in the use of 'I' and 'We'

This section discusses other factors that may encourage or discourage the use of 'I' and 'We' in the students' essays. Firstly, 'I' and 'We', especially 'We', are a part of fixed expressions, for example, *as we have mentioned* and *as we can see*. Therefore, the frequency of 'We' is to some extent dependent on the frequency of this particular phrase. This is a characteristic peculiar to the use of fixed phrases. It is proposed that each of these fixed phrases is seen as one distinct unit with a certain meaning and should therefore be processed holistically.

Secondly, the limited information about academic conventions might discourage the students from using the two FPPs. The advice given about the academic conventions in the academic writing classroom might also discourage the students from using 'I' and 'We'. In my experience, academic conventions are summarised as 'do not use the first person pronouns'. Further, there is no instruction on when and where FPPs would be appropriate in academic texts. It is taken for granted by some academic writing teachers and most of the novice writers that the FPPs are subjective and face-threatening. Therefore, the students are advised to use other expressions. The most popular alternative is probably the passive voice. Alternatively, if the students choose the FPPs, they would prefer to use 'We' to 'I', as stated in the Principle section. The reason for this less than desirable advice is due to the shortage of time available for teaching academic writing in China. It may also be possible that the instructors of academic writing also consider the use of FPPs in an academic text as being too subjective and informal. The advice given may be construed according to the teachers' understanding, in which case, it may or may not necessarily convey an accurate assessment of when the use of 'I' and 'We' may be appropriate.

Thirdly, there could be a cultural factor that is involved in the choice of 'I' and 'We'. Chinese culture is more inclined to collectivism and stresses less on individualism. In China, self is mostly collectively constructed(Hyland 2002; Ramanathan and Atkinson 1999). Chinese people tend to use more 'We' than 'I' to present themselves in both spoken and written language. It is a sign of collective effort and a means of being humble, both of which are highly valued virtues in China. The greater number of instances of 'We' to interpret the research or express viewpoints in the students' dissertations might also be influenced by the highly valued Chinese collective culture. This culturally influenced aspect of 'I' and 'We' in academic writing needs cross-cultural examination, which is beyond the scope of this study.

7.5.3 The choice between inclusive 'We' and exclusive 'We'

There are several uses of 'We' in academic writing. According to Quirk et al. (1985, p.350), 'We' can be inclusive and 'We' could also be exclusive. In single authored academic text, inclusive 'We' can be the writer and the reader, or the writer and everyone else, whereas exclusive 'We' refers to the writer only. It is acknowledged that not all the instances of 'We' in academic text can be clearly differentiated between the inclusive and the exclusive use. Poncini(2002), for example, found that about half the instances of the 'We' are not definable in her corpus of business meetings of the company's international distributors. Charles (2004) reports that about 70% of the instances of 'We' in her corpora are interpretable as inclusive 'We' in her investigation of 16 theses from two disciplines. She argues that in some instances, for example, when the first pronoun collocates with modal verbs of uncertainty or with *if*, the use of singular FPP would seem rather "odd" and

"... thesis writers make use of this indeterminacy (*we*) in order to construct a stance which creates consensus with the reader, without relinquishing the writer's authority completely ... Inclusive 'we', then, is a powerful device by means of which thesis writers can construct a stance which is appropriate both for a candidate and for a professional in the disciplinary community"(Charles 2004, p.191).

Without the writers being present, the problem with 'We' is that the reader can only guess who 'We' actually are. Although the writers can be asked afterwards to recall who the 'We' were or was. However, by delayed interview they might forget, or they might change their idea about who 'We' actually was or were when they were writing the articles. There are two problems in determining the inclusiveness and the exclusiveness of 'We' in text(e.g. Harwood 2005): first, who is the 'We' in reality, and who is the 'We' in the discourse. For example:

Example 7-6: People's opinions of how best to satisfy their needs are various across cultures, as showing in Table 3-3 on varying priorities regarding sources of job-related satisfaction. From the table, *we* can see differences of motivational factors between American and Chinese cultures. (PGBM 0083)

In this sentence, the person who *sees* the difference in the text is the writer himself/herself when he/she is analysing the data and writing the thesis. Therefore, *we* is the exclusive 'We' in reality. On the other hand, when readers read this text, the discourse *we* in this example can be inclusive, i.e. the writer and the readers. This hypothesis will be true if the readers agree with the writer. Under this condition, *we* is inclusive 'We' because this proposition is believed as true by other parties. The inclusiveness and exclusiveness, is essentially dependent on the reaction of the reader. Only when the readers proceed and *see* what is going on in the text can they decide whether the proposition proposed is the inclusive or exclusive *we*. If the reader agrees with the writer's interpretation, 'We' is inclusive, if not, it is exclusive. It is primarily about who is involved in the process of reading, thinking and whether or not the interpretation is in line with the readers' understanding.

7.6   Comparison with previous research

As reviewed in Chapter 2, previous corpus-based studies on 'I' and 'We' either explore indeterminate length of text(e.g. Kuo 1999; John 2005) or focus on the verbs that collocate with 'I' and 'We'(e.g. Fløttum et al. 2006). Like Fløttum, I have taken the pronoun-verb collocation as the key indicator of the discourse functions. But I extended that to look at the phrases of 'I', 'We' and their verb collocates. Introducing the phrases of 'I', 'We' and their verb collocates could be a useful addition to Fløttum et al.'s approach.

The other controversial issue of this CLC study could possibly be the comparison between the learners' subcorpora instead of making comparison between native and non-native learners or between novice and expert texts. The findings of this research indicate that this methodology is helpful to explore specific language features in the learners' texts and also offers an additional perspective to the investigation of learner language in its own right, which in turn, justifies the methodology used in the study.

This study also confirms the discourse functions proposed by most of the previous research(e.g. Kuo 1999; Hyland 2002; John 2005; Harwood 2005, 2007). In general, the expressions of 'I' and 'We' are mostly used for discourse organising, recounting research procedure and elaborating personal opinion in the students' texts of this research. Similar functions, though under different labels, appear to work well in my data. What this study adds is the use of the FPPs to report epistemic knowledge, which is probably unique to the students' academic writing.

In terms of 'I', 'We', their phraseology, discourse functions, and the writer identity reflected by the FPPs, previous research does not look at the continuity of these issues. The examinations are either on 'I', 'We' and writer identity (e.g. Tang and John 1999), 'I', 'We' and discourse functions(e.g. Harwood 2007), or lexical bundles(considered as a type of a phraseology here) and discourse functions (e.g. Staples et al. 2013). This research synthesises these issues and adds to our knowledge of their correspondence to the students' academic discourse. The relativeness is listed as follows:

- There is correspondence between the identified frequent phraseology and the proposed discourse functions of 'I' and 'We' in the novice writers' academic texts. Specifically, a textual function can be served by one or two phrasal frames of the two FPPs.

- There is a relativity between the discourse functions and the writer identities of the FPPs phrases. In other words, writer identities can be identified by specific discourse functions in the academic texts.

This relativeness could help to identify the discourse functions and writer identity of 'I' and 'We' by looking at the phrasal frames of the FPPs in academic discourse studies.

With my Chinese background, my educational background as an EFL learner, and my professional background as an EAP teacher, I propose a simplified categorisation of the four discourse functions, three writer identities, a set of principles and some other factors that may influence the students' choices of 'I', 'We' and other impersonal expressions. Together with the findings of the phraseology and the discussion of the appropriateness of the uses of the FPPs, this pedagogically oriented study provides some new insights into the teaching and learning of academic writing in EAP classrooms(see Chapter 8).

7.7   Conclusion

In this chapter I have firstly synthesised the results presented in Chapters 4, 5 and 6. The discourse functions, the phrasal patterns, the disciplinary and academic level varieties and choices of the FPPs are discussed in the context of the whole corpus. Three writer identities are discussed in relation to the discourse functions in the students' texts. A set of principles that push student writers to choose either 'I' or 'We' has been proposed. At the same time, the other factors that influence the employment of the two FPPs are also discussed. Indeed, for the novice writers, the phrases including the FPPs, the concepts of the principles, writer identity and discourse functions are all important to them. The awareness of these notions would direct their choices of 'I', 'We' and other impersonal impressions before and during their academic writing process. The pedagogical implication of this study is further discussed in Chapter 8.

CHAPTER 8
CONCLUSION

8.1   Introduction and outline of the Chapter

The main findings of this research have been summarised and discussed in Chapter 7. In this chapter, I shall consider the implications of the research. Section 2 focuses on how 'I', 'We' and their verb collocates function in EFL learners' academic discourse. This section answers RQ1, RQ2 and RQ3 raised in Chapter 1. Section 3 is devoted to the discussion of the learning and teaching of the proper usage of 'I' and 'We' in EFL academic writing classrooms. This section answers RQ4 from applied pedagogical perspective. In Section 4, limitations of this study are pointed out. Directions for future research are suggested in Section 5. Section 6 is made up of my closing remarks in relation to my views of this research undertaken from my multiple identity, specifically that of an EFL teacher, an EFL academic discourse writer and a researcher of applied linguistics.

8.2   The implications of this study

This section discusses the implications of this research, focusing on the discourse functions of the phrases of 'I', 'We' and the verbs that collocate with them. The findings of this research provide the following insights into the EFL academic texts:

1) In the Chinese students' academic texts, the phrases of 'I', 'We' and their verb collocates serve four major discourse functions to achieve interpersonal purposes: *organise discourse*, *construe knowledge community*, *report research*, and *interpret research*.

I started this research with the identification and categorisation of the functions of the phases of 'I', 'We' and their verb collocates in the student writers' academic text. Initially, the four discourse functions proposed were used to facilitate the comparisons of the phrases between disciplines and between academic levels. I attempt to give them simple labels with the purpose of applying the findings of this research to teaching academic writing in EFL classrooms. After the texts across the disciplines and academic levels were examined, it was found that these four categories were quite helpful in recognising and differentiating the pragmatic functions of 'I' and 'We' in the students' dissertations. Thus, although the functional categorisation proposed in this study is exploratory, these identified discourse functions may be applicable to the exploration of academic discourse of other genres and disciplines.

2) The phrases of 'I' and 'We' that perform the four discourse functions can be generalised into to a few phrasal patterns: *I + V-ed*, *I + base form of the verbs*, *I/We + have + past participle*, *I/We + will + base form of a verb*; and *we + modal verb + verb*.

First, these phrasal patterns show that the expressions of

'I' and 'We' are highly formulaic when they serve the discourse functions in the students' academic texts. Second, this research raises the question of the extent to which there is one-to-one correspondence between the identified phrases and the discourse functions. It is found that each function is realised by one or two phrases (see Table 8.1). For example, the phrase *I/we + have + past participle* is always used for text organising. On the other hand, some of the phrases may serve more than one function. For example, *we know that* can be an expression of construing knowledge community or an expression of research interpretation. The functions of these phrases need to be defined via wider contexts. Third, the verbs in some of the identified phrases are not restricted to one semantic category even though the discourse functions of the phrases remain the same. For example, both expressions *we can find* and *we can know* may be used to interpret research findings, whereas, *find* is an activity verb and *know* is a mental verb according to Biber et al. (2002). Therefore, this study suggests that the semantic classification of the verbs in academic discourse involves considerable attention to their immediate and expanding contexts.

   3) Three issues are interrelated in academic writing: the discourse functions, the students' writer identities and the principles of using or not using the FPPs.

As mentioned in Section 7.5.2.1 of Chapter 7, the three issues of 'I' and 'We' discussed in this study can be differentiated from the time line of the writing stages. It is suggested that the students are influenced by a number of principles, for example, the Modesty Principle and the Alignment Principle. These principles govern their usage choice of 'I' or 'We' or alternative expressions. These principles operate at each particular point of writing. Before a sentence is written, the students are following these principles and making decisions to determine which expression they are going to choose. After the students have determined which principle to follow, the writer identity is made manifest by these decisions relating to the usage of 'I', 'We' and their verb collocates. The discourse functions are the post writing textual effects that the writers intend to achieve. However, whether the pragmatic effects have been

Table 8.1   The discourse function and phrases

Discourse functions		Phrases	Examples
organise discourse		I/we + have + past participle	*I/we have discussed/mentioned*
		I/we + will + base form of a verb	*I/we will discuss/mention*
construe knowledge community			*(as) we(all) know(that)*
report research	report study or internship	I + V-ed	*I read/learnt/worked*
	recount research procedure		*I collected/analyzed/found*
interpret research	interpret research results	we + possibility and ability modal verbs + verbs	*we can/could/will see/know*
	argue for/against viewpoints	I + base form of the verbs	*I think/believe/argue/hope*
		we + obligation and necessity modal verbs + verbs	*we should/must learn/know*

achieved is not known until the writing is read by readers. These functions, in return could match with the respective writer identities proposed in this study, *self as text organiser*, *self as research reporter* and *self as evaluator*. These three issues have been discussed according to the pre-, mid-, and post-chronological writing process. I would suggest however, a reversed order of these three elements, *discourse function*, *writer identity* and *principles* that need to be introduced to students in academic writing classes. I will elaborate on this point in Section 8.3.

8.3 Pedagogical implications

The findings of this study would shed some light on the teaching and learning of academic texts in EFL context. In this section, the pedagogical implications are discussed by reorganising the findings into a few interrelated combinations. The aim of the discussion on the discourse functions and the phrases is to suggest how and what to teach in the EAP classrooms. The interpretation of the interrelatedness of the discourse functions, writer identity and principles jointly work towards raising the awareness of using 'I', 'We' or other impersonal expressions in academic discourse. I also discuss the possibility of combining data driven learning and intensive reading of academic writing samples, which could help the students to identify the phraseological features, as well as the effective use and the ineffective use of the FPPs.

8.3.1 Discourse functions and phrases

As has been discussed in Chapter 7, it is found in this study that the students use a few phrasal patterns to serve the four major discourse functions in their academic discourse. As illustrated in Table 8.1, there is a correspondence between the phrases and the functions. Each function is realised by one or two phrasal frames of 'I' and 'We'. This indicates the expressions of the FPPs are highly formulaic when they serve these discourse functions. In the EAP classrooms, teachers could introduce the use of the FPPs in terms of the functions they realise and in what phrases they can do so effectively.

The disciplinary difference that is found in this study also calls for more specific disciplinary instructions in EAP classrooms. It is found in this study that different disciplines may use the phrases including the FPPs to reflect different epistemic experience. This may suggest that the students have accommodated themselves to the conventions of the disciplines, with or without instruction. However, I do think students would benefit from being more aware of what 'I' and 'We' mean in their disciplines. It would help them to understand what pragmatic effects of the FPPs on the readers are in their academic texts. For example, students of Business and Management should know that if they use the 'I' phrase(e.g. *I used/collected*) to report research procedure, it would distinguish their methodology from other peoples' research methodology. Therefore, the expression would stress the newsworthiness of the research(cf. Harwood 2005). If students of English Literature use 'I' phrases(e.g. *I read ... as*) to interpret research findings, they should be aware that they stress personal understanding and evaluation of the original literature. These phrases would present their originality and authoritativeness of their research.

The comparison between the academic levels suggests that the students of the more advanced academic level, the postgraduate students in this study, may still need explicit instruction on the appropriate use of the FPPs. The academic level variations presented in this study suggest a greater degree of objectivity in the texts of the postgraduate students than those of the undergraduates. This observation becomes apparent from the fewer instances of the FPPs and more alternative impersonal expressions utilised in the postgraduate texts. However, it was also found that the postgraduate students tended to replace 'I' with 'We' to avoid criticism and challenge. This finding relates to the effective and ineffective use of 'I' and 'We' in the students' texts, which has been discussed in detail in Chapter 7. The postgraduate students' misconception that 'I' and 'We' are interchangeable needs to be pointed out by EAP teachers and more formal instructions should be given on the appropriate use of the FPPs. In this specific case, the postgraduate students may need to be notified clearly that the plural 'We' also projects authorship and implies authority. The replacement of 'I' with 'We' is not always the best strategy for avoiding face-threateningness.

As discussed in Chapter 7, the phrases of 'I' and 'We' are identified because they are widely used in the students' texts in this study. However, these expressions or even the other impersonal expressions that are used to replace them may or may not be appropriately used in their academic texts. This point may be explained by the low level of awareness of the discourse functions of 'I', 'We' and the lack of the conception of writer-reader interactivity in academic texts, which will be addressed in the next section.

8.3.2　Discourse functions, writer identity and principles

I have discussed the interrelationship between the discourse functions, writer identities and the principles proposed in this study in Section 7.2. Both discourse functions and writer identity in academic writing texts have been explored in varies ways respectively(e.g. Fetzer 2014; Harwood 2005). However, they have not been introduced as interrelated concepts to students in academic writing classes. In actual practice, these three entities would help the students' conceptualisation of the uses of the FPPs. In order to pass on this knowledge, EAP teachers first of all, must become sensitive to these three concepts and be knowledgeable about the uses of the FPPs in academic discourse.

In practice, these three issues can be introduced to the students in a reversed order in the EAP classrooms. Teachers could start from the reader's point of view, focussing on the discourse functions. This introduction will equip learners with the knowledge about what pragmatic effects their language use could have on their readers. For example, the expressions of 'I' and 'We' could help the readers to see the manner in which the text has been organised. It could also help to build solidarity with the readers, to claim their own authority or alternatively, place them in an awkward situation of being questioned or challenged by the readers. Then writer identity may be introduced. When realising the pragmatic functions, the students are no longer their autobiographical selves in the text. They become reporters, text organisers and evaluators. They present themselves and concurrently communicate with the readers. These different identities would raise the students' awareness that they assume multiple roles when writing academic texts. These writer identities would also remind the students that they need to interact with the readership. Then the student would need to know that during the interaction with the readership, there are principles and other factors that may influence their choice of using 'I', 'We' and various other impersonal expressions. An example of one of the principles that the student may already be aware of is the Modesty Principle. If they want to sound modest, they would probably choose either 'I' or 'We' or other expressions. However, students may be unaware of other factors such as the Authority Principle and the influence of the concept of collectiveness enshrined in the Chinese culture. In order to sound affirmative, the Chinese student writers may use 'We' instead of 'I' even though the essays are single authored. Their decisions in turn, will lead to either successful or face-threatening pragmatic effects. Therefore, the students should be informed that they have choices at their disposal, of utilising either 'I' or 'We' or other impersonal expressions. What matters is that different decisions would result in different pragmatic effects. They would need to decide between keeping themselves from being challenged and taking the risk of claiming authority. Following the steps of introducing these three issues, the student writers would have a better understanding of why and when to use or not use the FPPs in their academic texts.

8.3.3   Data Driving Learning and intensive reading

The assistance of data driven learning and intensive reading of sample disciplinary texts help the students in the EAP classrooms with the following two aspects: to let the students identify the phraseological features of 'I' and 'We'; and to let them be aware of the quality of using the FPPs in their academic text.

Firstly, by using DDL, the student can explore the formulaic features identified in the concordances, and compare them with their own writing. Recently, scholars started to employ CLC technology in language classrooms, particularly, academic writing classrooms(Charles 2012, 2014; Flowerdew 2015; Lee & Swales 2006; Su 2019; Zhang & Zou 2022). The technology of corpus linguistics is especially useful in terms of looking for conventionalised features, including collocations and phraseology. At the same time, by building their own disciplinary corpora, students can turn to them for comparison and reflective studies. Personalised corpus of one specific discipline can meet the requirement of exploration of different genres, for example, term papers, research report and thesis of varying competence levels. Charles(2014) explores the DIY corpus assisted academic writing teaching and suggests that this method may be applied to most of the higher education academic classes. The use of DDL in EAP classrooms will not only help the students to realise the conventions of certain genres, but also the conventionalised rhetorical practice and preferences of their academic community. In this sense, the exploration of the discourse functions, collocations and phraseology of 'I' and 'We' and many other issues in academic writing would be assisted by corpus technology.

Secondly, the intensive reading exercise of both disciplinary expert research papers, essays written by the students themselves and essays of their peers(with authorisation) could help the student writers observe effective and ineffective use of the FPPs. In classrooms, teachers could also help the students to compare and explore those impersonal expressions that serve the same textual function as 'I' and 'We' in expert writers' texts. The combination of DDL and intensive reading would not only provide the students opportunities to look at frequent expressions in corpora, but also make them realise that the expression of 'I' and 'We' could be both an effective and ineffective device of self-representation in academic texts.

8.4 The limitations of the study

In this research, I compared the disciplinary differences between BM and EL, and the variation between the academic levels, UG and PG. The manipulation of these subcorpora (UGBM, UGEL, PGBM and PGEL) is to enable the two-dimensional exploration of the disciplinary and academic level difference. As introduced in Chapters 1 and 3, this study is designed to look at general divergence of the disciplines and academic levels. The limitation of this approach is the discipline differences at each distinct academic level have not been accounted for in this study. In each comparison there is either a mixture of academic levels or a mixture of disciplines.

However, considering that the collected theses were all accepted for either a Bachelor's or a Master's degree, I would argue that the disciplinary difference is better explored by regarding that all the texts are up to acceptable standards and can be compared. This method also makes it manageable for me to look at the academic texts of undergraduate and postgraduate levels from a broader perspective than to examine the four sub-corpora at the same time. Nevertheless, this is not to say that there is no difference between each of the four subcorpora. Closer examinations between the two disciplines of the same academic level and between two academic levels of the same discipline would be a research activity that I would hope to pursue after this study.

The second limitation of this study is that I did not examine all the verbs that collocated with 'I' and 'We' in the corpus. The verbs extracted for examination are limited to those that collocate with 'I' no less than 5 times and/or collocate with 'We' no less than 10 times across at least three texts in the corpus. This is because the aim of this research is to investigate the discourse functions of 'I' and 'We' by looking at the verbs that collocate with them. The frequency thresholds serve the purpose of examining those frequently used verbs in the students' texts. The drawback of this approach is that those infrequent verbs that collocate with 'I' and 'We' are not included in the categorisation step of this research. However, during the analysis stage, some of those infrequent verbs are presented when the phrasal patterns are examined(see Chapter 7). It is observed that even though these verbs are not shortlisted for categorisation, most of them fit well into the discourse functions and phrasal patterns proposed in this study.

Thirdly, I would have to acknowledge that the categorisation of the verbs and the discourse functions of the collocations are highly subjective. I am not an expert in either Business and

Management or English Literature. Whenever necessary, my colleagues in the Business and Management and English Literature Departments were specifically asked for help.

Fourthly, the corpus of this research is made up of final versions of the EFL student writers' dissertations. We do not know if there has been any intervention from the students' supervisors about the FPP use in their texts. Supervisors' interventions and the effect of revision during the process of writing up would be worth exploring after this study.

8.5 Suggestions for future research

This learner corpus based study did not use a reference corpus, neither was any form of comparison undertaken between native speaker and non-native speaker nor between novice writer and expert writer of the same discipline. My intention was to avoid the assumption that the observed language features in learner corpus are common to the native speaker's or expert writer's corpus. I have discussed this point in Chapters 1 and 3. The findings of this research suggest that comparing learners' texts written by writers of differing levels of exposure to expert texts or academia would be helpful in finding out the phraseological divergence between novice writers and more advanced academic text writers. I have identified a few frequently used phrasal patterns with corresponding pragmatic functions in this study. In the next study, I would possibly look at PhD texts of the same discipline to evaluate if the more experienced EFL academic writers use the same phrases to serve the same discourse functions or if they did not. With the observed differences between writers of different academic levels we are likely to have a better understanding and appreciation of what the next pedagogical aim should be in EAP classrooms. This could be one direction worthy of further investigation.

Most of the research on 'I' and 'We' in academic discourse so far is largely quantitative and based on the researchers' observation. A few exceptions such as Hyland (2002) and Işık-Taş(2018) did a few interviews with the writers, but they are a small part of the whole study. Harwood (2007) presents a different perspective of looking at the research papers by interviewing the writers and the writers' peers. However, the interactive effect of the FPPs in academic discourse from the reader's perspective is not explored extensively. In fact, it is not known to writers whether or not the readers would choose to agree or disagree with them, or acknowledge their authorships. The pragmatic purposes of the rhetorical strategies are attempted but not necessarily achieved. Hence, it would be interesting to find out what readers think and feel when they encounter 'I' and 'We' in these students' academic texts. Some people may approve some of the uses of 'I' and 'We', like the participants agreeing with their peers' usages in published research papers in Harwood's(2005) interviews. Others probably would consider the expressions of 'I' and 'We' as informal or too subjective in academic texts. All things considered, it would be beneficial to the writers of academic articles to know what the readers' reaction might be when the FPPs are used. In the context of this research, further study on the teachers' or supervisors' reaction of these EFL students' dissertations could help us to know what is expected, approved or disapproved of from the readers' perspective. This understanding will increase awareness and credibility on the writer's side when they construct their self-images in their discourse, as well as author more readable and friendly academic articles.

Another issue raised in this study is how to be authoritative in academic discourse. In essence, being authorial is not a one-sided activity, but is an interaction between writer and reader with awareness of who their counterparts probably are. Being authorial is about evaluating an entity or proposition, expressing the writer's own opinion, seeking solidarity, and claiming originality and contributing to academic discourse. These discourse functions can be achieved by 'I' and 'We' as well as many other expressions in the academic context. From the observation of the usages of 'I' and 'We', the Chinese EFL writers in this study do not display much confidence in presenting themselves and their work to their readers.

In this study, the interactivity between writer and reader of academic text has only been observed and interpreted from the perspective of two words, 'I' and 'We'. The question itself is likely to be more complicated than these two FPPs and worth further exploration in the EAP field. The examination of the alternative expression of 'I' and 'We', for instance, *it is ... that*, adverbs, evaluative adjectives and some subtle language expressions suggest more complex perspectives on writer-reader interaction (cf. Charles 2004; Hunston 2004; Hyland 2010). Therefore, the textual function and individual persona in academic discourse is only viewed through a microscope in this study. I did not explore the issues mentioned above further in this study. Those issues are certainly worth further exploration in the future.

8.6 Closing remarks: my writer identities as an EFL teacher, an academic discourse writer and an EFL PhD student of applied linguistics

I started this research with the question of how the FPPs are used in EFL academic texts. With a specific goal in mind, I wanted my research to be of pedagogical significance and to have practical applications in a classroom setting. This decision was obviously influenced by my career as an EFL teacher. The other two identities that I am well aware of during my PhD study are those of an EFL academic text writer and a researcher in applied linguistics. Both of these identities helped and shaped my book writing during the whole research and writing up process. I wrote with awareness and caution and was mindful about when, where and how I would need to present myself and how I would like myself to be presented in discourse. However, as a Chinese EFL writer influenced by the principles that are discussed in Chapter 7, I have probably both overused and at times avoided the use of 'I' and 'We' unconsciously in my drafts. On several occasions, I was advised by my peer reviewers and Susan, my PhD supervisor, to either replace the FPPs with other expressions or rephrase a few expressions by using 'I' and 'We', particularly 'I' in this book.

Taking myself as an example, I want to stress here the importance of self-representation in EFL academic discourse. The use of the FPPs is problematic, not only in the sense of the difficulty associated with the presentation of the writer in the discourse but also a more complicated conundrum of how to use, when to use and which FPP to use in academic discourse. The question of 'how to use' relates to the collocation and phraseology of the FPPs, 'when to use' relates to the intended discourse functions, and 'which one to use' relates to the choice between 'I', 'We' and other impersonal expressions. All of these would affect the quality and strength of self-representation in the academic texts.

This study and my three identities throughout my research and writing process amplifies the point that with progress in academic experience, the skill of using the FPPs appropriately hinges on explicit awareness and instruction. This study sheds some light on the issue of 'I' and 'We' in disciplinary EFL academic discourse. It is hoped that the findings of this research could inform the practice of researching, teaching and learning the FPPs in academic contexts. Further, it is hoped that this study can raise the EFL learners' and EAP teachers' awareness of various aspects of the FPPs in academic discourse.

REFERENCE

Ackermann, K., & Chen, Y. H. (2013). Developing the Academic Collocation List(ACL)—A corpus-driven and expert-judged approach. *Journal of English for Academic Purposes*, *12*(4), 235—247.

Ädel, A. (2006). *Metadiscourse in L1 and L2 English* (Vol.24). John Benjamins Publishing.

Başal, A. & Bada, E. (2012). Use of first person pronouns: A corpus based study of journal articles. *Energy Education Science and Technology Part B: Social and Educational Studies*, *4*(3), 1777—1788.

Bazerman, C. (1984). Modern evolution of the experimental report in physics: Spectroscopic articles in Physical Review, 1893—1980. *Social Studies of Science*, *14*(2), 163—196.

Becher, T. (1989). *Academic Tribes and Territories: Intellectual Inquiry and the Cultures of the Disciplines*. Milton Keynes: SHRE/Open University Press.

Bestgen, Y., & Granger, S. (2014). Quantifying the development of phraseological competence in L2 English writing: An automated approach. *Journal of Second Language Writing*, *26*, 28—41.

Biber, D. (2006). *University language: A corpus-based study of spoken and written registers* (Vol.23). John Benjamins

Publishing.

Biber, D. (2009). Corpus-based and corpus-driven analyses of language variation and use. In B. Heine and H. Narrog (eds.), *The Oxford Handbook of Linguistic Analysis*. Oxford: Oxford University Press.

Biber, D., S. Conrad, and G. N. Leech. (2002). *Longman Student Grammar of Spoken and Written English*. Harlow: Longman.

Biber, D., Conrad, S. and Cortes, V.(2004). "If you look at ...": Lexical bundles in university teaching and textbooks, *Applied Linguistics 25*:371—405.

Biber, D., & Barbieri, F. (2007). Lexical bundles in university spoken and written registers. *English for Specific Purposes*, *26*(3), 263—286.

Biber, D., Conrad, S., & Reppen, R. (1998). *Corpus Linguistics: Investigating Language Structure and Use*. Cambridge: Cambridge University Press.

Çandarlı, D., Bayyurt, Y., & Martı, L. (2015). Authorial presence in L1 and L2 novice academic writing: Cross-linguistic and cross-cultural perspectives. *Journal of English for Academic Purposes*, *20*, 192—202.

Charles, M. (2004). The construction of stance: a corpus-based investigation of two contrasting disciplines. Unpublished Doctoral Dissertation. University of Birmingham.

Charles, M. (2006). Phraseological patterns in reporting clauses used in citation: A corpus-based study of theses in two disciplines. *English for Specific Purposes*, *25*(3), 310—331.

Charles, M. (2014). Getting the corpus habit: EAP students' long-term use of personal corpora. *English for Specific*

Purposes, *35*, 30—40.

Chau, M. H. (2015). From language learners to dynamic meaning makers: a longitudinal investigation of Malaysian secondary school students' development of English from text and corpus perspectives. Dissertation. Unpublished Doctoral Dissertation. University of Birmingham.

Chen, M. (2013). Overuse or underuse: A corpus study of English phrasal verb use by Chinese, British and American university students. *International Journal of Corpus Linguistics*, *18*(3), 418—442.

Chen, Y. H., & Baker, P. (2010). Lexical bundles in L1 and L2 academic writing. *Language Learning & Technology*, *14*(2), 30—49.

Coxhead, A. (2000). A new academic word list. *TESOL quarterly*, *34*(2), 213—238.

Crismore, A., Markkanen, R., & Steffensen, M. S. (1993). Metadiscourse in persuasive writing: A study of texts written by American and Finnish university students. *Written Communication*, *10*(1), 39—71.

Davies, M. (2008). *The Corpus of Contemporary American English*. BYE, Brigham Young University.

Ellis, N., R. Simpson-Vlach, and C. Maynard. (2008). Formulaic language in native and second-language speakers: Psycholinguistics, corpus linguistics, and TESOL. *TESOL Quarterly*, *42*(3), 375—396.

Erman, B. & Warren, B.(2000). The Idiom Principle and the Open Choice Principle. *Text-Interdisciplinary Journal for the Study of Discourse*, *20*(1), 29—62.

Fetzer, A. (2014). I think, I mean and I believe in political discourse: Collocates, functions and distribution. *Functions of language*, *21* (1), 67—94.

Firth, J. R. (1957). A synopsis of linguistic theory 1930—1955. In *Studies in Linguistic Analysis*, pages 1—32. The Philological Society, Oxford. Reprinted in Palmer (1968), pages 168—205.

Fløttum, K., Dahl, T., & Kinn, T. (2006a). *Academic voices*: *Across languages and disciplines* (Vol.148). John Benjamins Publishing.

Fløttum, K. Kinn, T. and Dahl, T.(2006b). "We now report on ..." versus "Let us now see how ...": Author roles and interaction with readers in research articles, in Hyland, K. and Bondi, M. (eds.) *Academic Discourse across Disciplines*. Frankfort: Perter Lang.

Fortanet, I. (1998). Verb usage in academic writing: reporting verbs in economics research articles in English and in Spanish. In *Proceedings of the 11th European Symposium on Language for Special Purposes. LSP Identity and Interface Research*, *Knowledge and Society*. Copenhagen: Copenhagen Business School, LSP Centre, 231—240.

Fortanet, I. (2004). I think: opinion, uncertainty or politeness in academic spoken English? *RAEL*: *Revista Electrónica de Lingüística Aplicada*, 3, 63—84.

Geertz, C. (1988). *Works and Lives*: *The Anthropologist as Author*. Stanford University Press.

Geoffrey, L. (1983). *Principles of Pragmatics*. London and New York: Longman.

Granger, S. (1994). The learner corpus: a revolution in applied linguistics. *English Today*, *39* (3), 25—29.

Granger, S. (1998). Prefabricated patterns in advanced EFL writing: Collocations and formulae. In A. P., Cowie(ed.), *Phraseology: Theory, Analysis and Applications*, Oxford: Oxford University Press, 145—160.

Granger, S. (1998). The Computer Learner Corpus: A Versatile New Source of Data for SLA Research. In S., Granger(ed.), *Learner English on Computer*. London & New York: Addison Wesley Longman, 3—18.

Granger, S. (2003). The international corpus of learner English: a new resource for foreign language learning and teaching and second language acquisition research. *TESOL Quarterly*, *37*(3), 538—546.

Granger, S. (2007). A bird's-eye view of computer learner corpus research. In W. Teubert & R. Krishnamurthy (eds.), *Corpus Linguistics: Critical Concepts in Linguistics*. London & New York: Routledge.

Granger, S., Hung, J., & Petch-Tyson, S. (eds.) (2002). *Computer Learner Corpora, Second Language Acquisition, and Foreign Language Teaching*(Vol.6). John Benjamins Publishing.

Granger, S., & Bestgen, Y. (2014). The use of collocations by intermediate vs. advanced non-native writers: A bigram-based study. *International Review of Applied Linguistics in Language Teaching*, *52*(3), 229—252.

Gries, S. T. (2008). Phraseology and linguistic theory: A brief survey. In S. Granger & F. Meunier(eds.), *Phraseology: An Interdisciplinary Perspective*, 3—25.

Gries, S. T. (2013). 50-something years of work on collocations. *International Journal of Corpus Linguistics*, *18*(1), 137—166.

Groom, N. (2007). Phraseology and epistemology in humanities writing: a corpus-driven study. Unpublished Doctoral Dissertation. University of Birmingham.

Gui, S., & Yang, H. (2002). *Chinese Learner English Corpus*. Shanghai: Foreign Language Education Press.

Halliday, M. A. (1994). *An Introduction to Functional Grammar*. London: Edward Arnold.

Handl, S. (2008). Essential collocations for learners of English: The role of collocational direction and weight. In F. Meunier, & S. Granger(eds.), *Phraseology in Foreign Language Learning and Teaching*, 43—65.

Harwood, N. (2005a). 'Nowhere has anyone attempted ... In this article I aim to do just that': A corpus-based study of self-promotional *I* and *we* in academic writing across four disciplines. *Journal of Pragmatics*, *37*(8), 1207—1231.

Harwood, N. (2005b). 'We do not seem to have a theory ... the theory I present here attempts to fill this gap': inclusive and exclusive pronouns in academic writing, *Applied Linguistics 26*(3), 343—375.

Harwood, N. (2006). (In) appropriate personal pronoun use in political science: A qualitative study and a proposed heuristic for future research. *Written Communication*, *23* (4), 424—450.

Harwood, N. (2007). Political scientists on the functions of personal pronouns in their writing: An interview-based study of 'I'and 'we'. *Text & Talk*, *27*(1), 27—54.

Howarth, P. (1998). Phraseology and second language proficiency. *Applied Linguistics*, *19*(1), 24—44.

Hunston, S. (1993). Professional conflict: Disagreement

in academic discourse. In M. Baker, G. Francis & E. Tognini-Bonelli (eds.). *Text and Technology: In Honour of John Sinclair*. Amsterdam: John Benjamins Publishing, 115—134.

Hunston, S. (2002). *Corpora in Applied Linguistics*. Cambridge: Cambridge University.

Hunston. S. (2003). Lexis, word form and complementation pattern: a corpus study, *Functions of Language*, 10 (1) 31—60.

Hunston, S. (2004). Counting the uncountable: problems of identifying evaluation in a text and in a corpus. In A. Partington, J. Morley & L. Haarman (eds.), *Corpora and Discourse*, 9, 157—188.

Hunston, S., & Francis, G. (2000). *Pattern Grammar: A Corpus-driven Approach to the Lexical Grammar of English*. John Benjamins Publishing.

Hyland, K. (2000). *Disciplinary Discourses: Social Interactions in Academic Writing*. London: Longman.

Hyland, K. (2001). Humble servants of the discipline? Self-mention in research articles, *English for Specific Purposes* 20, 207—226.

Hyland, K. (2002). Authority and invisibility: Authorial identity in academic writing. *Journal of Pragmatics*, 34 (8), 1091—1112.

Hyland, K. (2004). Disciplinary interactions: Metadiscourse in L2 postgraduate writing. *Journal of Second Language Writing*, 13(2), 133—151.

Hyland, K. (2005). *Metadiscourse*. London: Continuum.

Hyland, K. (2008). Academic clusters: text patterning in published and postgraduate writing, *International Journal of*

Applied Linguistics 18(1), 41—62.

Hyland, K. (2010a). Community and Individuality: Performing identity in applied linguistics. *Written Communication*, *27*(2), 159—188.

Hyland, K. (2010b). Constructing proximity: Relating to readers in popular and professional science. *Journal of English for Academic Purposes*, *9*(2), 116—127.

Hyland, K. (2012). *Disciplinary Identities: Individuality and Community in Academic Discourse*. Cambridge: Cambridge University Press.

Hyland, K. (2015). Genre, discipline and identity. *Journal of English for Academic Purposes*, *19*, 32—43.

Hyland, K., & Jiang, F. K. (2017). Is academic writing becoming more informal? *English for Specific Purposes*, *45*, 40—51.

Hyland, K. & Tse, P. (2004). Metadiscourse in academic writing: A reappraisal, *Applied Linguistics*, *25*(2), 156—177.

Hyland, K. & Tse, P. (2005). Evaluation that constructions: Signaling stance in research abstract, *Functions of Language*, *12*(1), 39—63.

Hynninen, N., & Kuteeva, M. (2017). "Good" and "acceptable" English in L2 research writing: Ideals and realities in history and computer science. *Journal of English for Academic Purposes*, *30*, 53—65.

Ivanic, R. (1998). *Writing and Identity: The Discoursal Construction of Identity in Academic Writing*. Amsterdam: John Benjamins Publishing Company.

Ivanič, R., & Camps, D. (2001). I am how I sound: Voice as self-representation in L2 writing. *Journal of Second Lan-*

guage Writing, *10*(1—2), 3—33.

John, S. (2005). The Writing Process and Writer Identity: Investigating the Influence of Revision on Linguistic & Textual Features of Writer Identity in Dissertations. Unpublished Doctoral Dissertation. University of Birmingham.

Kaszubski, P. (1998). *Learner Corpora: the Cross-roads of Linguistic Norm*. Presented at the Teaching and Language Corpora(TALC 98).

Kilgarriff, A., Baisa, V., Bušta, J., Jakubiček, M., Kovář, V., Michelfeit, J., ... & Suchomel, V. (2014). The sketch engine: ten years on. *Lexicography*, 1—30.

Kjellmer, G. (1987). Aspects of English Collocations in Proceedings of the Seventh International Conference on English Language Research on Computerized Corpora. *Costerus*, *59*, 133—140.

Kuo, C. H. (1999). The Use of Personal Pronouns: Role Relationships in Scientific Journal Articles. *English for Specific Purposes*, *18*(2), 121—138.

Leech, G. (1983). *Principles of Pragmatics*. London and New York: Longman.

Leech, G. (2000). Grammars of spoken English: New outcomes of corpus-oriented research, *Language Learning 50*(4), 675—724.

Li, J., & Ye, T. (2023). Patterns and functions of *I* in academic writing: From a local grammar approach. *Journal of English for Academic Purposes*, 61, 101186.

Liu, D. (2003). The Most Frequently Used Spoken American English Idioms: A Corpus Analysis and Its Implications, *TESOL Quarterly 37*(4), 671—700.

Lorés-Sanz, R. (2011). The construction of the author's voice in academic writing: The interplay of cultural and disciplinary factors. *Text & Talk-An Interdisciplinary Journal of Language, Discourse & Communication Studies*, *31*(2), 173—193.

Martinez, R. & Schmitt N., (2012). A Phrasal Expression List. *Applied Linguistics*, *33*(3), 299—320.

Martin, J. R., & White, P. R. (2003). *The Language of Evaluation*(Vol.2). Basingstoke: Palgrave Macmillan.

Mauranen, A. (1993). Contrastive ESP rhetoric: Metatext in Finnish-English economics texts. *English for Specific Purposes*, *12*(1), 3—22.

McEnery, T., & Hardie, A. (2012). *Corpus Linguistics: Method, Theory and Practice*. Cambridge Textbooks in Linguistics.

Meunier, F. (2015). Developmental patterns in learner corpora. In S. Granger, G. Gilquin, & F. Meunier(eds.), *The Cambridge Handbook of Learner Corpus Research* (Cambridge Handbooks in Language and Linguistics, pp.379—400). Cambridge: Cambridge University Press.

Millar, N. (2011). The Processing of Malformed formulaic language, *Applied Linguistics*, *32*(2), 129—148.

Myers, G. (1989). The pragmatics of politeness in scientific articles. *Applied Linguistics*, *10*(1), 1—35.

Myers, G. (1991). Lexical cohesion and specialized knowledge in science and popular science texts. *Discourse Processes*, *14*(1), 1—26.

Nattinger, J. R. and DeCarrico, J.(1992). *Lexical Phrases and Language Teaching*. Oxford: Oxford University Press.

Nesi, H., Gardner, S., Thompson, P., & Wickens, P.

(2007). British academic written English corpus. *Retrieved* October 12, 2014.

Osborne, J. (2008). Phraseology effects as a trigger for errors in L2 English. In E. Meunier and S. Granger(eds.), *Phraseology in Foreign Language Learning and Teaching*. Amsterdam: John Benjamins Publishing Company, 67—83.

Oxford English Dictionary Online. Retrieved 11 November 2017 from https://en.oxforddictionaries.com/.

Paquot, M. (2008). Exemplification in learner writing: A cross-linguistic perspective. In E. Meunier and S. Granger (eds.), *Phraseology in Foreign Language Learning and Teaching*. Amsterdam: John Benjamins Publishing Company, 101—119.

Paquot, M. & Granger, S. (2012). Formulaic Language in Learner Corpora. *Annual Review of Applied Linguistics*, 32, 130—149. Cambridge University Press.

Pérez-Llantada, C., Plo, R., & Ferguson, G. R. (2011). "You don't say what you know, only what you can": The perceptions and practices of senior Spanish academics regarding research dissemination in English. *English for Specific Purposes*, *30*(1), 18—30.

Poncini, G. (2002). Business relationships and roles in a multicultural group: an investigation of discourse at an Italian company's meetings of its international distributors. Unpublished Doctoral Dissertation. University of Birmingham.

Quirk, R., Greenbaum, S., & Leech, G. and Svartvik, J. (1985). *A Comprehensive Grammar of the English Language*. London and New York: Longman.

Ramanathan, V., & Atkinson, D. (1999). Individualism,

academic writing, and ESL writers. *Journal of Second Language Writing*, *8*(1), 45—75.

Simpson-Vlach, R., & Ellis, N. C. (2010). An academic formulas list: New methods in phraseology research. *Applied Linguistics*, *31*(4), 487—512.

Sinclair, J. (1991). *Corpus*, *Concordance*, *Collocation*. Oxford: Oxford University Press.

Sinclair, J. (2004). *Trust the Text*: *Language*, *Corpus*, *Discourse*. Routledge.

Sinclair, J. (2005). Corpus and text-basic principles. In M. Wynne(ed.), *Developing Linguistic Corpora*: *A Guide to Good Practice*. Oxford: Oxbow Books, 1—16.

Sinclair, J. (2008). The phrase, the whole phrase, and nothing but the phrase. *Phraseology*: *An Interdisciplinary Perspective*, 407—410.

Su, H. (2019). Patterns, local grammars, and the design of English teaching materials. *ELT Journal*, 74(1), 1—10.

Swale, J. (1990). *Genre Analysis*: *English in Academic and Research Settings*. Cambridge: Cambridge University Press.

Swetnam, D., & Swetnam, R. (2000). *Writing your Dissertation*: *The Bestselling Guide to Planning*, *Preparing and Presenting First-Class Work*. Hachette UK.

Tadros, A. (1994). Predictive categories in expository text. In M. Coulthard(ed.) *Advances in Written Text Analysis*. London: Routledge. 69—82.

Tang, R., & John, S. (1999). The 'I' in identity: Exploring writer identity in student academic writing through the first person pronoun. *English for Specific Purposes*, *18*, 23—39.

Thompson, G., & Yiyun, Y. (1991). Evaluation in the

reporting verbs used in academic papers. *Applied Linguistics*, *12*(4), 365—382.

Tribble, C. (2017). ELFA vs. Genre: A new paradigm war in EAP writing instruction? *Journal of English for Academic Purposes*, *25*, 30—44.

Vyatkina, N., & Cunningham, D. J. (2015). Learner corpora and pragmatics. In Granger S. & Meunier F. (eds.) *The Cambridge Handbook of Learner Corpus Research*. Cambridge University Press. 281—305.

Wang, Y. (2018). As Hill seems to suggest: Variability in formulaic sequences with interpersonal functions in L1 novice and expert academic writing. *Journal of English for Academic Purposes*, *33*, 12—23.

Wray, A. (2002). *Formulaic Language and the Lexicon*. Cambridge: Cambridge University Press.

Zhang Q., & Zou, Y. (2022). Application of data-driven learning in foreign language teaching and learning, *Journal of Changchun University of Science and Technology*, 35(6):181—185.

图书在版编目(CIP)数据

语料库与学术语篇作者身份短语研究/邹艳丽著
.—上海:上海三联书店,2024.3
ISBN 978-7-5426-8324-3

Ⅰ.①语… Ⅱ.①邹… Ⅲ.①英语-短语-研究
Ⅳ.①H314.3

中国国家版本馆 CIP 数据核字(2023)第 242327 号

语料库与学术语篇作者身份短语研究

著　者 / 邹艳丽

责任编辑 / 殷亚平
装帧设计 / 徐　徐
监　　制 / 姚　军
责任校对 / 王凌霄

出版发行 / 上海三联书店
　　　　　 (200041)中国上海市静安区威海路 755 号 30 楼
邮　　箱 / sdxsanlian@sina.com
联系电话 / 编辑部: 021-22895517
　　　　　 发行部: 021-22895559
印　　刷 / 上海颛辉印刷厂有限公司

版　　次 / 2024 年 3 月第 1 版
印　　次 / 2024 年 3 月第 1 次印刷
开　　本 / 890mm×1240mm　1/32
字　　数 / 260 千字
印　　张 / 9.75
书　　号 / ISBN 978-7-5426-8324-3/H·131
定　　价 / 68.00 元

敬启读者,如发现本书有印装质量问题,请与印刷厂联系 021-56152633